TWENTIETH-CENTURY WOMEN NOVELISTS

Twentieth-Century Women Novelists

Edited by
Thomas F. Staley

BARNES & NOBLE BOOKS
TOTOWA, NEW JERSEY

First edition 1982
Reprinted 1985

First published in the USA 1982 by
BARNES & NOBLE BOOKS
81 Adams Drive
Totowa, New Jersey, 07512

ISBN 0-389-20272-X

Printed in Hong Kong

Library of Congress Cataloging in Publication Data
Main entry under title:
Twentieth century women novelists.
Includes index.
1. English fiction — Women authors — History and
criticism.   2. English fiction — 20th century — History
and criticism.   I. Staley, Thomas F.
PR888.W62T9   823′.914′099287   82-1740
ISBN 0-389-20272-X   AACR2

Contents

Notes on the Contributors   vii

Introduction   Thomas F. Staley   xi

1   Passionate Portrayal of Things to Come: Doris Lessing's recent fiction   *Sydney Janet Kaplan*   1

2   The Wages of Intellectuality . . . and the Fictional Wagers of Iris Murdoch   *Kingsley Widmer*   16

3   Olivia Manning: witness to history *Harry J. Mooney, Jr.*   39

4   Women Victimised by Fiction: living and loving in the novels of Barbara Pym   *Barbara Brothers*   61

5   Cold Enclosures: the fiction of Susan Hill *Rosemary Jackson*   81

6   The Clinical World of P. D. James *Bernard Benstock*   104

7   Women and Children First: the novels of Margaret Drabble   *Gail Cunningham*   130

8   Muriel Spark: the novelist as dandy *William McBrien*   153

9   Edna O'Brien: a kind of Irish childhood *Darcy O'Brien*   179

10   The Masculine World of Jennifer Johnston *Shari Benstock*   191

Index   218

Notes on the Contributors

Thomas F. Staley is Provost and Vice President for Academic Affairs at the University of Tulsa, where he also edits the *James Joyce Quarterly*. He has written and edited books on James Joyce and other modern writers such as Italo Svevo and Dorothy Richardson. His essays on a wide range of modern authors have appeared in *Commonweal, Genre, Journal of Modern Literature, Twentieth Century Literature, Etudes Anglaises*, and many others. With Hugh Kenner he is editing the centennial volume on James Joyce. His most recent book is *Jean Rhys: A Critical Study* (1979).

Sydney Janet Kaplan is an Associate Professor of English at the University of Washington. Her publications include *Feminine Consciousness in the Modern British Novel* (1975), and articles on Doris Lessing, Katherine Mansfield, and a review essay on women's studies in literature and criticism for *Signs: Journal of Women in Culture and Society* (spring 1979). She recently returned from New Zealand where she was studying the Katherine Mansfield papers at the Alexander Turnbull Library in Wellington, in preparation for her next book, a critical re-evaluation of the fiction of Katherine Mansfield.

Kingsley Widmer, raised in midwestern small towns and educated in diverse labours and several state universities, teaches English at San Diego State University. Among his varied writings are books of literary study — on D. H. Lawrence, Herman Melville, Henry Miller, Nathaneal West and Paul Goodman, and on issues of modernism, literary rebellion and cultural dialectics.

Harry J. Mooney, Jr. is Professor of English at the University of Pittsburgh. His principal areas of teaching and study are the Continental and English novel of the nineteenth and early twentieth centuries. His publications include *Katherine Anne Porter: A Critical Study* (1957), James Gould Cozzens: *Novelist of Intellect* (1964), *The Shapeless God* (essays in the modern novel, edited with Thomas F. Staley, 1968), and *Leo Tolstoy: The Epic Voice* (1969). He is currently at work on a study of the treatment of colonial and political themes in the English novel during the period 1895–1975.

Barbara Brothers is Associate Professor and Chairman of the Department of English at Youngstown State University. Her articles and reviews have appeared in *Boundary II, Mosaic, ADE Bulletin, James Joyce Quarterly, Journal of Beckett Studies, Pi Kappa Pi Journal, Sean O'Casey Review* and *ACIS Newsletter*. She is presently at work on a book on Henry Greene's novels.

Rosemary Jackson graduated in 1973 from the School of English and Comparative Literature, University of Warwick, then wrote a D.Phil. thesis on 'Dickens and Gothic tradition' for the University of York. Until 1981 she had a full-time lectureship in literature in the School of English and American Studies, University of East Anglia. She is now a freelance lecturer and is particularly interested in feminism, fantastic literature and the relation between these in terms of subverting traditional cultural assumptions. Her book on *Fantasy* is to be published shortly.

Bernard Benstock teaches detective fiction, as well as James Joyce and other modern writers, in the Department of English and Program in Comparative Literature at the University of Illinois. He has published four books on James Joyce and two on Sean O'Casey, and a recent publication is *Who's He When He's at Home: A James Joyce Directory*, co-authored with his wife, Shari Benstock. In preparation is a study of crime fiction, *The Necessary Murders*, and a collection of essays on the major practitioners of the genre, *Essays in Dectective Fiction*.

Gail Cunningham is Senior Lecturer in English at the Middlesex Polytechnic. She is the author of *The New Woman and the Victorian Novel* (1978) and is currently preparing a book on Margaret Drabble.

William McBrien, editor, since 1974, of the scholarly journal *Twentieth Century Literature*, is at work on a critical biography of Stevie Smith, *Me Again: Uncollected Writings of Stevie Smith*. He is Professor of Modern British Literature at Hofstra University in New York and the author of many essays and reviews on this subject.

Darcy O'Brien is Professor of Modern Letters in the Graduate Faculty, the University of Tulsa. His novel, *A Way of Life, Like Any Other*, received the Ernest Hemingway Award in 1978. A second novel, *The Silver Spooner*, will appear this year. His previous books include *The Conscience of James Joyce, W. R. Rodgers* and *Patrick Kavanagh*. He has written numerous essays on Irish literature and has done articles on Irish politics and other subjects for the *New York Times Magazine* and *New York Magazine*. In 1978 he was awarded a Guggenheim Fellowship for fiction writing. Currently he is at work on *The Emergency*, a novel set in Ireland during the Second World War.

Shari Benstock has published on various modern authors from James Joyce and Djuna Barnes to Harold Pinter and T. S. Eliot, and is co-author of *Who's He When He's at Home: A James Joyce Directory* (1980). When not engaged in her administrative duties in medical sciences at the University of Illinois, she is at work on a study of the distaff expatriates in Paris between the world wars, and chapters on the relationship between modernist literature and post-impressionist art. The first section, on James Joyce and Henri Matisse, was published in 1981.

Introduction

The first two novelists in F. R. Leavis's *Great Tradition* are women, and, while nearly everyone would add others, no serious student of the English novel would eliminate Jane Austen or George Eliot. The achievement of women writers of the British novel is a significant one, and the major talents within this tradition have been recognised. Besides Austen and Eliot, there are the Brontës, possibly Dorothy Richardson, and certainly Virginia Woolf. But there are others, too, who have only recently engaged wide critical attention: Elizabeth Gaskell, Mrs Humphry Ward, May Sinclair, Jean Rhys, to name only a few. In Leavis's pantheon Austen and Eliot rank with Conrad and James, and by later critical standards Woolf would rank with Lawrence, but it would be difficult to name an equally imposing quartet of women novelists of the same generation to rank with Scott, Thackeray, Meredith, or Hardy, to say nothing of Dickens. The reasons for this disparity have only recently been discussed seriously by critics such as Elaine Showalter and Ellen Moers among others. One point that I believe the essays in this volume make collectively is that those who study the British novel of the last half of this century will recognise that women novelists in this tradition have come into their own, if not dominated, during the sixties and seventies.

During the period of the 1960s and especially the 1970s there has been a dramatic change in the reception given to serious women novelists generally. They have achieved much wider recognition both critically and popularly than at any other time in the history of British fiction. The reasons for this recognition are, of course, social as well as literary. Unlike the generation of women novelists such as Woolf and Dorothy Richardson who began writing during the early half of this century, women novelists of this period, and male novelists too for that matter, are not bold experimentalists in form or technique; their achievements rest on other claims. The themes they have inaugurated have grown out of new experiences. For example, as Gail Cunningham points out in her essay, Margaret Drabble's literary roots are clearly Victorian and Edwardian, but her heroines provide a careful portrait of the contemporary woman with crises and conflicts unknown to her predecessors. This is not to say that their personal conflicts are greater or any more frustrating, but they do reflect a much more complex engagement with the social and economic order. Women novelists of this period, like Drabble, bring to the fictional worlds they create an obviously wider range of experience from the world outside. The cataclysmic social changes and radical cultural alterations in the last twenty years have brought new freedom and along with it awesome responsibility to women. And these changes in cultural, social, and economic patterns are so significant that they have both expanded and altered the nature of reality for women. This entire phenomenon has raised some of the deepest philosophical and psychological questions of our age, and it is inevitable that these questions are embodied in the fiction of the period, and equally inevitable that they be probed by women.

The 1960s and 1970s have seen enormous changes in the ways in which some women, especially educated ones, have the opportunity to live their lives. Such opportunities have created a diversity and choice for women, but this new experience and awareness has obviously introduced new problems and frustrations. In spite of the many social advances and economic opportunities that have seemed to develop, however, like all revolutions, this one has been marked by as much pain as joy, as much guilt, frustration, and setback, as triumph, freedom, and promise. The questions of identity, career, motherhood, marriage, sexual and economic freedom are all the more complex as they become matters for active decisions rather than merely subjects for hope and speculation. And because women are beginning to enter the social world in most of its aspects, the social effect on men is also a subject of importance. These are only a few of the questions with which a new generation of women are confronted as they enter the public world and face responsibilities from which earlier generations of their sex have been 'protected'. The feminine social world portrayed in Virginia Woolf's novels, for example, with all of its sophistication was not that much larger than that of Woolf's immediate predecessors. *A Room of One's Own* was a meagre ambition in light of female experience today. The turmoil, the triumphs, the accommodations, the anguish of these new circumstances have become the subject matter of some of the most important novels written by women during the 1960s and 1970s, and the problems that the female in the contemporary novel confronts were hardly concerns of Woolf's female characters simply because the world for them was much smaller, more enclosed. The themes and subjects, and the characters in these later novels reflect a far larger world with its shape much less clearly defined.

Perhaps the most remarkably distinguishing characteristic of the contemporary novel such as those written by the novelists discussed in this volume is the ability to create women not in some image to conform or conflict with the masculine world, but clearly as themselves.

We are, however, both comforted and frustrated that artists seldom, if ever, conform to our expectations and rarely explore the popularly predictable. And so it is with the women novelists whose careers began in the 1960s and reached their mature artistry or recognition in the 1970s, or who only began their careers, as some of the writers discussed in this volume, in the 1970s. In the novels of several of these writers it would seem on the surface of things that little has changed. For example, Barbara Pym's four elderly characters in *Quartet in Autumn* build fragile defences for their lonely, meagre lives which allow them a quiet dignity and tender meaning in a dull, faceless world. Yet we can ask that had it not been for the changed atmosphere and new awareness, would her work have come to the attention of critics and, even if it had, would the reading public have so readily recognised the quiet triumph of this beautiful work? As Barbara Brothers's essay makes clear, however remote Pym's characters seem from the modern world, and however dim their prospects, they reveal their author's sensibility and her deep understanding of human nature — a sensibility surely attuned to the struggle of the female in the modern world with its larger circumference.

This portrayal of the female in the novels of women has quite properly been the central focal point of critical discussion, but another important development in the advancement of women's fiction, and one that has received too little attention, has been the depth of understanding and wider range of sensibility women novelists have shown in their creation of male characters and their willingness to deal with the consciousness of the male directly. The creative energies of women novelists are now revealed in their characters of both sexes. This is not to say that it is only the new status of women that has brought about this new confidence; genius has its influence over time and social conditions, and these present novelists write out of a tradition inspired by George Eliot's portrayal of Tertius Lydgate in *Middlemarch*, but this masterful creation of a male figure was a rare and brilliant exception. The male experience in the contemporary world is now an integral part of the woman novelist's domain. She is no longer restricted to the deepest probing of the feminine consciousness only to leave the male nature to the surface reality of dialogue and plot, or have male motives and passion filtered through the consciousness of a woman character. This emergence is nowhere better revealed than in the work of Iris Murdoch, who also brings an intellectual quality to her work that has few parallels in the contemporary novel, as Kingsley Widmer's discussion makes abundantly clear. The most intimate concerns of mind, sexuality, and relationships of males are frequently taken up directly, confidently, and convincingly by contemporary women novelists, and literary criticism which often grudgingly and belatedly follows literature has, except in its more backward habitats, become aware of the enormous cultural and aesthetic value of women novelists.

The novelists discussed in these essays vary widely in their concerns, their subjects, and their themes, and this in itself is testimony to the broad development in female fictions. Their subjects are not predictable. Jennifer Johnston, as Shari Benstock points out in her essay, is deeply concerned with form and narrative technique. Her novel, *How Many Miles to Babylon*, among other things, evokes the atmosphere of the trenches of the First World War with brilliant detail as it deals at the same time with questions of loyalty, family, and self. Muriel Spark's fictions seem to come from another era, and at times, another world, as William McBrien suggests in his discussion of her themes and especially her style, which draws from another era. P. D. James is more than an heir to the tradition of Agatha Christie and Dorothy Sayers; her characters are more deeply drawn and her themes of good and evil are more resonant and complex than her predecessors. Her fiction, as Bernard Benstock suggests, transcends our expectations of detective fiction. James's latest novel, *Innocent Blood*, which was published after Benstock completed his essay, confirms her growing strength as she enlarges the social and moral frame of her work. As Rosemary Jackson comments, the work of Susan Hill, 'does not seem to be primarily concerned with the subject, or the subjugation, of women'. Yet Jackson makes a convincing argument for a feminist approach to her fiction. Although Darcy O'Brien sees distinct limitations in Edna O'Brien's fictions, he recognises her achievements in the frank exploration of the sexual dimensions of her women characters. This diversity, expected in fiction by male novelists, is now a characteristic of women's fiction. When given the opportunities of a full world women novelists will write of that new world; their vision till now has only been restricted by the limited lives afforded them.

A testimony to the rich and diverse achievement in the contemporary British novel is the difficulty in making too many critical generalisations. Women novelists have always had the uncanny ability to create a small world that is a true microcosm of the conflicts and relationships, both historical and personal, that affect society. Olivia Manning's *Balkan Trilogy* is a work that deals with a small group of Englishmen engulfed in the turbulence of the Second World War, and, although her stage is deliberately confined, these novels, as Harry Mooney shows, reflect in their acuity and understanding the concerns of an entire generation of people who lived through a war that tested their ideals along with their lives. And as Olivia Manning vividly recreates a particular time and place in history, Doris Lessing, as the title of Sydney Janet Kaplan's essay suggests, passionately portrays things to come. However bleak the predictions and the elegiac tone of Lessing's recent fiction, her literary career, which began with the exploration of the feminine consciousness and has turned to predictions of a cataclysmic demise for all of us, in a curious way exemplifies the willingness of women novelists to engage the largest questions that confront all human beings. The battles for women's freedom have by no means been won, and many women novelists are deeply concerned with the problems which the victories as well as the defeats present. But with this emergence has come a more significant aspect, and that is the challenge of art that women's fiction now gives to the world − not in a partial or secluded way, but in a total one.

This volume can make no claims to completeness in its discussion of living writers, for there were a number of others who could have been included and Barbara Pym and Olivia Manning have died since this volume went to the publisher. At the time it was conceived Jean Rhys and Antonia White were still alive, and Beryl Bainbridge's work is clearly as important as several of the writers discussed. The attempt was not to be exhaustive, but representative; to show collectively the considerable vitality of the contemporary British novel written by women in a series of essays which each treat the works of one author. It is appropriate to devote a volume of criticism to such a subject, because, first of all, it gives special focus to a significant development in the contemporary novel, and, further, directs our attention to the particular problems, approaches, and insights which the richness of this literature generates. The title of this book is more ponderous than I like; yet the diversity of these writers left thematic descriptions inaccurate or less than complete.

In the 17 October 1918 issue of *The Times Literary Supplement* there appeared a review of a now obscure book by R. Brimley Johnson, *The Women Novelists*. The reviewer praised the volume for the very interesting things it had to say about literature, but also the even more interesting discussion about the particular qualities of the literature that is written by women. The reviewer was Virginia Woolf. Today these 'particular qualities' that we find in serious women's fiction are not limitations or confined insights but rather revelations of art and experience for all of us.

August 1981   Thomas F. Staley

1 Passionate Portrayal of Things to Come: Doris Lessing's recent fiction

Sydney Janet Kaplan

> If genius is the power of anticipation, the passionate portrayal of things to come, then your work carries the mark of genius and over and above its artistic ventures it is a moral phenomenon.
>
> (Thomas Mann to his brother Heinrich, 1941)

If it is dangerous to assess the work of a living author, it is especially so with Doris Lessing, who is twenty steps ahead of us whenever we try to place her in a critical framework or predict the direction of her work. Her own attitude towards her critics is highly ironic and she has questioned students about wasting their time dissecting only one book or even the works of a single author.[1] As a critic then, I must face the fact that my current attempts to interpret Lessing may later appear foolish, but I also know that this body of work of hers is worth being foolish over. It intrigues me, worries me, infuriates me. How I hope her vision of the future will not come true! The clarity of her depiction of the dissolution of society, with its prediction of world-wide destruction and catastrophe makes many of her readers long to reject her prophesies, her rejection of the way most people live their lives.

Some years ago I thought I saw a pattern unfolding in Lessing's development as a novelist, and I sensed that with the novels beginning with *The Four-Gated City* (1969)[2] she was leaving behind that intense struggle for sexual definition that had made her earlier

1

work so remarkable, especially *The Golden Notebook* (1962). At that time I believed that Martha Quest's death brought the whole question of 'feminine consciousness' to its end in Lessing's fiction, and that her newer work would take her 'away from the concerns of feminism'.[3] Lessing had commented in an interview in 1969: 'I'm impatient with people who emphasise sexual revolution. I say we should all go to bed, shut up about sexual liberation, and go on with the important matters.'[4] The 'important matters' for Lessing relate to the very future of the human race, to her apparent certainty that catastrophe is inevitable. In the same interview she flatly stated: 'I believe the future is going to be cataclysmic'.

A growing sense of urgency thus marks Doris Lessing's writing over the past decade, and her creative methods have become more experimental in order to convey that urgency. *Briefing For a Descent Into Hell* (1971), with its epigraph: 'Category: Inner-space fiction / For there is never anywhere to go but in',[5] allows Lessing to intensify her exploration of states of consciousness by incorporating into the realistic novel elements usually ascribed to the genres of fantasy, romance, and science fiction. In her most recent novel, *The Memoirs of a Survivor* (1974),[6] Lessing envisions — in relentlessly convincing detail — the world we will surely inhabit *after* the destruction of our present civilisation. At the same time as Lessing forces our attention on speculations about the future, the accuracy of her awareness of the psychology of human relationships and her grasp of the specifics of political and social realities never falters. As one of her reviewers has remarked: 'The most frightening aspect of Doris Lessing's *The Memoirs of a Survivor* is that her "bad times" could so easily stem from the conditions we have had a taste of in the last few years. We have had only intermittent shortages of sugar and toilet rolls, but Lessing's people live by barter and bargaining.'[7] In this context it is interesting to discover that Doris Lessing is presently working on a series of novels of a type she calls 'space-fiction'.[8]

Not only do these later works reveal Lessing's concern with humanity's future, but they also demonstrate her concurrent involvement with the study of Sufism,[9] which began to surface in her fiction as early as *Landlocked* (1965). For Lessing, the Sufi Way is a source of wisdom that could help people come to terms with the current sense of crisis and fear of social and personal dissolution.

In *The Four-Gated City* Lessing describes Martha's struggle to develop innate but limited extra-sensory powers which might help her to forecast the oncoming disaster and allow her to make preparations to escape from it. The novel ends with the appearance of mutant children who are born with such powers fully realised, indicating at least a possible hope for the survival of human life, as well as a concept of the direction of its evolution. Such notions appear to be in accord with certain Sufi beliefs that Lessing makes explicit when she quotes from Idries Shah's *The Sufies* at a crucial juncture in *The Four-Gated City*:

> Sufis believe that, expressed in one way, humanity is evolving towards a certain destiny. We are all taking part in that evolution. Organs come into being as a result of a need for specific organs. The human being's organism is producing a new complex of organs in response to such need. In this age of the transcending of time and space, the complex of organs is concerned with the transcending of time and space. What ordinary people regard as sporadic and occasional bursts of telepathic and prophetic power are seen by the Sufi as nothing less than the first stirrings of these same organs. The difference between all evolution up to date and the present need for evolution is that for the past ten thousand years or so we have been given the possiblity of a conscious evolution. So essential is this more rarefied evolution that our future depends on it. (p. 492.)

But people who appear to be developing these new organs are often misunderstood by others with more limited capacities. In *Briefing For a Descent Into Hell* Charles Watkins is declared 'insane' by his doctors when he begins to experience higher states of consciousness. Charles becomes aware of interconnections between all things and envisions human life as part of a larger whole. His vision also communicates to Lessing's readers a painful, last-chance appeal to change before we destroy ourselves and the planet that is our home, because 'some sort of a divorce there has been somewhere along the path of this race of man between the "I" and the "We", some sort of a terrible falling away. . .'. (p. 103.)

The most profound moments of Charles Watkins's interior journey parallel innumerable descriptions of 'the highest state of consciousness' expressed throughout the centuries by visionaries from diverse cultures and traditions. While Lessing's approach appears to be through Sufism, her uninitiated readers might be able to grasp at least a part of her intent through a more generalised description of the concept of mind-expansion, such as the following by John White:

> . . . all are agreed in calling it the highest state of consciousness: a self-transforming perception of one's total union with the infinite. It is beyond time and space. It is an experience of the timelessness which is eternity; of unlimited unity with all creation. One's socially conditioned sense of 'me' is shattered and swept away by a new definition of the self, the I. In that redefinition of self, I equals all mankind, all life and the universe. The usual ego boundaries break down and the ego passes behind the limits of the body.[10]

The consciousness behind and within Lessing's fiction strains those boundaries in *Briefing For a Descent Into Hell*, while in *The Memoirs of a Survivor* it dissolves them completely, as its narrator and those who are linked with her pass 'out of this collapsed little world into another order of world altogether'. (p. 182.)

Within this context of earthly calamity and psychic evolution the Lessing novel interceding between *Briefing* and *Memoirs* almost seems like a throwback to much earlier concerns. When I first read *The Summer Before the Dark* (1973)[11] I thought that it might imply Lessing's return to her earlier focus on the role of women in society, sexual relationships and the problems of independence for intelligent women. But I quickly realised that this apparent 'return' was not to the same questions at all. For if this seemingly 'conventional' novel is viewed within the contexts of Lessing's concern with the collapse of present systems and the evolution of consciousness it may even be recognised as one of her most deeply revelatory works. Its deceptively simple story about a middle-aged woman's attempts at self-discovery actually complements the more overtly grand vision of the novel which preceded it. Kate Brown's journey, in its geographical locations alone, hints at a connection with Doris Lessing's overriding concern with spiritual evolution. Istanbul and Spain, the two 'foreign' destinations of Kate's initial wanderings, are both centres of ancient Sufi wisdom. Watching a bird fly past her window in Istanbul, Kate feels 'that subtle approaches were being made to her from an unknown world'. (p. 53.)

Many of the first critical reviews of *The Summer Before the Dark* focused on the external level of plot: the question of what Kate Brown should *do* with her empty days. Alison Lurie, for example, complained about the novel's ending:

> . . . Kate herself, now restored in health and looks, cannot think
> of anything to do but return home − like the seal in her dream,
> whom she has finally restored to the sea. The only apparent
> result of all Kate has gone through is a resolve not to dye her hair
> any more.
>   It is a puzzling, unsatisfactory conclusion to what up to this
> point has been a brilliantly realistic, wise, and courageous
> novel. Perhaps I have missed the point; but both this fatalistic
> ending and the title seem to suggest that for most women there is
> no escape from the prison constructed for them by society and
> their own sexual vulnerability. Yet this ending is as incomplete
> as any of the earlier ones would have been, because Kate is an
> incomplete character . . . A woman like Kate, provided with
> exceptional intelligence, courage, energy, and charm . . .
> would surely have some interest, some ambition in life. Having
> achieved freedom, she would have something better to do with it
> than go into 'the dark'.[12]

While there may be for Kate a 'return' to the world of ordinary women, a 'return' to everyday living and mundane problems (and it may seem more of a return stylistically after penetrating the extraordinarily rich interior world of Charles Watkins in *Briefing*, or the depiction of political and psychological complexities in *The Four-Gated City*), I do not believe that such returning signals a failure in Doris Lessing's realisation of Kate Brown's level of awareness.

Since the evolution of consciousness in Lessing's fiction is towards the universal, it necessitates a change in her methods of characterisation as well, if she is to express the immediate relationship between the illusion of a self-contained ego and the reality of universal forces, powers, currents, and cosmic energies. Alison Lurie's complaint about Kate's incompleteness may be relevant here. Lurie notices something unfinished in terms of Kate's 'ego'. She might also be responding to a rather peculiar flatness of style apparent at times in this novel. For everything does seem pared down, stripped of inessentials, the diction and syntax reminiscent of those in parables, fables, archetypal myths. But Kate Brown is not merely a symbolic 'Woman'. Lessing allows us to know Kate through specific details from her personal life as well; we see her children and know their ages; we see the lawn of her suburban house; we explore Kate's memories of chocolate cake, daisies on her daughter's dress. Small, 'trivial' details? Doris Lessing has remarked elsewhere: 'At last I understood that the way over, or through this dilemma, the unease at writing about "petty personal problems" was to recognise that nothing is personal, in the sense that it is uniquely one's own'.[13] These words do not differ very much from John White's comment: 'Enlightenment reveals that *what is most deeply personal is also most universal*.'[14]

There is a return to ordinary life then, in *The Summer Before the Dark*, but the ordinary is no longer what it once was in Doris Lessing's fiction. For all Kate Brown's sense of unease, there is yet none of that anguished panic over being bombarded by so many conflicting feelings, perceptions, possibilities in experience, fears, and unresolved crises that packed the pages of the earlier volumes of *Children of Violence*, and was ready to explode *The Golden Notebook* right out of its package. The return to ordinary life is presented to us in prose equally clear and simple. It is a prose corresponding to the style of our own stately dreams, that have – even with all their ramifications of longing, violence, and incongruities – that sharply delineated outline, that surrealism so clearly defined to make us yearn for their hidden meanings, their suggestions of what we really know but have forgotten. Such dreams are 'crafted' with the genius we associate with the perfectly executed objects of a time before individualism, before industrialisation: the gems and tapestries, the royal robes, crowns, those carefully wrought, beautiful objects made to last forever, containing a lifetime in their making, the communal consciousness of a people, way of life, time of being. Unique but also, 'impersonal'. Yet certainly not 'depersonalised'.

Here is a crucial distinction, and I would like to use Roger Wescott's definitions as a guide toward understanding it, although other frameworks might be equally suggestive.[15] Wescott recognises three kinds of 'impersonality': 'Prepersonality': 'the impersonality of nonhominian animals and of hominian infants'; 'depersonality': the alienated condition of modern humans 'in which personality has been eroded or destroyed by excessive regimentation'; and 'transpersonality': 'a relatively sudden and transitory experience of spiritual growth, too dramatic in nature to be called "learning" in any ordinary sense'. The 'transpersonal' results in an 'illuminated self always . . . larger, more cosmic, and less personal than the common self'.[16]

Kate Brown's journey of discovery also corresponds to the traditional paradigm of spiritual journeying, familiar to the Romantic poets, that M. H. Abrams described as a journey both circular and linear, 'the ascending circle, or spiral'.[17] The end of Kate's journey is a 'return'. Back to her home, her husband, her family. But it is not a return to her old 'depersonalised' self, nor is it a return to an idyllic 'prepersonal'. Kate returns, but on a higher plane of understanding and experience — in fact a plane on which are incorporated all the stages of the journey. She has insights during her journey that push her close to the 'transpersonal', not that she achieves it totally. But the novel shows us her path through the most difficult stage of the process. Her dream about the seal may be the pattern of her answer. When Kate reaches the ocean and sets the seal free, it joins the others in the collective unconscious. Kate then recognises the possibility of letting go that burden of 'personality' she has carried around and protected for so long. The time to do so will come and Kate is no longer afraid of it.

What Kate has undergone is a breaking through in her recognition of 'depersonality', a crucial stage on the way towards the transpersonal. Westcott suggests that:

> . . . both the prepersonal and the transpersonal states are apparently free of anxiety, while the depersonal state is typified by a complex of wholly negative emotions, ranging from resignation through apathy, depression, and intimidation to impotently rebellious rage. In emotional tone, depersonality resembles personality more than it resembles either of the other two forms of impersonality. For, although personality is affectively more variable than depersonality, exhibiting considerable, if sporadic exhuberance, its most persistent mood is one of apprehension. And this, after all, is only what might be expected in view of the fact that personality, being both transitory and self-conscious, inevitably anticipates and fears its own dissolution . . . What makes depersonality painful, of course, is the element of more or less overt coercion involved in it.[18]

Kate's understanding of how she has become depersonalised,

allows her to recognise the illusion of personality as well. Her answer should not be to create a new personality — the response Alison Lurie seems to want from her — but a going beyond personality altogether: to move on to that higher state of consciousness, transpersonality.

Doris Lessing puts Kate Brown's journey into a social, economic, biological, and political perspective — as she does with all her characters, in all her novels — and in this regard Kate's discovery and potential must be examined. Wescott is helpful here as well, because he sees the transpersonal as 'the wave of the future'. Not because more people might be experiencing it, but due to 'an obvious and increasing sense of personal malaise among the most highly educated and economically secure members of the industrialised societies'.[19] Wescott insists that 'one must have known the waking state before he can attain the released state, since *striving for release can occur only in one who has achieved awareness of confinement*'.[20]

Kate Brown reaches 'the waking state' by the end of *The Summer Before the Dark*. She is at the point where she clearly understands that her past life was 'entranced' (Wescott lists the stages of consciousness from the bottom up: sleeping, dreaming, entranced, waking, released); that is, she has been operating on conditioning, patterned reflexes, responding to pressures automatically. Awake by the end of the novel, Kate is catching a glimpse of 'release' (or that highest stage of consciousness the Sufies call 'fana'), although she does not attain it. Her dream's ending reveals its possibility when the seal re-enters the ocean. *But the dream is not the release itself.* Leaving behind her depersonalised self is the essential condition for one who would approach it. Kate recognises now the *possibility* of release because she 'has achieved awareness of confinement'.

Kate's process of seeing through her depersonalised self involves primarily, a growing awareness of her 'role' as a wife and mother, and how she was conditioned into it. As usual, Lessing gives us her always larger framework to see this process within. Individual and collective are interdependent: 'Because — while everything seemed so personal, and aimed at her . . . in fact it would be pressures from the other, the public, sphere, pressing on her small life, that would give what she experienced its urgency'. (p. 12.) Through Kate's son Tim, that 'public sphere' becomes a prediction that 'the end of civilisation was close, and that we should shortly be looking back from a world-wide barbarism formalised into a world-bureaucracy to the present, which would, from that nasty place in time, seem like a vanished golden age'. (p. 81.) Kate's possibilities for an individually realised new freedom become then even more problematic.

It is fitting that Doris Lessing develops Kate's awakening with her realisation that the words we use to communicate our experiences are slogans, parcels handed to us ready-made, to which we react accordingly. Lessing focuses upon the very *unsuitability* of all those common expressions by which we attempt to define our experiences: '"trying on" ideas like so many dresses off a rack'. (p. 7.) This is the language of our modern life: the clichés, the jargon, the empty expressions. The analogy is perfectly apt; for what other activity is more boring, more ultimately frustrating and defeating than clothes shopping, that drug of middle-class female existence? 'Like so many dresses off a rack' reminds us that ready-made dresses rarely fit, were never intended to fit a body but rather a concept. Lessing begins with these ill-assorted dresses, and also a 'woman' who is just that any-woman or every-woman who tries to make a choice between objects that are *all* unsatisfying. Never the *right* dress, never the *ideal* dress. For, after all, *we live in a world that has no respect for craftsmanship*, or *things aren't made the way they used to be*, or *whatever happened to that little dressmaker who* — our responses become clichés which merely evoke other clichés. The ready-made phrases slide back and forth along the rack.

But we must remember that something has changed. There aren't so many dresses on the racks any more. There are shortages, not enough cotton, a drought in India perhaps. Some patterns, but not in all sizes. Kate Brown's spiritual awakening is in the midst of these material shortages. As the figure of 'Kate' gradually emerges out of the unspecific 'a woman' at the start of the book, we see that she is making small, reconciling movements toward adjusting to these increasing scarcities and interferences in the smooth-running consumption of goods and services of our time. The novel begins with a power cut, and Doris Lessing makes a connection between it (the diminishing supply of 'energy' available to us), and increasing world starvation (the deprivation of food — energy that makes humans run). She also makes an implicit connection between impoverishment in physical goods and services and impoverishment of language, which has become as 'ready-made' and skimpy as the dresses on the rack.

The days of made-to-order tailoring have ended. That is, except for the exquisite few, 'stars' like that beautiful couple at Kate's London hotel. Remember the hundreds of hand-sewn buttons on that young woman's dress? (pp. 134—5.) The original detailing — tiny stitches that did not show but had such strength that a fabric might last for years, enabling a garment to belong to its wearer for life — is gone, and as far removed from the experience of most of us as that 'rare vintage' Tim evokes with such nostalgia and longing. (p. 81.) And gone too is language that once was rich and decorated, spangled and embroidered, sequined and over-wrought. Such fullness not mere ostentation, but the result of an over-abundant richness of imagination and irrepressible bubbling energy. But even its opposite, spare and precise, enduring Pilgrim's grey, fitting so well and lasting even longer, that is gone too. Both fashions resulted from a system of learning so difficult, so life-absorbing, that even their remnants appear to us like works of genius: those fragile bits of Coptic textiles, Chilkat blankets, Ladik carpets.

The power cut at the beginning of the novel serves to underscore one of Lessing's basic themes: the question of energy, physical and spiritual. Or perhaps I should not even speak of them in separate terms, for in Lessing's view 'energy' is what it is all about — everywhere and in everything. Nancy Hardin quotes Lessing as stating: '*Now the real question is this: Where do you get your energy from? What kind of energy is it? How do you husband it? How do you use it?*'[21] In the case of the world Kate Brown inhabits energy appears to be displaced, or inconsistent — in the wrong places and concentrated unhealthily, as in a pancreas shooting forth too much insulin before it collapses and diabetes sets in. There are, for example, those airline stewardesses Lessing describes so well. They are overstimulated, in fact, so much so that they are 'ready to explode with the forces of attention [they have] absorbed'. (p. 58.) Everything is intensified, speeded-up:

There was the feeling abroad, irrational or not, that these events, once high and rare (or had they ever been, was that just false memory?), were moving into the first place of everyone's experience, as if an air that had once been the climate of a distant and cataclysmic star had chosen to engulf our poor planet [an image reminiscent of Watkins's vision in *Briefing*]. The crucial experiences, when you came to think about it, were for more and more people: invasion, war, civil war, epidemic, famine, flood, quake, poisoning of soil, food and air. For these, the allotted attitudes were even more stereotyped. None go much beyond: '*We ought to be doing something about it*, or *Oh woe, alas*'! (p. 9.)

This speeding-up relates to Kate herself as well. Her growing old won't be gradual: '. . . Kate Brown was going to get the whole thing over with in a few months'. (p. 12.) At the end of these months it may no longer be for Kate a taking of choices, an active assertion to *do* one thing rather than another: 'It is always a question, when in a cul-de-sac, a trap, of seeing what there is for you; one has to be listening'. (p. 97.) And Kate is listening. Alison Lurie was disappointed that 'the only apparent result of all Kate has gone through is a resolve not to dye her hair any more'. Nonetheless, if that decision appears trivial, banal, certainly not a dramatic resolution to Kate's problems, it is still a highly significant symbolic action. It informs us that Kate has reached the end of functioning at the level of conditioned responses to the world. She will no longer allow herself to be an entranced object for another's pleasure and satisfaction regardless of her own spiritual and biological evolution. As Lessing explains in her *Vogue* essay: '"You will have to learn through that most banal of all things", says the Sufi to the would-be student, "you must learn through ordinary life". And he is likely to have nothing to say to people looking for excitements and sensational experiences'.[22] And elsewhere Lessing comments: 'you cannot approach Sufism until you are able to think that a person quite ordinary in appearance and in life can experience higher states of mind'.[23]

Lessing intimates these higher states of mind through the device of Kate Brown's serial dream about a seal that she rescues and struggles to return to the sea. The dream provides us with a dynamic inner structure that allows us to infer the spiritual countermovement to the novel's action. The dream begins 'like the start of an epic, simple and direct', (p. 34) and its individual episodes conform to a consistent archetypal pattern. Kate must overcome the obstacles posed by the adversity of nature and the backwards pull of human desires on her perilous journey to return the seal to the ocean. The animal's suffering in its bitterly cold environment away from the sea corresponds with a description of Kate sitting with 'her shoulders hunched: they were set to withstand the sort of cold a living animal must feel if its skin is ripped off . . .'. (p. 50.) The general movement within the dream — Kate dragging and carrying the heavy seal in her arms — symbolises Kate's growing awareness that during the years of being conditioned into her role as lover, wife and mother:

> . . . all that time she had been holding in her hands something else, the something precious, offering it in vain to her husband, to her children, to everyone she knew — but it had never been taken, had not been noticed. But this thing she had offered, without knowing she was doing it, which had been ignored by herself and by everyone else, was what was real in her. (p. 126.)

Kate recognises that 'walking into the winter that lay in front of her she was carrying her life as well as the seal's . . .'. (pp. 130–1.)

I tend to believe, however, that the symbolic weight of the seal is meant to suggest more than a metaphor for Kate's self ('self' distinguished from 'ego' in Jungian terms). A characteristic feature of dream logic is the way images may actually be condensations of clusters of associations. An image could suggest the object it depicts (in this case the particular animal Kate visualises — whose very amphibious nature, incidentally, connotes a stage of evolution *between* two levels of existence), but that same image might also refer to the *word* for that image, a word with several very different denotations. A 'seal' is an animal, true enough, but the same word denotes a mark or a brand; it can be 'a sign of ownership and individuality — of differentiation'.[24] In this respect the seal symbolises what is unique in Kate, what is most deeply herself. Additionally, the word 'seal' also means 'to decide irrevocably (the fate of a person or thing)'; in this way it suggests the inevitability of Kate's aging, death, and possible transcendence. Finally, the word might have hidden or esoteric connections: the sealing of one's lips, vows of secrecy and silence. For all we know, Lessing has encoded a secret message here, an allusion to Sufi knowledge.

Kate's growing self-knowledge permits her to establish a relationship with Maureen, the young woman from whom she rents a room after recuperating from the illness that was the catalyst for her awakening. Kate functions as a guide or teacher for Maureen. Now awake, Kate works toward awakening Maureen from *her* own confinement. Kate's dream about the yellow bird in its cage, which she says is Maureen's dream, indicates that Kate is helping Maureen to start on her own journey. But Kate knows that Maureen is not to be alone, releasing herself to fly anywhere. Enlightenment proceeds in stages, and Doris Lessing appears to believe that these are in accordance with biological stages and needs as well. Lessing's earlier experience with Jungian therapy surfaces here.

During an interview soon after the publication of *The Summer Before the Dark*, Lessing remarked: 'we're very biological animals. . . . It's hard for many people to take, but 90 per cent of our . . . thoughts are in fact expressions of whatever state or human stage we're in. . . .'[25] Such comments are reminiscent of Jung's discussion of the stages of life and the need for humans to be involved with the tasks of generation during the first half of life.[26] In the same interview Lessing mentioned young women 'who don't want to get married or have children, and very vocal they are about it. Well, they're trying to cheat on their biology.'

In this context Lessing's analysis of Maureen's particular stage of development includes a prediction that Maureen will marry to complete her biological needs. Kate understands this when she imagines Maureen and William 'in their large house in Wiltshire or somewhere, deep in plentiful horses, children, and dogs, everything according to the pattern, including their humorous comments on it'. (pp. 240–1.)

Kate's perception of Maureen's future is kindly ironic, but she no longer has Maureen's illusions of unlimited possibilities. When Kate watches Maureen go out to buy a dress (and how often are dresses significant in this novel!), Kate realises that Maureen 'could come back as anything at all; she might just as well be wearing a nun's habit as a belly dancer's . . . envy, oh yes, this was envy all right. Maureen could choose to dress as a gipsy or as a young boy or a matron in the course of a day: it was some kind of freedom.' (p. 212.)

But only 'some kind'. Notice how Lessing associates material abundance with abundance of *choices*. For some there are full meals, a variety of different and delectable foods. For others there are the bread and soup from relief vans, now lining the streets of London, and signalling the end of abundance and the future material shortages Lessing predicts in *The Memoirs of a Survivor*. Correspondingly, Maureen's youth and money, her relatively un- completed self offer her choices among so many things; she has so many hours, so many days and years ahead. But Kate's vision is narrowed. It is her summer before the dark, and her need is to complete *one* dream — *one* dream only.

Other dreams may fitfully enter her consciousness: the one about the turtle going the wrong way into the arid desert to die, for example. But it really is Jeffrey's dream, insinuating that Jeffrey turns away from the ocean, wrong-headedly forging inland, becoming sicker as he goes. Kate does not want to complete her 'Jeffrey's dream', for that occurs too early in her journey, before she is ready to become anyone's teacher. Her relationship to Jeffrey 'in retrospect . . . would seem to her all dryness and repetition'. (p. 71.)

Later Kate is more willing to receive Maureen's dream, to use it to help awaken the younger woman. Moreover, when Kate begins to probe her own memories, she finds that 'the things she remembered were because of Maureen's interest . . . It was Maureen who was doing the choosing.' (p. 216.) The storytelling becomes then almost mythic. Incidents from Kate's past become 'tales', as they are repeated over and over while Maureen begs for them like a child longing to hear how 'once upon a time . . .'.

As Kate approaches the transpersonal, repetition is fundamental. It is all part of the multiple—single; the adding—subtracting; the abundant and scarce; the youthful and aging polarities that tease us throughout the novel. Those memories, those dreams, are they then all part of that storehouse of memories? Dreams stacked in rows, memories sliding by on racks, words in phrases? Kate's one dream ends in a return to the multiple; but it also connects her with a singular image as well, to *one* moment of ecstacy: the skate swimming in its little pond: 'It was playing. It held itself in the fresh stream and it waved and rippled and seemed to dance: it was intoxicated with the air coming in from the world outside the tank.' (p. 233.)

NOTES

1. D. Lessing, 'On the Golden Notebook', *Partisan Review*, XL (Spring, 1973) 14–30; *The Golden Notebook*, (London: Michael Joseph, 1962).
2. D. Lessing, *The Four-Gated City*, vol. five of *Children of Violence* (London: MacGibbon & Kee, 1969).
3. S. J. Kaplan, 'The Limits of Consciousness in the Novels of Doris Lessing', *Contemporary Literature*, XIV (Autumn, 1973) 536; *Feminine Consciousness*

in the Modern British Novel (London: University of Illinois Press, 1975) pp. 136–72.

4. J. Raskin, 'Doris Lessing at Stony Brook: An Interview', *New American Review*, no. 8 (1970) 175.

5. D. Lessing, *Briefing For a Descent Into Hell* (London: Jonathan Cape, 1971).

6. D. Lessing, *The Memoirs of a Survivor* (London: Octagon, 1974).

7. J. Mellors, 'Island Styles', *The Listener*, XCIII (23 January 1975) 126.

8. The first volume of Lessing's new series of novels, *Canopus in Argos—Archives*, has just been published: *Shikasta* (London: Jonathan Cape, 1979).

9. For discussions of Lessing's interest in Sufism, see: R. Rubenstein, *The Novelistic Vision of Doris Lessing* (London: University of Illinois Press, 1979); N. Hardin, 'Doris Lessing and the Sufi Way', *Contemporary Literature*, XIV (Autumn, 1973) 565–81; and D. Seligman, 'The Sufi Quest', *World Literature Written in English*, XII (1973) 190–206.

10. J. White (ed.), *The Highest State of Consciousness* (New York: Anchor Books, 1972) p. vii.

11. D. Lessing, *The Summer Before the Dark* (London: Jonathan Cape, 1973).

12. A. Lurie, 'Wise Women', *New York Review of Books*, 14 June 1973, pp. 18–19.

13. D. Lessing, 'On the Golden Notebook', p. 21, op. cit.

14. J. White, p. xiv, op. cit.

15. R. W. Wescott, 'States of Consciousness', in J. White (ed.), p. 26, op cit.

16. Ibid., pp. 26–7.

17. M. H. Abrams, *Natural Supernaturalism* (New York: Norton, 1973) p. 184.

18. R. W. Wescott, p. 27, op cit.

19. Ibid., p. 28.

20. Ibid., p. 33.

21. D. Lessing, New School for Social Research Lecture, 25 September 1972, quoted by N. Hardin, p. 565.

22. D. Lessing, 'An Ancient Way to New Freedom', *Vogue*, CLVIII (July 1971) 98.

23. D. Lessing, 'In the World, Not of It: On Sufism', *Encounter*, XXXIX (August 1972) 62.

24. J. E. Cirlot, *A Dictionary of Symbols* (New York: Philosophical Library, 1962) p. 268.

25. J. Hendin, 'Doris Lessing: The Phoenix 'Midst Her Fires', *Harper's Magazine* (June 1973) pp. 84–5.

26. C. G. Jung, 'The Stages of Life', in J. Campbell (ed.), *The Portable Jung* (New York: Viking, 1971) pp. 3–22.

2 The Wages of Intellectuality . . . and the Fictional Wagers of Iris Murdoch

Kingsley Widmer

> The original *felix culpa* is thought itself.
>
> (*Henry and Cato*)

Plato, Iris Murdoch writes in her carefully learnéd and sympathetic study of his moralistic aesthetic (*The Fire and the Sun*, 1977), presented the 'most uncompromising declaration ever made by a major philosopher of the equality of the sexes. Women can even do philosophy.' And what is it they will philosophise about? Almost everything, of course, but not least about the inadequacies of men. Murdoch's novels do, and often do-in, philosophical claims, but almost obsessively they do, and do-in, self-deluded and self-destructive intellectual males. While quite a variety of women hardly escape the author's contemptuous wit, there seems to be an insistent cerebral delight in catching out her male protagonists — most often English upper-middle class intellectual men with the sexual and moral perplexities of middle-age — in their comic-horrific muddles. 'Muddlers' (a favored term of hers) may be Murdoch's great specialty. Yet she is in several senses a 'philosophical' novelist who seeks to go beyond muddle, not only in disciplined intellectual-artistic self-consciousness but in an affirmative ancient concern for the True, the Good and the Beautiful.

16

Murdoch's reflexive sophistication leads to elaborate play around the no longer quite credible absolutes and the post-modern uncertainty about any extended qualities of goodness. Murdoch's ironic gaming of morality both proposes and undercuts some larger, possibly transcendent, qualities of the Good, which are reached after yet never really confirmed. Hence, for her fictional dialectics, the absolute, and not least the absolute negation, provides illusions with rich possibilties. Intellectual game-playing around the largest meanings furnishes much of the reader's pleasure in her novels; there is almost always the delight of observing a rangingly curious and ingenious mind at work. But because of the daring intellectual play, the moral muddle seems unresolvable, or, at most, cleverly replayable into an exalted conventional love-ethic — the higher muddle. The Murdochean fictional patterns, of course, often do not appear that simple amidst her finely observed detailing and her sensitively probed relationships. Thus her moral order, like the Nietzschean God, may be mostly present in its absence; love opens up into an endlessly complicating labyrinth; and most exalted ethics cover self-delusions. Or perhaps it is all really the other way around, as one so often feels in turning her pages, for she is the mistress of gamesmanship's reversed reversal, the intellectual's art for transcending by defeating intellect, which thus falls back on ordinary decency and muddle.

Take a simple example from one of her minor fictions, *The Unicorn* (1963), where, recurrent theme, the immanent sense of death leads to the affirmation of life. Effingham Cooper, cultivated and muddled upper-civil servant, in a kind of vacationing lunacy has persuaded himself that he is the courtly lover of a reclusive half-mad, half-religious, beautiful mythomaniac, Hannah. According to his old Platonist teacher (a defeatingly passive figure, as usual with Murdoch's wisemen), Hannah must be understood as a 'beautiful unicorn', such a mythic being as was Christ, 'our image of the significance of suffering' which we must simultaneously apprehend as our ideal and, by our own suffering, make real. Misinterpreting, Effingham takes as his heroic duty the kidnapping, with the help of an earnest lady, of the unicorn-Hannah from her semi-captivity. He botches it, with the incursion of yet another eccentric lady-love, and in chagrin short-cuts home through a bog, gets lost, and is sinking to his death in the dark. Asking himself what meaning was left in the last moments of his failed life, he concludes:

What was left was everything else, all that was not himself, that object [the bog] which he had never before seen and upon which he now gazed with the passion of a lover. And indeed he could always have known this for the fact of death stretches the length of life. Since he was mortal he was nothing and since he was nothing all that was not himself was filled to the brim with being and it was from this the light streamed. This then was love, to look and look until one exists no more, *this* was the love which was the same as death . . . with the death of the self the world becomes quite automatically the object of a perfect love.

It appears as a moment of individual and symbolic illumination at the point of death almost worthy, one is briefly tempted to say, of Tolstoy. But the foolish-become-wise Effingham unfortunately has his literal life saved, and, shortly later, when he attempts an exposition of his new found mystical wisdom, with the help of considerable recuperative Scotch and three doting women, he gets it hopelessly garbled. Without following out all the Murdochean ironies, we can note that the enlightened one becomes even more ineffective and self-indulgent. Indeed, he has been illuminatingly saved not from self but for the smug egotism with which the book ends, his comically muddled and brutally self-complacent affirmation of 'the big well-lighted world'. To see the unredeemable saved, and then even more thoroughly unsaved, illuminates the sardonic author and the reader as surely as it illuminates the character.

Murdoch's tough intelligence seems to triumph here; however, the considerable failure of *The Unicorn* as a fiction − it is grotesquely overdone for its genteel characters with two suicides, two murders, quite a variety of erotic twistings, and too many allegorical convolutions around guilty romanticism and love-as-suffering − must partly defeat the ironist. We are left with a manipulatively shaded vision in which the irony of the 'automatic' love turns a hard light back on the authorial machine.

Here, I am making a partly negative, but I hope not unfair, case about the weaker novels of Murdoch, which I see as including such forays into Gothic melodrama. Granted, melodrama seems to be a congenial form for the philosophically insistent writer (as we recall from Marlow, Dostoyevsky, Sartre) perhaps because it allows the highlighting intrusion of ideas into the dull round of commonplace reality. And its Gothic manner allows entry for the forbidden and subterranean. But the isolated castles and dark demons, obscene grottos and hysterical recluses, strange wills and secret crimes, lingering curses and mad loves, all of which Murdoch employs, cannot help but be a machinery of too portentous incongruity when combined with a refined upper-middle class English milieu. The morals and manners of such an intelligentsia provide Murdoch's materials, and, I suspect, moral limitation.

Another in the Gothic genre, *The Italian Girl* (1964), combines antithetical artist-brothers (for her frequent pairing/contrasting/reversing), the perverse will of a rapacious mother, an hysterical reclusive wife and a fey daughter (both pregnant by a demonic refugee), 'dark' and 'light' Jews (suffering and success, to be reversed), and other such mechanisms. The elder brother discovers in his corruption that all is 'muddle' until one is 'broken and made simple by a knowledge of mortality', until one recognises his 'evil is a sort of machinery' to be replaced by suffering 'acceptance of death that alters the soul. That *is* God'. Or, as the young brother discovers, all is muddle until one transcends the puritanic in the romantic fate of taking the mothering nurse, the Mediterranean dark lady of passion *(la belle dame sans merci)*, the 'Italian girl' of tabooed erotic dreams. Though clever and suggestive in its play with love and death, the fiction's style as well as form slide into the murkily portentous, and the Gothic game-playing produces the satiated sense of intellectual exercise.

The labyrinth of reflexive artistic will often turns the profound into the parodistic. *The Time of the Angels* (1966) Gothicises several important existential ideas. One is represented by a muddled philosophical headmaster doing a book, *Morality in a World Without God* – he, apparently like Murdoch, is a 'Christian fellow-traveller' – in a 'demythologising of morals' to rescue Good from both theological metaphor and crude atheistic denial of moral decency. But he collapses into the larger indecency of substituting a self-indulgent 'love' for morality. That 'revelation' partly came by way of a misunderstood blow from his brother, an Episcopalian Rector who has become a 'priest of no God' and holds that the atheism of 'all is permitted' is not enough. This down-converted religious attempts to go further: 'Suppose the truth were awful, suppose it was just a black pit, or like birds huddled in the dust in a dark cupboard?' (I find this less effective than its probable source, Stavrogin's eternity as an outhouse full of spiders.) 'The death of God has set the angels free', but they are awful angels since there 'is only power and marvel of power, there is only chance and the terror of chance'. So, in his Gothic rectory and weirdly reclusive ménage, the priest pursues evil, meanly rejecting one daughter and copulating with another (product of his revenge-seduction of his brother's wife), having previously driven his wife and brother mad, and trapping his would-be saint of a black housekeeper in a religious-sexual slavery, while morbidly musing on Heideggerean ontological meaninglessness. But Murdoch rather shoddily mocks this 'machine' of malevolence by also reducing him to an arrogantly playful adolescent immersed in saccharine Tchaikovsky. Fearing exposure, the Rector commits suicide, abetted by his rejected daughter who has learned 'the utter and complete absence of God' and life as a crippling trap. Murdoch's deployment of the existential ideas, then, emerges both serious and farcical, aware but overloaded with mystification of the diabolist, much rather digressive satire of only slightly related eccentrics, and inappropriately tricky shock effects.

But when the sense of outrageous incongruity shows comic discipline, the extremity becomes delightful. Comedy, after all, was her starting place as a novelist. The Gothic, I suspect, was partly a series of artistic wagers for superseding the comic with a darker moral view. During an elite-academic career (Oxford), Murdoch published a scattering of quasi-Platonic essays (some collected later in *The Sovereignty of Good*, 1970) and a book on the early writings of Jean-Paul Sartre (*Sartre: Romantic Rationalist*, 1953). That critical literary argument concluded with the aesthetic moral that Sartre's Hegelian ideological abstraction failed to recognise that 'the human person is precious and unique'. For Murdoch, it later becomes clear, such recognition points to eccentrics and to love.

Her first novel, about eccentrics and love, *Under the Net* (1954), was a polite picaresque (an example from that time of the more lively impolite picaresque might be J. P. Donleavy's *The Ginger Man*). It centred on the maturation of a supposedly unique London bohemian writer who moves from translating the French and philosophical dialogues (loose analogue to the author and echoing of Sartrean motifs) toward becoming a richly responsive novelist accepting the strange muddle of himself and the world. The magic later to be over-exploited in Gothicism appeared in the never resolvable 'guises of love', in absurdist masquerading, and in a grotesque 'enchanter' figure, obsessively recurrent in her fictions. Usually, the enchanter appears as a rich wiseman serving as ambiguous catalyst for the sense of 'destiny' of others. This seems to be Murdoch's left-handed image of the need for God. In her second novel *Flight from the Enchanter* (1956), a more expansive but sadder and less certain comedy of confused identities, the ambiguous play around the *deus ex machina* expands to the witty eccentrics, amoral refugees, diabolical manipulators, yearning women, learned recluses, precociously dangerous adolescents, pathetic outcasts, and muddled male intellectuals who will provide the cast of much of her fictional world. Love also displays considerable perversity, more cerebral than sensual.

Murdoch's third novel, *The Sandcastle* (1957), confined comedy closer to wryly sensitive conventional realism than any of her other nineteen novels (to 1980). It centres around the defeat by conventionality, personified by a wilful wife, of an intellectual schoolmaster in the provinces who fails in his summer 'sandcastle' demi-romance with an alien artist because a 'lifetime of conformity was too much . . . his whole previous life contained him like a straitjacket'. Also approximately within the realistic modes was her fourth novel, *The Bell* (1958), though rather contrived and thin on character genesis, perhaps because of the author's tone of superiority. This takes a ragged group in a lay religious community – a middle-aged, upper-class, would-be religious trapped in homosexual guilts; a suicidal would-be nun; an impulsive bohemian would-be artist; etc. – who collectively toll human confusion and the difficulty of religious life in the contemporary world, an insistently recurring theme.

It is not, I think, until Murdoch's fifth novel, *A Severed Head* (1961), that the concern with upper-middle class manners, a tough realism about unique character, the religious sense as part of moral transcendence, and the witty play with the bizarre come together in full comic provocation. The narrative intensely confines itself to the point of view of her usual befuddled and self-deceived intellectual fortyish male, a London wine merchant and amateur military historian, Martin Lynch-Gibbon, caught in the games of 'civilised adultery'. In spite of ironic treatment, Martin seems the first of Murdoch's protagonists significantly growing in awareness and erotic power.

A Severed Head deploys drawing-room comedy – the seduction games, the clever repartee, the upper-middle class types, the urbane detailing − plus sophisticated Freudian casuistry. Yet the more central sources may be the witty perceptions of eroticism-as-war in the brilliant eighteenth-century *Les Liasons Dangereuses*, to which this is a worthy successor, and D. H. Lawrence's images of passion as the confrontation of aliens who acknowledge 'the dark gods'. But the gods work oddly. Martin's dear American psychoanalyst friend, Anderson, conquers complacently married Martin's Bloomsbury-elegant wife, Antonia, who has also been carrying on an affair with Martin's charming amoral artist brother, Alexander, who seduces Martin's young and desperate donnish mistress, Georgie, who finally runs off to America with her therapist, Anderson, who leaves friend Martin to replace him in his incestuous affair with his half-sister, Honor, after Martin ironically dumps his unfaithful wife on his unfaithful brother − not to mention underlying erotic threesomes and foursomes. It's a bit much, but hilariously so, with well-timed reversals and credible motivations for the erotic musical chairs. The deceptions, doubled and reversed, not only come out of adulterous yearnings/revenges but out of insights about wives as maternal surrogates (and thus their lovers as admired substitute fathers for the cuckolded), about siblings as lover-rivals (and thus their endless replacement of each other), about heterosexual seductions as homosexual substitutions (and thus the delight in being deceived), and even about actual incest as surrogate for symbolic incest! It will not do, of course, to take these Freudian patterns literally. Psychoanalysis in Murdoch's hands exposes its glibly closed postulates as infinite regresses. That which can 'liberate' can, by exactly the same logic, enslave (and which is which?). The most compulsive neurotic seducer is the analyst (his disease his trade). And the will to discover ambivalent motivations may defeat the will to be motivated (to be one's self). But Murdoch does not counter with the old moral will since right-and-wrong also too easily reverse. Instead we have the transcendent fusion of desire and moral identity. The action does tend to confirm Anderson's dictum: 'On the whole "do what you want" costs others less than "do what you ought"'.

To break through the 'sheer weight of mess and muddle' bearing Martin down requires a new force. Says anthropologist Honor Klein, 'Being a Christian you connect spirit with love', but others more wisely connect it 'with power'. And that comes by way of the otherness represented by 'the dark gods'. (Less definable, they are not morally objectionable, unlike the Christian God responsible

for this cruel world.) The dark-visaged, darkly alien Jewish Honor,
an allegorical character, connects with the dark gods and promises
new erotic possibility and its new identity. Suddenly recognising,
after initial rage, his dark passion for the awesome and tabooed
Honor, Martin sees commonplace objects in 'a strange sudden
glory, such as is said to invest the meanest object in the eyes of
those who claim to experience the proof of the existence of
God *e contingentia mundi*', Murdoch follows the transforming
moment, naturally, with irony, Martin's next rumination: 'Like
one of Köhler's apes, my cluttered mind attempted to connect . . .' But we are to see the God/ape irony paradoxically
dissolving in the gestalt of a new passionate purpose.

What also follows for Martin is a denuding of the old self — the
loss of wife, brother, mistress, best friend, even beloved *objets
d'art*, and his past ordered world: 'The talent for a gentler world
. . . had now died in me. It had been at best no saintly talent;
merely a quieter mode of selfishness'. The transcending selfishness, the openness to an extreme passion, becomes a love not easily
bound by society and personality, something almost monstrous.
Thus Murdoch played with images of the primitive 'severed head',
the Medusa, passion's masks, and other devices of 'strange knowledge', along with the symbolic incestuousness that 'procreated
monsters' and the love-hate rages. The Scots-English businessman-
historian's impersonal passion for the bizarre Jewish anthropologist will serve, in the confined British upper-middle class
milieu, for the neo-Kierkegaardean leap into an unknown faith.
'This', Honor at the end coolly assures Martin (alone together in
his new home), 'has nothing to do with happiness, nothing whatever.' It is the disturbing and sundering chance of going for a new
destiny.

In spite of all the mockery, then — or rather, into and beyond
the irony — this is a romantic tale by an anti-romanticist. Passion
becomes erotic combat for a new being, power, of the self. No
doubt it remains equivocal since the free-flowing ironies can
hardly be turned off, including the labyrinthine ones of seduction-
adultery-homoeroticism-incest out of which the passion came.
Resting on violation, it includes recognitions that 'freedom'
consists of 'betrayals', virtue of more ambitious vices, fuller
humanity of a 'centaur' half-bestially prepared, as Martin may be,
to half-kick his way out of the moral order. But as Honor declares
in her savage-intellectual way, 'you cannot have truth and

what you call civilisation'. Surely such passion remains problematical — and rather uncertain for the given character of Martin. In part, the fiction remains problematic, too, with the twisting of comic conventions into philosophic revelations, the sometimes portentous tone ('my whole being is prostrate before you'), and the sometimes forced metaphors (such as the Jewish don as the dark lady, an intellectually primitivised Rebecca in a parochial philoSemitic mythicising). Murdoch's intellectuality here achieves more than superior wit and a well-made form; the muddled middle-aged intellectual male comes out almost heroic, his greying head almost severed from his too-confined world.

After the highly disciplined romantic absurdism of *A Severed Head* — never fully repeated in her other novels — Murdoch appears to have artistically wagered on fusing the irrational with the class and consciousness confines of her English order by the machinery of Gothic fiction (above), by her one attempt at a non-English milieu in an Irish historical novel around the Easter events, *The Red and the Green* (1965; probably her weakest as well as least characteristic fiction, which I will ignore), and by trying yet another reversed direction in *An Unofficial Rose* (1962) — back to the nineteenth century. This family drama, almost a generational saga, centres on a mid-sixtyish retired Civil Servant, recently widowed, Hugh, and his touching search for a renewed romance. Also sharply present: his self-pitying, and therefore self-indulgent, middle-aged romantic-cad son, his nearly saint-in-everyday-life daughter-in-law, his ruthless adolescent granddaughter, and other comic-sad relations. Hugh sells his family heirloom, a small sensuous Tintoretto — traditional art works take a crucial metaphoric role in many Murdoch fictions in an affirmation of past transcendence — in order to finance his son's abandonment of his rose-nursery and family for a romantic escapade. In the usual convoluted plot, Hugh's partly selfish motive is to regain the witchy mistress he had renounced a generation earlier for family convention. Fortunately, we are led to see, Hugh fails in his romanticism but is rewarded for his decent heroics by a genial affair with a neighbour. Murdoch again dramatises erotic twistings, the 'fantasies' and 'duplicities' that 'reside in the bosoms of quite ordinary people', and a full-scale unfolding (as in the early *The Sandcastle*) of the strength of traditional conventions (including convention-flouting) with a too-gentlemanly army officer, a sacrificing country-religious wife, etc.

But in spite of the modern candour and erotic play, much of the manner, as well as the house furnishings so lovingly described, seem antique. It is a parochial game with the faded literary roses of nineteenth-century love and duty, pretty nostgalgia and narrow moral order.

The old-fashioned moral fiction with an expansive cast is repeated by Murdoch. *The Nice and the Good* (1968) provides perhaps the most earnest version, not least in tying everything up, including half a dozen pairings, some rather improbable. That push toward equilibrium, with plotting as the moral machinery in a closed form, unfolds some lessons in 'loving what is good'. Romance subordinates to humble bourgeois virtue, and intellect to a manner frequently as ponderous as George Eliot's. 'No love is entirely without worth, even when the frivolous calls to the frivolous and the base to the base. But it is in the nature of love to discern good, and the best love is in some part at any rate a love of what is good.'

That complacent conclusion comes self-justifyingly to John Ducane as he takes to marriage the goodly mothering widow Mary, less as an erotic field than as 'a permanent moral background'. Mary, a repeated Murdochean stock figure of virtue, the good homemaker, believes that the way out of moral 'jumble' is that 'you just think about the decision and not about yourself' and thus allow the self-evident moral 'machinery' to work. John, a wealthy middle-aged barrister with a Scottish conscience, provides the more central case of niceness reaching towards goodness. Though 'a man who needed to think well of himself', he guiltily muddles into ambiguous flirtations while also dragging on a tormenting affair with a dependent bohemian (the also recurrent demi-artist female without a 'moral sense' in the promiscuous code of contemporary 'youth', treated by Murdoch with an intellectual's contempt). John's muddles supposedly dissolve by his letting his petty indiscretions be revealed, by the anguished charity of ordaining conventional morality for others, and by a revelation when he goes to save Mary's love-distraught adolescent son who has let himself get suicidally trapped in a sea cave. At the point of near death (like the scene in *The Unicorn* discussed above), John judges himself as 'a busy little scurrying rat seeking out its own advantages and comforts. To live easily, to have cosy familiar pleasures, to be well thought of.' But up against mortality, one realises that ratty niceness is not enough. 'Nothing is worth doing except to kill the little rat [of self], not to judge, not to be superior, not to exercise power, not to seek, seek, seek. To love and reconcile and to forgive, only this matters. All power is sin and all law is frailty. Love is the only justice.' Moral dialectics, then, dissolve into a vague secularised Christian *caritas* – the centre of the higher muddle.

Granted, thoughtful Murdoch suggests several other dimensions to this piety, including 'the other face of love, its blank face'. But she finesses around them. When John and her son are feared dead, already bitterly widowed Mary discovers that while there 'is only one absolute imperative, the imperative to love', when put up against mortality 'it must be love of death and change'. But in her giving this revelation to a conventionally good woman, we get less a heroic *amor fati* than the pathos of the balancing reassertion of everyday niceness. The novel variously, and rather heavily, under-scores such moralisms. For example, a guilt-wracked Jewish refugee-scholar explains happy virtue as the 'ordinary everyday mode of consciousness . . . busy and lively and unconcerned with self. To be damned is . . . unremitting agonising preoccupation with self.'

John provides the larger application in completing his assigned criminal investigation which, in the usual ornate plotting, also serves the reverse pursuit of his own moral style. In contrast to the pettiness and tawdriness of wilful evil, 'The great evil, the dreaded evil, that which made war and slavery and all man's inhumanity to man lay in the cold self-justifying selfishness of quite ordinary people, such as . . . himself'. No doubt such sermonic moments seem decorously enlightening in moralistic earnestness, even a touch improving in the otherwise not much questioned traditional order in all its immorality. John's good marriage to Mary – the tone does at times descend into gross sentimentality – will be very nice, indeed.

The 'dark gods' of *A Severed Head* and the dark irrationalities Murdoch played with in her Gothic fictions have, in this moralistic sunniness, shrunk to distant part-time images. Says a submissive woman in *The Nice and the Good*, on the way to re-marrying her brutal and deceitful husband, one must accept 'the deep dark logical injustices of forces which govern us at our most extreme moments and which, though they have nothing to do with morality, must sometimes be recognised in all our lives like gods'. How sane and humble on the way to seeing that 'loving matters most', how utterly nice!

John Ducane in *The Nice and the Good* displays Murdoch's fictional wager on an old-style positive protagonist, affirmatively seen from the dull inside as an upper-class representative of traditional moral decency. Elsewhere in this expansive novel appear some lovely bits of Murdochean irony, such as an elderly refugee unexpectedly copulating with his friend John's ex-mistress on John's bed and explaining to her, 'This is sacrilege . . . A very important human activity'. And Murdoch plays her perceptive wit on some variety of everyday erotic criss-crosses and other emotional perversities, from aged wisemen through cruel adolescents even unto cats and dogs. But she tries to treat her central John without much of the irony he deserves, sympathising with his petty moral muddles and resolving them in the higher muddle of niceness-cum-love. The results include happy John and Mary on their way in his Bentley, a concluding scene of laughing children, and a skillful sentimental moralistic fiction. Could it be in repentant reversal of devastating intelligence?

Niceness only partly wins out in Murdoch's later wager on the old familial order, *Henry and Cato* (1976), because she includes in her double-plot her dominant later theme of obsessional guilt, which in this case envelopes Cato, a convert Catholic priest (focus of some intriguing theology), who behaves in an ugly and cowardly way and kills someone he loves and so ends a remorsefully yearning atheist. But the parallel story of moral sentimentality takes a thirtyish second-son of landed gentry, Henry, a second-rater of muddle (and a second-class at Oxford) who has committed the extreme vulgarism of becoming an American college professor (and part of a cute *ménage à trois*). He unexpectedly inherits and returns to England for a siege of one-upmanship with his ruthless matriarch, affiancing his late-brother's supposed tart and selling-off the family estate, which, of course, undergoes the usual witty Murdochean reversals. Though not quite persuasive as the rebel-son (perhaps because the needed childhood scenes are missing), this up-dated squire shows touchingly earnest yearnings ('We lesser folk just sponge on the God that holy men invent'). He ends up properly rich (for a while he planned to give his wealth away), properly married (to a good virginal neighbour, quickly pregnant), properly decent (for part of his estate goes for low-income planned housing), and thus conventionally 'doomed to be a happy man'. Though not without its ironies, the fiction holds that the nice upper-class values continue to work in some facsimile of contentment, and control. But what moral alternative is there? As the highly contrived paralleling religious plot demonstrates, few show capacity for relevant belief and suffering. 'Morality', the shattered priest discovers, 'is nothing but self-esteem . . . simply affectations of virtue and spiritual charm'. That gone in crisis, there is only the 'fury of unbridled egoism'. How much better, then, the fideistic author dramatically argues, to affirm moral muddle, the conventionally happy and sunny world.

Yet a similar morality applies to the less sunny (indeed, quite rainy even unto a flood) *Bruno's Dream* (1969), which strongly shows Murdoch's increasing novelistic turn towards morbidity and bleakness. The pathetically solipsistic centring figure of the darkened comedy, Bruno, is an almost-ninety, dying invalid surrounded by his valuable stamp collection (a materialism lost in the flood), his scholarly concern with spiders (a life-long hobby), his unloving poet son and his loving business-successor son-in-law (and their quasi-saintly women), his bizarre servants and his commonplace ancient sexual remorse ('selective guilt'), and his pervasive self-pity in a London world spun by a 'spider god'. Here turns less the existential death-of-God than the melancholy 'God is death'. Life is a dream of 'mislaid' happiness. As usual in Murdoch, the fiction deploys some perspicacious erotic paradoxes (including a low-keyed repeat of the Martin-Honor passion of *A Severed Head*), some speculative play with metaphors from an enchanter-god (though more appropriately peripheral in the guise of a harlequin-saint gay servant), and some witty reversals. Even so, the mortal pathos and religionised moralisms take control of the fable. One saintly woman advises Bruno: 'Leave your self. It's just an agitating puppet . . . think about anything that's good.' At the end Bruno slowly learns that he 'had made a muddle of everything by not loving unselfishly and enough'. By then the saintly sister has ironically gone over, and to bed, to the *homme moyen sensual* son-in-law, but the conventional homemaker daughter-in-law, transformed in her devotion to the dying man, saintishly concludes the book: 'Yet love still existed and it was the only thing that existed'. This pushed Murdochean bet on moral salvaging insists on the ancient illogic by which love answers death, and all else.

In another of her more expansive later novels, *A Fairly Honorable Defeat* (1970), a somewhat less sentimental intelligence again works out the exposure of obvious male self-deception. Here appears a much less forced claim on the love-ethic; indeed, one of the more objective characters reasonably enough summarises: 'Almost all human love is bloody selfish'. But a partial exception appears in Murdoch's least skittish approach to a modern saint-liness with Tallis Browne, though there is some of her condescension to a figure of lower-class origins. This middle-aged marginal man's goodness combines with nearly pure muddle, except in moral decency. An impoverished teacher of working-class adults, a pacifist and earnest social reformer, he genuinely and unjudgmentally tries to help everyone. And he suffers everyone – his patronising better-class friends, his impoverished neighbours, his misanthropic father dying of cancer, his hysterically unfaithful wife. A man anguished with his own weakness as well as the suffering of others, further burdened with strange guilty visions, Tallis exhaustedly lives in mucky squalor, his life 'just a mess', a holy figure of muddle in Murdoch's almost-caricature of honourable moral defeat.

In the 'refined and lofty muddle' of his errant wife, Morgan, we may see a parody of romantic morality; she spouts, says an ex-lover, 'about freedom and love and about loving without bonds or convention like a noble savage'. This selfishly indulgent mannish woman has intellectual pretensions; engaged in the psuedo-science of fashionable modern linguistics, she ends as an academic in California (one of Murdoch's most hostile slashes). She cheats husband Tallis of money as well as hope, her sister of her husband's affections, her brother-in-law of his self-respect, her nephew of honest eroticism as well as concern – all from nicely exalted motives such as 'freedom'.

Her brother-in-law, Rupert, upper-civil servant and would-be moral philosopher who lives in a complacent marriage of hedonistic altruism, presents yet again the pathetically self-deceived intellectual. Like Murdoch, he has a 'deep age-old confidence in the power of goodness', though he 'disapproved of belief in God', and has spent years writing a conventional defence of the Good. His son, believing he has discovered his father in an adulterous affair with his beloved Aunt, willfully destroys the manuscript. Exposed in his confused duplicity, Rupert is rejected by righteous, sweet wife, disturbed son, selfish lover, and in his own shattered vanity, dies in a suicidal accident. Essentially, his moral pretensions killed him.

Murdoch presents her self-deluding moral muddlers with considerable descriptive sensitivity. With more persuasive sympathy,

she explores the insecure relations of a devoted homosexual pair —
often a deftly treated subject — who end as the only enduring
lovers in the story. Less effective, yet again, is her *deus ex
machina*, Julius King (née Kahn, a sort of spiritual Ghengis
Kahn), her recurrent charismatic 'enchanter', a wealthy Jew who
spent the war in Belsen and has become a cultivated *flaneur*, an
amoral scientist working on germ warfare projects, and a cynical
diabolist. Full of intellectual scorn — in protective modesty,
Murdoch's strongest arguments often come from perverse figures
— he mocks Morgan's pseudo-scientific linguistics, savages
Rupert's Kantian philosophy of the Good ('the top of the structure
is completely empty'; 'the metaphysical search is always the sign of
neurosis'; hardly anyone could be 'really gentle and selfless'), and
he tries puncturing almost everyone's affection and decency.
Dramatically, the saintly Tallis serves as a partial, however messily
ineffective, refutation of the satanic King. But, in common
Murdochean over-kill, the cynical enchanter comes out easily self-
refuted, yet another pretentiously self-deceived aging intellectual
male, since he believes himself an 'instrument of justice' when he is
mostly an opportunistic and self-indulgent con-man obtuse about
his victims and unable to acknowledge his effects and motives.
Presented externally as an allegorical figure, King carries a burden
of nineteenth-century gentlemanly satanism which undercuts the
moral dialectics as well as the social verisimilitude. While King's
bemused attempts to disprove love by damaging the homosexual
relationship show some psychological aptness (including his own
sadistic sexuality), the elaborate plotting for undermining Rupert,
his wife and Morgan requires purloined letters, forgeries, ornate
lies and strange coincidences; it becomes farcical. True, the
elaborate tricking of the good Rupert and the romantic Morgan
depends on their high-falutin vanity; each, convinced of his/her
morally free superiority, can generously do wrong while thinking
of self as 'innocent' and even good. Says King shrewdly, 'mix up
pity and vanity and novelty in an emotional person and you at once
produce something very much like being in love'.

Still, much seems forced, even Tallis' not-quite-in-time intervention on the side of decency. With the reversals, too, the tone
goes smugly wrong, as, after the debacle, King pleasantly enjoys
Paris, in a restaurant recommended by the now dead Rupert, and
concludes that 'Life was good'. It is essentially a moralist's cheap
shot. What went wrong with this frequently perceptive but, as so

often, too glibly tricky novel? Perhaps the fictionally defeating manipulation expresses an intellectuality not really wanting to admit the power of the cynical arguments which it must, for decency's sake, parodistically reduce rather than confront. Also, undeceived goodness has all too intelligently been reduced to pathetic messiness. Murdoch may be altogether too astute, too superior to mere characters and ideas, to allow seriousness free reign in meeting the comic-horrible dilemmas of her vestigially moral world — an artistic egoism.

Most of the Murdoch novels of the seventies could be viewed as variations around one issue: aging male intellectual egoism. Her muddled egoists become more obsessional, her novelistic tone often more grim, her moral dialectics sometimes over-insistent, claustrophobic. The last, and I suspect least interesting, is also the longest of her novels (over five-hundred pages), yet it is narrow in scope: *The Sea, The Sea* (1978). The endless confession of a sixtyish successful theatrical director at sea in his sea-side retirement, it raises various monsters of contradictory eroticism, a 'sea serpent of jealousy', a mad obsession with the frowsy housewife who was his rejecting 'first love', and a mixed flood tide of regrets, vanities, fears, mystical yearnings, and compulsions. Though sinking in aged disillusions at his semi-reclusive end, there is little escape from his, and Murdoch's, obsessional preoccupations.

Of more interest may be several of the related earlier studies, such as *An Accidental Man* (1971), which I think is one of her better novels. Not without some of her usual wit — including several new formal devices, set-pieces, such as elliptical party conversations, and epistolary sections (in eighteenth-century vein, she loves to use letters wryly), which expand the actions to off-stage characters — the dominant mood of *An Accidental Man* is melancholy. Several suicides fail, as do other moral choices. Curiously, the decisive actions come from a young American historian, Ludwig. He struggles through, giving up an Oxford fellowship and his plans to marry a wealthy English girl, choosing to return to the States as a non-religious Conscientious Objector to the American-Vietnam War ('absolute wickedness') and probable imprisonment. Though I detect some false notes in the responses of this supposed American, Murdoch suggestively plays the issue, one of her very few political-moral concerns. Ludwig shows moral failure in his submission to the obtusely self-centred girl, in his thinking too well of English society and Oxford, and in his failure to respond to a suicidal woman who needs his concern, yet we see the fine seriousness of his 'undoctrinated need to bear witness'. Not just moral anger at political viciousness, it also serves impersonal 'accidental' self-definition, a true ethical action: 'This is how the world is, so this is what a man must do'. The link between the two assertions, the moral oughtness, remains partly obscure but none-theless real, as does his possibly heroic role as 'a solitary con-scientious American'.

But little other heroism appears in *An Accidental Man*, with most of the characters trapped in messy contingencies. Even Murdoch's enchanter here, a somewhat cynical retired diplomat with Buddhist yearnings, is treated with bitter-sweet realism — for a wise change. Too worldly, Matthew has been rejected as contem-plative; too unworldly, he never quite adequately responds to his muddled mistress, desperate sister-in-law, suicidal old friend, or to the vengeful brother who messes up his life and even gratuitously destroys all his fine rare Chinese porcelain. Matthew finally recognises that his meddling in other people's lives comes from ambiguous sexual-religious drives and that he is morally 'mediocre'. Unlike other enchanters, he understands the limits of understanding, the 'dark which lies beyond the lighted area of our intentions'. As disenchanted moralists, however, Matthew and Murdoch are not beyond affectionate choices; Matthew surpris-ingly goes to America with Ludwig to help in his brave resistance — an enchanter finally well-employed.

But the focus of the novel is on the entitling 'accidental man', Austin Grey, horrendously 'accident prone', who vampirishly plays variations on 'the role of victim'. A middle-aged educated failure in jobs and relationships, he anxiously lives in his self-pitying fantasies and, unlike his brother Matthew, believes in 'imagination', for which he makes others pay real prices. In American parlance, he's 'a real loser' of the exploitative sort. His mischances and 'accidents' become his advantages as he lives 'simply by egotism' and 'never seemed to doubt his own self-importance'. Dramatising his miseries, charming in his pitifulness, he attracts good women whom he exploits. Even when they recognise him — 'Austin's handsome, cunning face, radiant with complicity' in guilt and weakness — they take him in. After all, it is bad luck, it was an accident, he couldn't help it. Poor Austin kills a child in a drunken car accident, robs and brutalises his mistress in blubbering fears, in cowardly rage permanently cripples someone else, and messes up the lives of a good many others. He may have murdered his first wife, in a jealous fit worked-up in imagination against his brother, though he much 'loved' her; he certainly has some responsibility for his 'beloved' second wife − a schizophrenic he married to sentimentally tyrannise (and then to partly abandon) − in her suicidal accident. Murdoch gives a devastating portrait of an ultimate muddler, carefully placed in the insularly aggrandising society to which he belongs, a man with little possibility of awareness or change, even by accident. That's the moral truth.

In her most mature work, then, Murdoch's evil is not Gothic horror but self-deluded egoism become a fated mechanism. *The Sacred and Profane Love Machine* (1974) exposes another egoist muddler. Blaize Gavender, middle-aged psychoanalytic therapist, appears complacently married to his Oedipally 'sacred' Harriet, older and 'so kind and good' (and wealthy upper-class), but for nine years has had a second family with his profane Emily, young and sluttish (and resentful lower-class), who not only satisfies his sexual peculiarities (never clear) but his essential vulgarity. He creates grotesque love machinery, first of a double-domestic duplicity, then of an absurd complicity dependent on his wife's forgiveness and generosity, and finally of an exploitative and self-rationalising lubricity. In response to his wife's 'mercy', 'I am unworthy, he said to himself, blinking and grinning at the wonder of it all', but while he saw the 'black balloon of grief and possible catastrophe', he 'tapped it away' with the insouciance of the self-indulgent egotist whose getting away with something convinces him to feel really 'innocent'. Through a series of the usual Murdochean reversals in which Blaize smugly 'redistributed the pain', he even sees himself (in a parody of ethical utilitarianism) as making several women 'happy', which is 'surely a good thing'.

While Murdoch deploys some of her usual erotic and philosophic wit − especially with her gallery of the writer-enchanter, a mythic sex-witch, a passive scholar would-be lover, and several outrageous adolescents − the main love machine grinds compulsively on. Blaize ends up partly crippled; his distraught fleeing wife dies absurdly, shot by terrorists while saving his bastard son (who becomes psychotic); his other son becomes totally alienated; a desperate patient dies (others, of course, improve without him); his mistress-become-wife, helped by the money from the first, ends lardy-dardy happy. The muddling psychiatrist has kindly let the good sacrifice themselves so he could become 'even more self-indulgent' in distributing pain and blame until 'he felt in himself a sort of achieved moral mediocrity, a resignation to being unambitious and selfish and failed which gave him a secret wry delight'. There is, then, not so much evil as anti-goodness. Taking his horrendous muddles as 'fated', Blaize can even righteously conclude, 'I don't have to think too badly of myself'. And for that obtuseness, there can be no reversal in this moral novelist's savaging of unsaving grace.

Murdoch employs here, and elsewhere as I have been noting, oddly insistent metaphors of the 'machine' of false-goodness, for an ethical voluntarist a surprising determinism which allows only very limited moral possibility. This seems to increase in the later novels. The automatisms of these fictions, hardly able to be overcome by love-goodness, deploy the traditional vices modernised into obsessions, such as moral complacency, self-pity, greedy lust and resentment. *A Word Child* (1975) expands the classical moralist's points that remorse is the most useless of passions and resentment the most destructive. Here the extreme case of self-centred 'pure obsession' appears in the guise of Hilary Burde, a burdened-with-guilt fortyish bastard reared in an orphanage, whose polyglot knack got him to and through Oxford. His fellowship there, and much else, ends when he kills, in a suicidal car 'accident', his adulterous love who had just rejected him for her upper-class husband, Hilary's Oxford mentor. Self-punishing for many years, he becomes in a hole-in-corner way a petty civil servant indulging his spleen in a pitifully rigid round of sado-masochistic humiliations with co-workers, an exploited mistress, and a dependent simple sister. While he has spent anguished hours for his 'crazed' love affair and catastrophe, it was 'a guilt which itself was a kind of sin', especially because it was fused with 'resentment and self-degradation'. But 'can sheer suffering redeem?' For Murdoch clearly not since goodness must go out of the solipsistic psyche into compassion for immediate others. Through endless rubbing of his one-sore reality, Hilary learns 'regret, remorse, that's the most selfish thing of all'. He decides that he has damaged others as well as himself 'out of sheer pique, out of the spiteful envious violence' of a bottom-dog history and its social-class resentments, perhaps, too, out of some of the 'ghastly revengeful sort of religion' of his Calvinistic early years, and surely out of the gruesome 'accidentalness' of the hopeless 'muddler'. Indebted to Dostoyevsky's 'underground man' – given an amusingly literal

application in Hilary's compulsively riding subways in circles —
Murdoch's is less metaphysically rebellious and profound because
it is confined to parochial concerns and some bland moral correct-
tion. English good sense defeatingly wins.

That is, of course, after some ingenious plotting to insist on the
obsessionality, a repetition of the earlier events: Hilary's mentor-
victim, now a top-dog civil servant remarried to a fancy lady, most
improbably comes back into linkage with him, adulterous
eroticism and all, ending again in the grotesque accidental death
of the woman. But this time Hilary goes beyond the self-
destructiveness of guilty despair (Murdoch *contra* many existen-
tialists) to recognise the new moral 'secret': 'Forgiving equals being
forgiven'. In dramatic confirmation, Hilary learns to spare others
— especially his loving sister Crystal, who refracts his virtue — by
no longer making his miseries their miseries. Of two suicides (the
schoolmaster who made him and his one intellectual friend), he
recognises they died of being 'unloved and uncared for', but rather
than stewing in 'remorse' for his complicity, he accepts 'solitude
and blankness'. He allows his sister to marry — on Christmas Eve,
yet — a doggy but actively decent man. Though the twice
aggrieved husband-mentor goes on to further successes (as do
others), our reformed protagonist forgoes the envy which gave rise
to the resentment which perpetuated the guilt. Taking a lowly
clerical job and returning to his submissive mistress, he appears to
accept the world as is, and to accept himself. The aging child of
the word has exhausted his underground obsessions. Yet the real
moral may be as grim as the wintry London scene and the
anguished tone: this intellectual middle-aged male muddler is —
to quote an aging failed writer from *Henry and Cato* — 'simply
one of those who have not and from whom will be taken away even
that which they have'.

This ancient moral apologetic may, in Murdoch's absurdist
contexts, be tasted as thin jelly on sour bread. In her involuted
fictions, it may also be seen as part of an absolute moral machine,
but one without deity. Yet whatever the reservations about
Murdoch's Pyrrhonistic morality, the intelligence of the art
remains. Thus there might be some metaphoric appropriateness
in concluding with several points from an earlier novel of
grotesque artistic obsession, *The Black Prince* (1973). This first-
person account of an aging novelist is complicated in a rather
Nabokovian manner (and there are other parallels to *Lolita*) by

two forewords and half a dozen postcripts by various characters. This, and infernally much other irony, does not allow the reader to simply take the novel's novelist as Murdoch (a romantic subjectivism of which she seems to sternly disapprove). But, of course, the recurrent figure of the mocked obsessive and failing writer also is Murdoch, and not least in the riddling solipsistic form here. Crucial concerns of the novelist within fit the novelist behind, such as the strange generalisation that 'All art deals with the absurd and aims at the simple'.

Absurdly, the fifty-eight-year-old Bradley Pearson, retired civil servant and rather precious aesthete of shopkeeper origins who has published several novels, becomes artistically and erotically obsessed. The primary object is Julian, the twenty-year-old daughter of his popularly successful protegé-competitor, the novelist Arnold Baffin. Playing with a murder-plot, Murdoch traps Bradley. The abused and jealous Rachael Baffin kills her husband and lets Bradley go to prison for it, where he writes this novel and dies. His fate confirms his view that 'human life is horrible' yet also a comedy ('God, if He existed, would laugh at his creation.').

Ambiguous art merges with sexual ambiguity. Dark Eros, which the novelist also dallies with as Shakespeare's Hamlet — the play implicitly read as a Murdochean dark comedy — includes the young girl in the role of the Black Prince to arouse the impotent old puritan. While Bradley's homoeroticism gets over-interpreted by a seedy psychoanalyst — a pathetic gay who insists that everyone else is gay — it does appear essential to his art as to his person, as with Shakespeare. More generally, art comes out as an ambiguous transcendence, both a grotesque heroism and an exalted perversion.

The complicated truth-telling which justifies the artistic eros and its manias yet turns about moral simplicities. Though perverse eros engendered his art, the old writer is rejected forever by the young girl when she learns that he has been dishonest and callous (he lied to her about his age and he deflowered her after learning of his sister's suicide). The muse was a callow moralist (appropriately, Julian ends as a morally evasive person and bad poet). But how can one justify any simple decency in an ugly and unjust world so fully characterised, as this one is, by too-mortal flesh, destructive marriage, wild obsession and endless muddle? The artist within can only salvage from it a belief in everyday

virtues by the paradoxical conclusion that 'all morality is ultimately mysticism'.

And the artist behind, a mystic as well. Further, Murdoch must
madly, though often with delightful wit, depend on *frissons* of
demonic complications, enchanter gods, outrageous reversals and
ceaseless ironies in order to claim intellectual truthfulness about
an absurd world. She is, then, in spite of longings for the
traditional and absolute, a very contemporary novelist of an
existential cast, however that be mocked. As another Murdoch
writer (the embittered mystic and detective fictionist in *The Secret
and Profane Love Machine*) explains: a writer's irony is self-
protective, a 'concealment' to hide one's true 'glee' in the
unacceptable. By such strategems within the old-fashioned forms,
Murdoch partly modernises traditional English fictions — the
novel of manners, the realistic comedy, the Gothic romance, the
family saga, the moral fable — with sophisticated disillusionments
and existential awareness.

Yet she wagers, as it were, that somewhere in the turnings of her
artful labyrinths and in the ironic interstices of her erotically
layered muddles, old fashioned morality, loving humanity, can be
found. By putting her moral agents (and ideal readers?) — mostly
obsessional middle-aged intellectuals — in unwinable games, she
bets they will desperately assert some facsimile of traditional
values. But more often than not, the games and the choices seem
acts of novelistic willfulness. Thus Murdoch's moral fictions must
be seen as an intellectual's gestures of bravado.

In the conflict of old moral simplicities and devastating absurdist intelligence, Murdoch can hardly take her self-deluded and
trapped moral agents, the class- and consciousness-bound English
males, quite seriously. The author cannot let them develop beyond
her patterned games, give them head as characters; they do not
have the freedom to find a different vision of themselves and
society. Consequently, readers may less remember her protagonists than her skillfully done scenes (especially London) and the
provocative experience of her relentlessly witty games. Sheer intelligence controls and mere mortal men are consumed in the
machine of the moralist's art.

The self-consuming fictional machine may be part of the price
of intellectual art, even of one dedicated to much of ancient forms
and virtues. But intriguingly, that game-playing seems to be how
the daring mind can find its way back to the traditional, how the

ironist achieves the intellectual catharsis which returns one to the conventional amidst wryly sad yearnings for a larger good. It would be hard to find such qualities, such sheer intelligence, of her best fictions — say, *A Severed Head* and *An Accidental Man* — in the work of any of her contemporaries. Murdoch's fictions often brilliantly fascinate though less often satisfy in wagering finally on fatal muddle as the *Ding-an-sich*.

NOTE

The date indicated parenthetically is the date of the first publication for each of the twenty-two Murdoch volumes. Page numbers are omitted, since the quotations are brief and are also from a variety of American as well as English editions.

3   Olivia Manning:
witness to history

Harry J. Mooney, Jr.

The ninth chapter of *The Great Fortune*, the first volume of *Olivia Manning's Balkan Trilogy*, begins:

> With late November came the *crivat*, a frost-hard wind that blew from Siberia straight into the open mouth of the Moldavian plain. Later it would bring the snow, but for the moment it was merely a threat and a discomfort that each day grew a little sharper.
>
> Fewer people appeared in the streets. Already there were those who faced the outdoor air only for as long as it took them to hurry between home and car. In the evening, in the early dark, there were only the workers hurrying to escape the cold. Taxis were much in demand. Run cheaply on cheap fuel from the oil fields that were only thirty miles distant, they charged little more than the buses of other capitals.
>
> At the end of November there came, too, a renewal of fear as Russia invaded Finland. Although his friends were inclined to hold him responsible for the Soviet defection, Guy's faith did not waver. He and Harriet heard the news one night at the Athenee Palace, where Clarence had taken them to dine. They found as they left the dining-room that the main room had been prepared for a reception. The chandeliers were fully lit, the tables banked with flowers and a red carpet had been unrolled throughout the hall.
>
> 'Germans', said Guy when he saw the first of the guests. The Germans and the British in Bucharest knew each other very well

by sight. This was Harriet's first real encounter with the enemy.
Guy and Clarence pointed out to her several important
members of the German Embassy, all in full evening dress,
among them Gerda Hoffman, a stocky woman whose straw-
coloured hair was bound like a scarf round her head. No one
knew what her true function was, but a whispering campaign
had given her the reputation of being the cleverest agent to
come out of Germany.[1]

I cite this passage at some length because I want to establish at the
outset of this essay something of Olivia Manning's distinctive
quality, and manner, as a novelist. Place is paramount in the
novels of *The Balkan Trilogy*; whether we are in the Bucharest of
the first two volumes or the Athens of the third, we understand the
experience of the characters to be altogether inseparable from the
two cities in which they find themselves. And these places come to
constitute, as we read, a time, a period, a history.

This is so primarily for two reasons. In the first place, Olivia
Manning knows her history so well that she can recreate it with
quiet control. Crucial to our reading of these novels is our developing sense that their atmosphere is something which we, like the
characters themselves, are constantly experiencing – until we are
in fact saturated in it. Secondly, the characters in the trilogy
witness as well as experience the history enclosing them. In the
above passage, for example, it is characteristic that the weather,
the 'frost-hard wind that blew from Siberia straight into the open
mouth of the Moldavian plain', is for a group of English men and
women and, surely, for their English author as well, unique. All
kinds of sharply defining, particularising details are, in Olivia
Manning's work, evocations of place, and therefore of a time in
history. The reason why a taxi, *here*, is almost as cheap as a bus is a
fine illustration of one part of her method.

But the November of 1939 is not merely November; it is, for
many of the characters in *The Great Fortune*, the occasion of a
new, historic fear; for some of them, because they are corrupt, it is
the occasion of no fear, but rather of impending alliance. For the
academic, buoyant, faithful Guy Pringle, it is the beginning of
what might be a long challenge to his left-progressive political
beliefs; for his wife Harriet it is her 'first real encounter with the
enemy', suddenly, boldly present in the group of Germans, and
especially so in the person of Gerda Hoffman, source of that

terrible 'whispering campaign'. Places and events unfold simultaneously because the characters of course experience them
simultaneously, scenes and occurrences dramatic with abnorm-
ality yet always threatening to become merely ordinary. Moreover,
they retain hidden and ominous qualities with which the
characters are forced to grapple. To make this last statement,
however, is to recognise the extent to which Harriet Pringle is the
novel's true and constant centre. Of Harriet's grapplings we are
certain: we know their nature because we know her mind so well.

To return specifically once more to the passage I have cited, we
discover in it two other important qualities fundamental to Olivia
Manning's work. The first is a kind of understatement which, to
an American at least, seems characteristically British. Historic
occasions are deliberately rendered in terms personal, casual, very
nearly unhistoric. (When, early in *The Great Fortune*, Harriet
speaks to Clarence Lawson of Stendhal, she perhaps provides a
clue to Olivia Manning's treatment of the historic; the author of
The Balkan Trilogy clearly understands the implications for the
development of the novel of the opening sections of *The Charterhouse of Parma*.) And the second is the special quality of auctorial
witness which Olivia Manning embodies in these novels. To the
laminating, accreting experience of the characters is added a reinforcing sense of the writer's own mind and eye. Though the
author never intrudes directly, and though her narrative presence
seems deliberately restrained, I often experience in reading her
work an odd, unsettling sense of George Orwell; she impresses me
as a writer whose experience as historical witness compels her to
creativity, though in a very different way from him. Her commitment is, after all, completely to the world of fiction, whereas such
an observation concerning Orwell would not begin to suggest the
nature of his achievement.

The Great Fortune commences by dramatising, in the assassina-
tion and funeral of Calinescu, some of the profound fissures in the
internal structure of Rumania, fissures ominous with meaning for
the near future: like the characters in the novel, we know from the
outset that we will apprehend a great deal in this strange country
sick with its own peculiar political disease. The novel closes with a
charade, a production, under Guy Pringle's direction, of Shakespeare's *Troilus and Cressida*, which, although it is filled with comic
irony, is surely not intended simply to comfort us. Meanwhile, Olivia

Manning analyses with great intelligence, partly by letting her characters become themselves and partly by maintaining our sense of a disengaged narrator who has the necessary overview to recreate for us the urgent history of the time, the multiple forces that are now converging on one vulnerable centre.

The Jews of Rumania are present in the solid, clannish, but wealthy and profiteering, Drucker family. One very careful chapter records Guy and Harriet's visit to them, Harriet's sense of their dramatic difference from the other Rumanians, and their own anxiety to secure exemption from service for the young boy, Sasha, should war come, as surely it must. Their conversation reveals a terrible awareness that, in leaving Germany for Rumania, they have only moved from one antisemitic social and political culture to the next. Now they exist, despite their money, precariously indeed, part of that vast force of Europe's people who are likely to be persecuted no matter what frontier they cross. The context in which their plight is treated provides a characteristic example of the way in which Olivia Manning, by understatement, arrives at complexity. Harriet hears the fears of the family expressed only after several of them have spoken in a manner in which Jews, just now at least, surely ought not to speak. She is listening to the banker, Drucker himself, and to his sisters and his brothers-in-law.

> Doamna Hassolel broke in aggressively. 'A banker', she said, 'upholds the existing order. He is an important man. He has the country behind him.'
>
> 'Supposing the order ceases to exist?' said Harriet. 'Supposing the Nazis come here?'
>
> 'They would not interfere with us', Flohr said with a swaggering air. 'It would not be in their interests to do so. They do not want a financial *débâcle*. Already, if it were not for us, Rumania would be on her knees.'
>
> Teitelbaum added somberly: 'We could a dozen times buy and sell this country'.
>
> Drucker, the only member of the family who seemed aware that these remarks were not carrying Harriet where they felt she should go, lifted a hand to check them, but as he did so his youngest sister broke in excitedly to urge the pace:
>
> 'We work, we save', she said, 'we bring here prosperity and yet they persecute us'. She leant across the table to fix Harriet with

her reddish brown eyes. 'In Germany my husband was a clever lawyer. He had a big office. He comes here — and he is forbidden to practice. Why? Because he is a Jew. He must first work for my brother. Why do they hate us? Even the *trasura* when angry with his horses will shout: "Go on, you Jew!" Why is it? Why is it so?'

This last query was followed by silence, intent and alert, as though, after some introductory circling over the area, one of the family had at last darted down upon the carcass of grievance that was the common meat of them all.

I cite this passage at some length because it seems to me important to emphasise how evenhanded Olivia Manning's characterisations are; they are the work of a novelist determined to tip no balance in order to achieve some point. *The Balkan Trilogy* therefore succeeds brilliantly in doing what all fine fiction should do, in creating the impression of a writer who always allows her characters the freedom to speak for themselves. Consequently, her Jewish characters in part betray themselves, and Harriet, herself a distinctive combination of judgement and compassion, is simultaneously dismayed by and fearful for them. Drucker's subsequent arrest, the dispersal of his family, and Harriet's own affecting relationship with the boy Sasha, whom, in *The Spoilt City*, the second volume of the trilogy, she hides out both in her apartment and on its roof, embodies both the history of a family and the moral challenge Sasha brings to Harriet. For Harriet herself must respond as best she can to what is perhaps at first merely surprising and mysterious to an Englishwoman suddenly living in Rumania, and yet soon turns out to be a dreadful, self-confirming reality. This dire Rumanian political and social sickness takes many forms: an antisemiticism long latent but now free to emerge actively; the corruption of the dispossessed and effete Rumanian aristocracy, attenuated now to its principal role as collective customer in the bar of the Athenee Palace Hotel; a government equally corrupt and, like the aristocrats, disasteful and ineffectual; a vast peasantry steadily neglected, on the one hand, and cynically exploited, on the other; and, in Bucharest, people of all classes long devoid of faith in any political institution and now dangerously adrift. In fact, what the first two volumes of the trilogy largely analyse are the complex (yet in the end clear) reasons why Rumania should emerge as the Germans' natural prey; here, at least, Hitler does not simply embody some uniquely German pathology. And, politically at least, these two novels have a second significant concern. Among their characters, only one excuse is ever offered for the Rumanian government's behaviour: its sponsorship, so to speak, by the British themselves. Towards the end of *The Great Fortune*, David Boyd, of the legation, is asked by Clarence Lawson, of the Propaganda Bureau, whether any change of official British policy might still be effective. His response carries weight, here and elsewhere in these novels, simply because he is the clearest, least compromised or deluded, of their political thinkers and talkers:

> 'Now, very little. We've left it too late.' David's argument was heated. 'But we need not play Germany's game for her.' Taking possession of the talk, David spoke with force and feeling. 'We support a hated dictatorship. We snub the peasant leaders. We condone the suppression of the extreme left and the imprison-ment of its leaders. We support some of the most ruthless exploitation of human beings to be found in Europe. We support the suppression of minorities – a suppression that must, inevitably, lead to a breakup of Greater Rumania as soon as opportunity arises.'

Unlike so many of the other voices in the trilogy, this one is authentic, compassionate, indignant in relation to larger causes. It is of course the voice of the traditional British left, and also, I feel fairly certain, that of the implied narrator of the novels.

With the rise of fascism in Germany and Italy, the impending dis-solution of Rumania, and the failure of British foresight and nerve, where are the possible reassurances, the sources of the dependable, in *The Balkan Trilogy*? Two such principles, of markedly different quality and meaning, emerge.

The first is comic, and eventually tragicomic, in a manner which is characteristic of one side of Olivia Manning's vision. It is embodied in the story of Yakimov, the penniless, cadging, alto-gether unscrupulous White Russian (was his overcoat *really* given to his father by the Czar?) whose adventures begin to interweave with those of Guy and Harriet in the second chapter of the first volume, and whose death, quite deliberately understated, occurs near the close of the third. Yakimov, occasionally charming and often desperate, is, when he insists upon the Pringles lodging him in their apartment, one of the trials which Guy imposes upon Harriet. This burden becomes especially clear when we consider it in relation to the apartment's other unexpected tenant, the young Sasha Drucker, in genuine danger after leaving the army and also of course a Jew, with whom Harriet forms what is probably the most satisfying relationship open to her in the course of the novels – until it too comes to its own ironic end under the direction of history. Yet, burden or not, it is finally appropriate that, in *Friends and Heroes*, the third volume of the trilogy, it should be Yakimov who provides Harriet, now forced to go on to Athens, with the comfort of the old and familiar discovered amidst the unexpected.

The second of these associating principles lies in the study of the Pringles' marriage, which, we are never in doubt, is central to all three novels in a manner which renders all other occurrences both peripheral and yet relevant to it. To begin with, the marriage is an illustration of the way in which political principles apparently of the most humane and enlightened kind do not always accord with important human relationships. Guy's convictions are convention-ally left, and they acquire a durability we view ironically when they are never seriously challenged, or even revised, by the Soviet behaviour of the period. Guy's principles constitute in fact a faith, a faith from which Harriet remains detached simply because she is immune to it. In Harriet, convictions arise from human relations, and especially from her relation to the husband she has married in England just before the opening of the novels and the onset of war. In Bucharest, Guy alarms her early on by staying out with Dudebat, an Englishman who has literally hitchhiked and walked his way from the collapse of Poland, and whose improvidence and spite have for Harriet a vaguely menacing quality, for she has begun to sense that, under the pressure of political crisis, nothing is quite what it seems, and also that perhaps in some persons only the worst will emerge. When Guy at last returns safely, Harriet exclaims, with utter sincerity, 'If the fifth columnists came for you, I'd murder them. *I'd murder them.*' But she has to contend with what she regards as Guy's 'faction', the group of persons, always it appears enlarging, who constitute his public and apparently his authentic life:

She reflected that he had asked Klein to try and discover what had happened to Sasha Drucker and because of this was meeting him with David at the Doi Trandafiri. He had never, as she felt inclined to do, let the matter drop. He was faithful to his friends, but (she told herself) indifferent to her. All these people — David, Klein, the Druckers, Dudebat and a host of others — were his faction: he bound them to himself. She had no one but her little red cat.

Yet her love for Guy causes her to warn Inchcape, the head of the overseas educational and cultural organisation, of her husband's contact with the mysterious Sheppy, quite likely a representative of MI5. When Inchcape in turn warns Sheppy away from his own men, the knowledge of his wife as the source of all this provokes Guy's first quarrel with Harriet.

It is therefore to another overseas Englishman, Clarence Lawson, who makes no secret of his attraction to her, that Harriet confesses what she is coming to feel Guy will never permit her to become; she would like to be simply 'what I am. The "I" that is obscured by my own feminine silliness.' When, however, Clarence speaks of his own early life, of his sadistic father and some more-than-usual horrors of his life at school, Harriet retreats from his indication of need, and retreats, quite naturally, to the comfortable solidity of Guy.

> She felt that by his confidence he [Clarence] had been making a claim on her. Involuntarily, she took a step away — not only from Clarence but from the unhappy past that overhung him. He had, she felt, been marked down by fear.
>
> He did not notice her movement. Still confiding, he said, 'I need a strong woman, someone who can be ruthlessly herself'.
>
> So Clarence believed her to be that sort of woman! She did not repudiate his belief but knew she was nothing like it. She was not strong, and she certainly felt no impulse to nurse a broken man. At the gate, she said she was meeting Guy at the Doi Trandafiri.

Yet even in her moment of withdrawal from Clarence and his view of her, she begins to see Guy as she will more and more frequently see him in the months to come: as at least in part an illusion.

> His size gave her an illusion of security — for it was, she was

coming to believe, no more than an illusion. He was one of those harbours that prove to be too shallow: there was no getting into it. For him, personal relationships were incidental. His fulfilment came from the outside world.

Later, though, when Clarence, speaking to Harriet, accuses Guy of squandering himself on the unworthy, Harriet, by the logic of her own temperament, her own developing sense of human relationships, now sees Clarence as a man who would wall her off in some totally private world. Furthermore, the contingent, even arbitrary, nature of human relationships during a period of crisis leading toward war, Olivia Manning quietly insists upon; at this same juncture in *The Great Fortune* she is writing, 'During this time there appeared in Bucharest an English teacher called Toby Lush who declared that all Bessarabia was in a ferment, the Russians being expected that very night'.

The Great Fortune closes with Harriet's yielding, by Guy's cunning design, in the matter of Yakimov's domicile, and in so doing recognising that Guy, 'seemingly reasonable and the most agreeable of men . . . always got his way'. Moreover, in the larger sense of the fourth and last section of the novel, Guy is shown in total command of a world both actual and metaphorical. For although his production of *Troilus and Cressida* ('The Fall of Troy', in the title of the novel's last section) both parallels and for a time obscures the reality of the fall of Paris, it constitutes its own reality; even Yakimov, the most antic of the novel's characters, has to agree to play Pandarus in lieu of the rent he cannot pay Guy for living quarters. (Following the production, Yakimov represents another side of Guy: he feels betrayed when Guy appears to have forgotten his contribution to the drama.) Guy reassigns Harriet's own role to Sophie, the young Rumanian woman of whom Harriet cannot help feeling suspicious if only because her husband once entertained the idea of marrying her, though only, he asserts, as a means of getting her safely out of the country; Harriet at first supposes that Guy might consider her own presence in the cast frustrating, a possible source of ridicule. Ultimately, however, she arrives at a more complicated view:

It was only later when everyone she knew was in it that she began to feel hurt at being out of the production. More than that, she was jealous that Guy should be producing Sophie in one of the chief parts of the play. Unreasonably, she told herself. She could no longer doubt that Guy had been perfectly honest about his relationship with Sophie. Innocent and foolish as he was, the idea of marriage to Sophie had been, nevertheless, attractive as an idea rather than as a reality. He was not, in fact, one to make a marriage of self-sacrifice. He was a great deal more self-protected − perhaps from reality − than most people realised. Realising it herself, she could only wonder at the complexity of the apparently simple creature she had married.

I examine in some detail Harriet's diverse and changing perceptions of her husband because they will bring me, a bit later, to what is for me, amidst all its strengths, the trilogy's only real weakness.

If *The Great Fortune* concludes in ambiguity, with the solace of Guy's production merging into the certainty that the fall of France is the prelude to the German rape of Rumania and therefore to the surrender of the national 'great fortune', *The Spoilt City*, the tautest and best of the three novels, opens in an atmosphere of unqualified menace. Against a background of Rumania's agreement to cede Bessarabia and Northern Bukovina to Germany, the Jewish economist Klein, until recently an advisor to Rumanian governments, analyses the way in which the trial of a prominent Jew like Drucker will provide the present government with a diversion to conceal from the people the reality of Bessarabia. Klein understands, on a deep empirical level, the way in which the earnest reactionary commitments of the government and many of the people will mean that Rumania will be cooperating with Germany in her own destruction, simply in the way in which natural forces having common purposes combine. Speaking to Harriet, he defines, by foresight, the terrible history of which *The Spoilt City* is in part the record. '"Ah, Doamna Preen-gul, was I not right? I said if you stayed here it would be interesting. More and more is it necessary to buy off the Germans with food. Believe me the day will come when this" − he touched the saucers of sheep-cheese and olives that came with the wine − "this will be a feast. You are watching a history, Doamna Preen-gul. Stay, and you will see a country die."' But Klein, acute diagnostician that he is, is far more than this: he is a Jew suddenly in hazard, and we are not surprised soon to learn that he has fled. Even when Olivia Manning's characters speak prophetically, they do so out of their own experience.

Dread. More than any other quality, this is the one that establishes the tone of Harriet's experiences in *The Spoilt City*. Unlike her husband, she has had from the beginning no anchor in political faith; Guy himself remembers her simple but challenging assertion, 'I cannot endure organised thought'. Harriet believes in the possibilities of personal relations, and in civility. These possibilities now emerge in her friendship with the fugitive Sasha, whom she and Guy have hidden away after he has deserted from the rapidly dissolving Rumanian army. Characteristically, she wonders whether her husband, 'fond of too many people', feels her own binding commitment to Sasha and his safety. And she now sees even in Yakimov an identity which demands her attention; restored to some bit of dignity by his role as Pandarus, he now feels abandoned by his director;

> The fact was, he had never grown up. She had thought once that Yakimov was a nebula which, under Guy's influence, had started to evolve. But Guy, having set him in motion, had abandoned him to nothingness, and now, like a child displaced by a newcomer, he scarcely knew what had happened to him.

Harriet's perceptions of Guy are just as level as her perceptions of the trap of political faith. She is nevertheless the embodiment of civilised hope, and the Bucharest of *The Spoilt City* rouses her to dread precisely because it represents the collapse of hope.

If I have suggested that it is Olivia Manning's method to write civilised comedy about the dismal end of a major period of our civilisation, two observations about the novelist's method are, I think, in order here. First, her comic sense in no ways prohibits her from arriving at a swift and devastating articulation of the awful. Here is Sasha Drucker, speaking to Harriet of the rapid triumph of antisemitism in the army from which he has just run away:

> We were on the train and he [Sasha's army friend, Marcovitch] went down the corridor and he didn't come back. I asked everyone, but they said they hadn't seen him. While we were waiting at Czernowitz — we stayed on the platform three days because there were no trains — they were saying a body had been found on the railway-line half-eaten by wolves. Then one of the men said to me: 'You heard what happened to your friend, Marcovitch? That was his body. You be careful, you're a Jew, too.'

And I knew they'd thrown him out of the train. I was afraid. It could happen to me. So in the night, when they were all asleep, I ran down the line and hid in a goods train. It took me to Bucharest.

Here, as elsewhere in *The Balkan Trilogy*, all experience is sharply particularised, individualised. General observations about anti-semitism or about anything else occur rarely. Moreover, the narrator of the novels is master of a broad range of experience and is on unblinkingly knowledgeable terms with evil. In the middle of *The Spoilt City*, in what I find the most shocking passage in the three novels, Yakimov appears in Hungarian-occupied Cluj, where he has gone on assignment, loosely speaking, for the English newsman, Galpin, who knows all too clearly the danger of the territory. But Yakimov has another reason for going to Cluj: to recapture his friendship with a man 'in an important post', the Nazi Gauleiter, Count Freddy Von Flugel, and thus to secure his safety from the other side. He does not hesitate to report the Pringles, the suspicious-looking young man they are harbouring, and the plan to destroy an oil well (given to Guy by Sheppy) which he has purloined from the Pringles' desk. The encounter between Yakimov and Von Flugel is a metaphor for the final stage of the collapse of the terminally enfeebled European aristocracy. And yet, complex and ironic as these novels are, we will occasionally sympathise with 'poor old Yaki', as he calls himself, although our sympathy probably has an edge of desperation to it.

Concerning my second point, I have already said that I find it appropriate that Harriet Pringle should have spoken, early on, of Stendhal. 'Politics in the novel is like a pistol shot at a concert. . . .' But of course Stendhal's famous comment really means that no novel worth the name will steer clear of the topic. And, although she does not of course achieve the depth or intensity of the author of *Le Rouge et le Noir* or *La Chartreuse de Parme*, a similar sense is at the heart of Olivia Manning's novels. Not only are they centrally about politics and its consequences, they also appear to explore the topic from as many angles as possible. Moreover, she shares the great Frenchman's conviction that large, public forces and even the events that embody them are best recorded through the chaos they impose on private life, a chaos too complex to be measured totally by either a comic or a tragic vision. When, in one of many intimidating gestures, the Germans summon the Rumanians to

Salzburg, a large group of Rumanians meet in the salon of the Athenee Palace. The meeting is in fact an Iron Guard reception, attended by some of Rumania's wealthiest citizens, and it terminates in a demand for the abdication of the king. Harriet, her bleak education proceeding apace, perceives the reality clearly: 'Here was Bucharest's wealthiest and most frivolous society standing, grave-faced, almost at attention, singing the Nazi anthem'. But the context of the passage is dense and ambiguous, for it opens with Dudebat, 'taciturn when sober, garrulous when drunk', indicting for Toby Lush the poverty of his own early years and indeed of the life of half the world; conscience and social protest are reduced to a drunkard's diatribe. In the crush following the meeting, it is Harriet, not the men, who leads her party out of the lobby; she does so by thrusting the pin of her brooch into the principal backside in the crowd before her, simultaneously recognising that an important-looking woman in the group is the wife of the ex-Minister of Information, 'who had been pro-British no longer'. Finally, in the street before the hotel, she sees Dudebat and Toby Lush running off like desperate children, fleeing without shame. It is Harriet's intelligent mind, antic but dependable, which orders, often if only by perception, the diverse experience of the novels, and Harriet's mind is the mind of spirit.

I suppose *The Spoilt City* is for me the best of the three novels because in it the pressure of events is greatest, and also because Olivia Manning is so completely in control of both their irony and their complexity. *Friends and Heroes*, by contrast, often appears to be an anticlimax after the two Bucharest novels, partly because its material is intrinsically less dramatic and partly, I should guess, by the novelist's intention. One short scene in *The Spoilt City* captures completely Harriet's attractive difference from Guy, and also the dialectic which brackets both the early period of their marriage and their experience of Rumania. Harriet is passionate in response to the sight of a peasant assaulting his bony horse with a whip:

> She sat down, exhausted, and gulped back her tears. Seeing the peasant vividly, his brutish face absorbed and horribly gratified by the outlet for his violence, she said: 'I can't bear this place. The peasants are loathsome. I hate them.' She spoke in a convulsion of feeling, trembling as she said: 'All over this country animals are suffering — and we can do nothing about

it'. Feeling the world too much for her, she pressed her face against Guy's shoulder.

He put his arm round her to calm her. 'The peasants are brutes because they are treated like brutes. They suffer themselves. Their behaviour comes of desperation.'

'It's no excuse.'

'Perhaps not, but it's an explanation. One must try to understand.'

'Why should one try to understand cruelty and stupidity?'

'Because even those things can be understood; and if understood they can be cured.'

The faith and conviction of Guy's final lines are of course those traditional to the rationalist. For Harriet, however, little of what she sees in Bucharest can be explained rationally. And later, in the Athens of *Friends and Heroes*, a novel about the wartime dispersal of a community, the weight of Harriet's experience shifts, becomes more diffused.

Whether in Bucharest or Athens, however, human beings continue to act in ways which, though according to some inner logic, are as often surprising as not. Toward the end of *The Spoilt City*, Harriet is dubious when Clarence announces his intention to depart, and to take with him, and marry, the half-Jewish Sophie. A moment later, angry when he pettily and pompously demands the return of some shirts which he has lent Guy from the Polish relief stores he controls, she walks to the balcony of the apartment and deliberately throws the shirts into the courtyard below — only to discover that Clarence has secured for Sasha a Hungarian passport. Angry at him just a moment before, she can now only embrace him. Shortly thereafter, she encounters in the street her rich compatriot Bella Niculescu, wife of a Rumanian. Bella's behaviour is unfortunately more predictable than Clarence's, but surely not of a sort to be enclosed within the secure and narrow confines of rationalism. Amidst so many departures from Rumania, Bella has elected to stay, safe in her own wealth — and in the impending German occupation. 'She had found a means of managing her situation: she was shuffling off her own identity and taking on an aspect of the enemy.' Just as so many wealthy Rumanians reveal themselves as the Germans' natural allies, so too does a wealthy Englishwoman. But even Bella, though she can never justify herself to Harriet, can make her uncomfortable.

'"Rumania has been unfairly treated. The Allies guaranteed her, then did nothing. *Nothing*."'

At the close of the novel, the Gestapo, according to Galpin, are openly present in the lobby of the hotel, watching, in an emblematic movement, even as the Princess Teodorescu enters the hotel. 'She had returned to Bucharest relying, like the others of her class, on German influence to protect her against the Iron Guard.' Although the alliances so naturally struck by the rich surely confirm Guy's theories, it is Harriet who observes them. And in the dense cross-hatching of detail which renders this novel so impressive, and which reaches an appropriate peak at its close, she learns from David Boyd that the Rumanian youth are being conscripted and sent off, apparently under the impression that they will fight for England. To Harriet's inquiring whether the Rumanians actually believe this, David replies, 'They don't think. When the time comes, they'll be told, "This is the enemy, fight!" And they will fight and die.' Even now, David continues to protest British failure to support progressive forces within Rumania, and to castigate Britain's role in Rumania's present plight. And he does so before Sir Brian Love, who, as chairman of an advisory committee sent to Bucharest from Cairo, is the very embodiment of imperial bureaucracy, and, in David's words, 'full of zeal'. Because we feel the justification for his anger, David once more appears to offer the most balanced political views of any character in the trilogy. Certainly his mind and voice, characterised by knowledge and an outraged sense of betrayal, are crucial to the politics of these novels.

The Spoilt City, as if in preparation for *Friends and Heroes*, concludes with an ironic and indicative movement from climax to anticlimax. When Harriet, David and Guy return to find the Pringles' flat entered, searched and left a shambles, and Harriet a moment later discovers Sasha's passport ripped in half, the men admit their fear, while Harriet simply succumbs to the exhaustion and shock which now seem the natural culmination of her stay in this strange, indecipherable city. In the final chapter, just arrived by plane in Athens, she has in one sense recovered her freedom, at least within the ironic norms of wartime existence. But free from the oppression and danger of Bucharest, she now feels bereft of both Sasha and her husband; concerning Guy, she experiences 'an appalled remorse that she had left him without reflecting on what she might be leaving him to'. And Athens, so different from

Bucharest, in one respect immediately resembles it, for Harriet almost at once meets Yakimov, desperately hard up and riding his bicycle as a sort of messenger boy for the Information Office. Although she realises in one uneasy moment that it is clearly Yakimov who purloined the oil-well plan from the apartment in Bucharest, she is nevertheless forced to accept him as a conduit to the Information Office and possible news of Guy. Newly arrived in Athens, Harriet is still circumscribed by the world of Bucharest.

The Athens of *Friends and Heroes* is just as brilliantly rendered as the Bucharest of the two earlier novels; once again, Olivia Manning's characters move in a highly specific context of time and place: the city in which the results of the fighting of the Greeks against the Italians in the mountains is announced by church bells until it is finally superseded by the dread announcement of the German declaration of war, and the city from which, at the novel's close, the central group of characters has embarked, more or less ingloriously, for Cairo.[2] I say 'more or less ingloriously' because the overseas English of *Friends and Heroes* are a morally enfeebled lot, overtaken by pettiness, calculation, and, above all, failure of nerve (there are clear implications of homosexuality among some of the minor male characters). But the novel is also about movement in wartime, about persons who rapidly assume refugee status and struggle for some kind of safety, however qualified. The eminent Professor Pinkrose, a character who has been comically central to *The Spoilt City* partly because the Organisation back home sends him out to Bucharest to lecture at the worst possible time simply because cancelling his visit would be to yield to fate by acknowledging its existence, arrives early in the novel in Athens. The Professor, scared to death in Bucharest, Guy now sees seated at a table in a cafe: 'Nothing of his person was visible but a blunt, lizard-grey nose: the nose of Professor Lord Pinkrose who had also bolted from the dangers of Bucharest'. Dobson, the head of the legation, many of his people, Clarence, and finally even Sasha arrive in Athens. Harriet's conversation with Sasha, late in the novel, stands in stark contrast to her relationship to him in *The Spoilt City*; his earlier innocence has been replaced by mistrust, his captors having suggested to him that the Pringles betrayed him. Harriet now sees in him a sad but logical version of one area of the future:

> Looking at his face, the same face she had known in Bucharest and yet a different face, she could see him turning

into a wily young financier like the Jewish financiers of
Chernowitz who still proudly wore on their hats the red fox fur
that had been imposed on them long ago, as a symbol of
cunning. No doubt he would remake the fortune that he had
signed away. That would be his answer to life. She did not
blame herself, but she felt someone was to blame.

She had mourned Sasha and with reason. She had lost him
indeed and the person she now found was not only a stranger,
but a stranger whom she could not like.

As much as any relationship in the three novels, this one reveals the
way in which Olivia Manning's irony illuminates the true complexity of human beings moving in the historical currents of their
time. Their individuality, although it may be forced in unexpected directions, maintains its own logic.

Friends and Heroes is dense with vitality, and among its many
new characters there is one who is both major and highly
attractive. Alan Frewen, the Information Officer (and therefore
Yakimov's 'boss'), provides his own mild dialectic in contest with
Guy. Frewen, like his retriever and constant companion, Dio-
cletian, who is, according to Alan, a Grecophil, is an unabashed
lover of the country and its people. 'I love Greece. I love the
Greeks. I do not want to see any change here.' Guy of course can
only brand such rejection of historical force, to say nothing of the
Greeks' economic need, as 'apolitical'. Alan himself has a deep
appreciation of the curious tangle which constitutes Guy. He says
to Harriet: 'You must accept him as he is. After all, his virtues far
outweigh his faults.' And Frewen's judgements and affections are
confirmed in broader, even more fundamental ways, for the
Greeks of *Friends and Heroes* are a singularly attractive people, as
honest and free from corruption as many of the Rumanians were
not, and generous, hospitable, romantic in the most engaging
sense of the term. They are also fighters, though tragically so
because they are fighting an inevitably losing cause. Vourakis, a
journalist acquaintance of Frewen's, describes the desperate
situation of the Greeks once the Yugoslav southern army has withdrawn:

And there were two forts that held the pass till the area could be
evacuated. A hundred men stayed in the forts. They knew no
one could rescue them, no help could come to them: they knew

they must die. And they died. The forts were destroyed and the men died. It was Thermopylae. Another Thermopylae.

Here, as elsewhere, the novelist proceeds by devastating juxtaposition: Pinkrose, next morning, following his lecture (given at last, though in Greece!) and the party after it, says to Frewen, whose presence he has missed: 'You were the loser. You missed an excellent party. I must say it was, indeed, glittering.'

I have said that I should return to what is for me the one weakness of these splendid novels. It is simply this: at far-too-frequent moments Harriet ponders, rather formally, her evolving relationship to Guy and her own shifting response to it. Although these passages become more and more repetitive, they are clearly, by their rhythm, quite deliberately intended by the novelist. Since, however, Guy and Harriet's relationship is acutely analysed in the spontaneous development of the trilogy, these expositions are unnecessary. Moreover, they tend to suspend Harriet (and occasionally Guy) in an unnatural posture of pure thought.

And *Friends and Heroes* demonstrates once more how well that relationship is dramatised. Disappointed in the extent, the inclusivity and indeed the randomness of Guy's concerns, Harriet finds herself attracted to a young English soldier, Charles Warden, and tempted to yield to what she hopes might be a developing relationship with him – except that Charles has been assigned to join the fighting. Now competing for Guy's attention with an impeccably left-wing journalist, Ben Phipps, who seems to her to 'have taken over Guy', Harriet recognises that she has stepped beyond her husband and sees around him:

> She remembered when she had wanted him to take over her life. That phase did not last long. She had soon decided that Guy might be better read and better informed, but, so far as she was concerned, her own judgement served her better than his. Guy had a moral strength but it resembled one of those vast Victorian feats of engineering: impressive but out of place in the modern world. He had a will to believe in others but the will survived only because he evaded fact. Life as he saw it could not support itself; it had to be subsidised by fantasy. He was a materialist without being a realist; and that, she thought, gave him the worst of both worlds.

Appropriately, if at first surprisingly, it is Clarence Lawson, just returned from Turkey where Sophie has remained behind ('She really was a little trollop'), who indignantly questions Harriet about her walking out with that 'bloody little pongo', and who asserts, as he quickly tells Guy, who, within earshot at the same table, is curious about their conversation, that he considers her husband '. . . the finest man I've ever known, . . . a great man, . . . a saint. And she's not satisfied. . .' But Harriet's feelings for Guy do not clarify themselves until, getting ready to leave Athens and unable to find her cat in the woods near the villa where they have been living, she startles her husband into a cry of distress by referring to the cat as 'all I have'. Now, for the first time, she is aware of Guy as a man who suffers. 'Reluctantly she moved over to him. During the last weeks she had almost forgotten his appearance: his image had been overlaid by another image. Now, seeing him afresh, she could see he was suffering as they all suffered.' Harriet, perhaps with less excuse since her concerns are *not* so random, has been nearly as guilty as Guy of overlooking the claims and needs of the other.

Near the close of *Friends and Lovers* (and that it is the close of the trilogy as well is indicated by the death of Yakimov, characteristically understated, as a careless victim of martial law), when Harriet briefly entertains the idea of flight from her husband, she feels 'the tug of emotions, loyalties and dependencies'. Finally, filled with dread and fear at having witnessed the return of wounded soldiers − 'a smell of defeat came from them like a smell of gangrene' − Harriet finds Guy in Constitution Square:

> At first she could not speak, then she tried to describe what she had seen but, strangled by her own description, sobbed instead. He opened his arms and caught her into them. His physical warmth, the memory of his courage when the villa was shaken by gunfire, her own need and the knowledge he needed her: all those things overwhelmed her and held her to him, saying: 'I love you'.

At the end, amidst the moral squalor of self-concern which constitutes a large part of the desperate British departure from Athens, Harriet, aboard ship for Cairo, finds in Guy a tentative hope, a small sense of the future which, by its very limitation, seems appropriate to their circumstances and to themselves: 'If

Guy had for her the virtue of permanence, she might have the same virtue for him. To have one thing permanent in life as they knew it was as much as they could expect.'

Such a passage, restrained, coolly and acutely realistic, properly contingent, marks a fitting conclusion to the world of *The Balkan Trilogy* and to the marriage which stands at its centre. And that marriage, we now realise, has become more and more important to us in the moral decay, the timid compromises, the fearful threats and the small margins for hope that comprise the terrain of a certain corner of Europe between the fall of 1939 and the beginning of 1941.

NOTES

1. The three novels which make up Olivia Manning's *The Balkan Trilogy* are *The Great Fortune* (1960), *The Spoilt City* (1962), and *Friends and Heroes* (1965). All three volumes were published by Penguin in 1974 and all page references are to the Penguin editions.
2. Eleven years after the appearance of *Friends and Heroes*, Olivia Manning resumed the story of the Pringles and their friends and acquaintances in *The Levant Trilogy*. These are sparer, leaner novels than those of *The Balkan Trilogy*, but they are once again fiction of a very high order.

ADDENDUM

Since this essay was written, in January 1980, Olivia Manning has died — in July of the same year. Her death occurred just a few months after she had completed the third volume of her second trilogy* concerning Guy and Harriet Pringle, their friends, acquaintances and antagonists, and the diverse adventures of the whole group during the years of the Second World War. I have written in my present essay that this second series (on the basis of the first two volumes at least; I have not yet seen the third) is sparer, leaner in both concept and structure than the first, but all the works are closely related by Olivia Manning's complex detachment, her dry, sharp, even brittle tone, and her deep, anxious historical awareness. In relation to the kinds of experience she chronicles, what really set the second series apart from the first is the remarkable set of chapters, realistic yet fiercely restrained, that delineate Simon Boulderstone's adventures in the North African desert war. I suspect that many readers, discovering in their own literary experience no equivalent for these passages, will find it hard to believe that the whole account was written by a woman.

To speak of Olivia Manning's detachment, complex though I may describe it as being, is nevertheless to raise an interesting speculation, for the novelist herself went out to Bucharest as a lecturer's wife on the eve of the war, was evacuated out of the Balkans (through Athens, surely?) to Cairo, only to end, eventually, in Jerusalem. At the end of *The Levant Trilogy*, Harriet, having travelled from Damascus to Jerusalem and through the Lebanon back to Cairo, has rejoined Guy just as the North African theatre of the war is being superseded by the invasion of Italy. Although it is still only 1943, Harriet and Guy, with the sense that much has been concluded, await the war's end and return to England. Consequently, my concept of Olivia Manning as a highly sophisticated 'witness to history' carries through all of these works in ways perhaps more personal than I might have intended in my original use of the phrase. What seems to me

---

* *The Danger Tree* (1977)
  The Battle Lost and Won (1979)
  The Sum of Things (1981)

(These are American dates, and may therefore vary slightly)

beyond dispute is that we have here an extraordinary body of work that should earn her a permanent place among the authors of that very considerable literature arising out of the Second World War.

6 September 1980

4 Women Victimised by Fiction: living and loving in the novels by Barbara Pym

Barbara Brothers

A woman's life is redeemed by love, or so we have been told in fairy tales, medieval chivalric legends, lyric love poems, and novels. Woman's destiny is to light a flame in a man's heart so that all he does in the world is a tribute to her of his passion. She is muse. For her a man sails the world, studies the heavens and the earth and its creatures, divines the laws of God, man and nature, writes books, composes poetry, and preaches sermons. A man lives in relation to the world; a woman in relation to a man. 'Love', as Virginia Woolf has summarised the portrayal of women's lives in literature, 'was the only possible interpreter'.[1]

As it has been in art, so it has been in life: for a woman so much depends upon love. It is for love, according to the conventions of our culture as well as the values of our fictions, that woman was created. Their role in history, to use Woolf's image, is to serve as 'looking-glasses possessing the magic and delicious power of reflecting the figure of man at twice its natural size', giving him the imaginative power, the 'self-confidence', to civilise the world.[2] Whether in life or literature, a woman's only hope has been to catch the eye of a man. How else can she expect a part in the play!

But what of those who never light a flame in a man's heart? Or what of those whose prince is really only a frog after all? Are their lives needless stories? Barbara Pym's eight novels − *Some Tame*

61

Gazelle (1950), *Excellent Women* (1952), *Jane and Prudence* (1963), *Less Than Angels* (1955), *A Glass of Blessings* (1958), *No Fond Return of Love* (1961), *Quartet in Autumn* (1977), and *A Sweet Dove Died* (1978) — tell the stories of women, and of men, too, who exist as characters, if at all, only on the periphery of life as depicted by writers of fiction.[3] Her '*excellent* women' are those 'who can just go home and eat a boiled egg and make a cup of tea and be very splendid'. (*Angels*, p. 108.) They are the women whose room of their own is a bed-sitting room with a gas-ring, women who are the twentieth-century counterpart of the Victorian governesses with 'no prospect of a romantic attachment to the widower master of the house or a handsome son of the family'. (*Quartet*, p. 77.)

Or if the women in Pym's novels do marry, their husbands are neither passionate nor profound, neither great lovers nor great thinkers. Married for over twenty years, Jane Cleveland reflects ironically on her husband's concerns when she recalls an un-married friend's remark about men's preoccupation with sex: 'If it is true that men only want one thing, Jane asked herself, is it perhaps just to be left to themselves with their soap animals or some other harmless little trifle?' (*Jane & Prudence*, p. 129.) To love and serve as the mirror for beings who are so frequently dull, self-absorbed, and pretentious may be an experience a woman could do without. Such, at least, is the observation of one of Pym's spinsters when she thinks of her sister's husband. (*Angels*, p. 36.)

In her novels, which sparkle with compassion, humour, and the wit of understatement, Pym contrasts her characters and their lives with those which have been presented in literature to mock the idealised view of the romantic paradigm and to emphasise that her tales present the truth of the matter. Though the men in her novels are not cast as heroes nor the women as goddesses of love and inspiration, the fantasy shapes the expectations of the characters. In Pym's novels women continue to be the 'second sex' more because of fantasy than because of political or social factors. Men, behind the mask of responsibility for society, make it little less than a 'holy privilege' for a woman to enter into their service. But that service lacks the rewards of love and meaning that adolescent romantic fantasies project for it. The life of a wife, Pym suggests, is little different from the life of the spinsters of the church who 'dote' upon the clergy. Love is not a flame, let alone a constant one. Men are more interested in their comfort and self-importance than in causes. And women, though not by nature self-effacing and good creatures, frequently pretend to be. Pym perceives that little has changed in the contemporary world: women are still psychic victims of what might be considered a self-serving, male-created myth that a woman fulfils herself only through love. She does not claim, however, as do some women's liberationists, that the world can be saved through women assuming roles of leadership. Women are neither more nor less heroic, original, petty or self-serving than are men. She attacks the myth because it has prevented both men and women from seeing and accepting themselves as they are.

Like Woolf and other feminists, Pym chides novelists for not telling the truth about women's lives. The sins of novelists in the world according to Pym are both sins of omission and sins of commission. In *Quartet in Autumn*, Letty no longer reads novels for there are none which reflect 'her own sort of life . . . [as] an unmarried, unattached, ageing woman'. (p. 3.) To read what is 'true', she now reads biographies. By not dramatising the life of the unmarried woman or that of the woman who is neither in love nor the object of some man's love, novelists, Pym suggests, have contributed to society's perception that such women have no lives of their own. What is more, the 'unattached' woman herself has been made to feel that she is a spectator of rather than an actor on the world's stage. Mildred Lathbury in *Excellent Women* thinks when questioned about her new next-door neighbours: 'I suppose an unmarried woman just over thirty, who lives alone and has no apparent ties, must expect to find herself involved or interested in other people's business'. (p. 5.) Since her life as a spinster is thought to be empty, she is presumed to live vicariously.

The consensus among Pym's characters is that such women, if they are to become participants in the drama of life, must find a way to serve others, though no one feels this is a necessity for the middle-aged or ageing bachelor. Dulcie Mainwaring, the central character in *No Fond Return of Love*, thinking of the oncoming Christmas holiday with her sister Charlotte and her family, anticipates with regret the role in which her family will cast her: 'she felt reluctant to uproot herself and be reduced in status to the spinster aunt, who had had an unfortunate love affair that had somehow "gone wrong" and who, although she was still quite young, was now relegated to the shelf and good works. When Dulcie wondered, did one begin to take up good works if they didn't come naturally? When – and how?' (p. 109.)

Pym maintains that while the silences of fiction have made it seem that the unmarried woman is a voyeur of life, the portrayal of women in fiction, on the other hand, has helped to create the image of woman as one who loves and serves. In *Jane and Prudence*, Jane Cleveland finds a model for her role as a clergyman's wife in the novels of Yonge, Trollope, and the other Victorians. But she is disillusioned with herself when she fails to be the 'gallant, cheerful' (p. 8) wife who manages the household on 'far too little money', gets along well with the parishioners, and rears a large family. Jane is ineffectual in running the house and in helping with church activities, and she doesn't 'feel so very much of a mother' (p. 66) since she has only one child. Her greatest gift is recalling quotations or analogies from literature which somehow always miss the mark. They seem as inappropriate for the situations she applies them to as do *Vogue* or the decorating magazines which her unmarried friend uses as models for her dress and apartment furnishings.

While fictive portrayals of clergymen's wives provide the standard by which Jane measures herself and her life, those portrayals so becloud Archdeacon Hoccleve's vision in *Some Tame Gazelle* that he forgets, on occasion, what his wife is really like. He remarks *without irony* when reminded that his wife has not had tea: 'It will please her not to have any . . . I wonder that you [Belinda] have had any. I thought women enjoyed missing their meals and making martyrs of themselves.' (p. 39.) He believes this in spite of the fact that his wife pays more attention to her clothing than she does to any of her wifely duties – cooking his meals, mending his clothes, or keeping a comfortable home. A good woman, as fiction tells us, always puts a man's needs first, and, of course, the Archdeacon knows that a man such as himself could have married only a worthy woman. Neither Jane nor Agatha Hoccleve fits the image of a self-sacrificing, efficacious, ever-attendant wife, but then their clergymen husbands are not great preachers bringing light and comfort to the people of the village either. The model that fiction has presented is mocked by the 'facts' as Pym presents them, yet the characters continue to accept that the paradigm reflects who and what they are or should be.

Pym makes the point in *Less Than Angels* that the education of women and women's liberation have done little to alter the expectation that women are to serve a man whose mission is thought to be to civilise the world. The 'changed position of the sexes', which we have heard so much about, means only that 'now . . . women . . . [are] more likely to go off to Africa to shoot lions as a cure for unrequited love than in the old days, when this had been a man's privilege' (p. 73) and women may select the plays to be attended rather than the men forming 'the women's tastes'. (p. 61.) Little, if anything, has happened to make 'the relations between men and women any more satisfactory', (p. 60) for their characters and their roles are still stereotyped. Though, as one young anthropologist observes, two people may live together in 1950 without being married, the parts they are expected to play and do play are still unchanged: 'It would be a reciprocal relationship — the woman giving the food and shelter and doing some typing for him and the man giving the priceless gift of himself . . . commoner in our society than many people would suppose'. (p. 76.)

Pym seems to feel that at least a part of the reason why education has not made a difference is that a woman's education is anachronistic, as Kate Millett has pointed out in *Sexual Politics*.[4] In *No Fond Return of Love*, published nearly ten years before Millett's book, Dulcie Mainwaring thinks 'sardonically' when her niece Laurel identifies her favourite subjects as English and history:

> how many a young girl must have given the same answer to that question! And really what did it mean? A sentimental penchant for King Charles the First or even Napoleon, or a liking for the poetry of Marvell, Keats, or Matthew Arnold? That was what it had been with her, but she had been fortunate in having an ambitious English teacher and parents who, rather bewildered by the whole thing, could afford to send her to Oxford. And now she was making indexes and doing little bits of research for people with more original minds than herself. What, as Miss Lord would ask, did it lead to? And what answer should a girl give now when asked what had been her favourite subjects at school? Russian and nuclear physics were perhaps too far advanced, as yet, but English and History would hardly do. (p. 50.)

Females are educated in the humanities and the social sciences;

they are taught the ideals of Renaissance humanism but not the facts of the hard sciences. That education, as Millett assesses it in *Sexual Politics*, becomes 'hardly more than an extension of the "accomplishments" they once cultivated in preparation for the marriage market'. What it leads to for more than one woman in Pym's novels is landing a husband because she has the 'learning' to do an index for his book! Though a man is writing the book and a woman indexing it, Pym leaves no doubt that his mind is no more original than hers.

At the Oxford class reunion that Jane and Prudence attend, Miss Birkinshaw's thoughts about her former students indicate that the perception of a woman's nature is still that she is an emotional, unanalytical, nurturing being and that therefore the world's doors have not really been opened to her: 'She liked her Old Students to be clearly labelled — the clergymen's wives, the other wives, and those who had "fulfilled" themselves in less obvious ways, with novels or social work or a brilliant career in the Civil Service'. (*Jane & Prudence*, p. 10.) What jobs are thought 'appropriate' are still determined by the supposed differences between the sexes: Dulcie's niece, Laurel, is surprised to learn that Monica Beltane is a lecturer in biology with a scientific interest in nature, while Paul Beltane, her brother, arranges flowers in a flower shop because he is 'very artistic and loves flowers for their own sake'. (*Fond Return*, p. 51.) Only in the fact that in the *Chronicle* of Jane and Prudence's college the 'women took precedence' (p. 8) by having their names listed first — 'the husbands existing only in relation to them: "Jane Mowbray Bold to Herbert Nicholas Cleveland"' — does their education seem to have made a ripple of a difference in their life histories. Love is still the 'interpreter' of a woman's life.

Pym depicts in detail what it means to be a man's muse or his 'looking-glass'. Her wives, spinsters, and young and middle-aged hopefuls spend their days washing surplices, arranging church jumble sales, darning socks, cooking boiled chicken with white sauce, typing manuscripts, compiling indexes and preparing tea for the clergymen, anthropologists, and historians, the men who do the 'real' work in the world. Women do those things that a man does not want to do, for everyone knows 'men did not usually do things unless they liked doing them'. (*Excellent Women*, p. 9.)

Though their lives as helpmates are unromantic, women cling to the notion that men and their world are as noble as they have been portrayed. When Dr Grampian says to Prudence that 'things have been rather trying lately', she wonders what things. 'Men did not have quite the same trials as women — it would be the larger things that worried him, his health, his work . . .'. (*Jane & Prudence*, p. 100.) Just as Hoccleve believes women like to be 'martyrs' even though there is nothing martyr-like about his wife, Prudence does not let 'facts' disturb the fictional paradigm. She does not perceive that which the reader perceives: as a single working women she has precisely the same problems that Arthur has.

In Pym's novels, so powerful is the mythic weight of man's responsibilities that her women fail to perceive not only that their jobs are often no different from a man's but also that a woman's needs are no different or less substantial. Jane Cleveland reflects with amusement on the woman in the café who insists on a 'man's needs' when she serves Jane one egg and her husband, Nicholas, two, and wonders why a man is thought to need more meat and eggs than does a woman. Her husband, however, finds nothing unusual about the portions: 'Nicholas accepted his two eggs and bacon and the implication that his needs were more important than his wife's with a certain amount of complacency . . .'. (*Jane & Prudence*, p. 51.) Women, after all, must be satisfied with less in return for being one of those things a man needs, even if only for such 'arduous or thankless' tasks as compiling an index. It is enough for them to be 'allowed to love' a man, as one of Pym's women puts it in *No Fond Return of Love*. (p. 75.)

Love is not portrayed as an intense sexual emotion in Pym's novels except, ironically enough, in the case of the affair that Ned and James have in *A Sweet Dove Died*. Instead, many women in Pym's novels have known 'love' only as caring for the needs of a younger brother or a widowed father. Winifred Malory, a 'tall, thin and angular' woman of forty with an 'eager face' looks after the vicarage and participates in the 'good works' of the church for which her brother is the vicar. (*Excellent Women*, p. 13.) Like Mildred Lathbury, who helps her widowed father until his death, she has never been 'really first in anybody's life'. (p. 39.) Why would Winifred, Mildred wonders, choose as her favourite poems those of Christina Rossetti; Winifred 'had not . . . had the experience to make those much-quoted poems appropriate'. (p. 40.) Nor do the women who have experienced being 'first' in some man's life find love to be what the poems they have read expressed it as being. Poetry has sung of love as undying passion: love transcends the mundane and makes the sun stand still. But, as

Jane Cleveland observes on looking in at her husband seated in his study: 'The passion of those early days, the fragments of Donne and Marvell and Jane's obscurer seventeenth-century poets, the objects of her abortive research, all these faded away into mild, kindly looks and spectacles. There came a day when one didn't quote poetry to one's husband any more'. (*Jane & Prudence*, p. 48.)

If a woman insists on love as it is idealised in literature, she will likely remain a 'sleeping beauty'. Jane believes that her friend Prudence seems doomed to go through life unmarried since she seems to have 'got into the way of preferring unsatisfactory love affairs'. (p. 9.) However, Prudence doesn't seek unsatisfactory love affairs so much as she finds love satisfactory only so long as it conforms to a romantic script. Fabian Driver, a distinguished-looking widower, seems a likely candidate for a husband; after all 'they would make a handsome couple', (p. 102) though Prudence is uneasy since his conversation is 'banal' and 'disappointing'. Somehow her evenings with him were never 'quite so sweet as [were] the imagined evenings [with Arthur Grampian] with their flow of sparkling conversation'. (pp. 101–2.) In the end she loses Fabian to a woman who has a more practical view of love: Jessie makes herself necessary to Fabian's comfort. Prudence is left with her reveries of past loves, each with his 'urn . . . deposited in the niche' on 'the shrine of her past loves' (p. 215) and visions of the 'eligible and delightful men' (p. 83) whose courting of her she can compose into a fitting scene and rewrite in the language of fiction:

> And yet it had been on one of those rare late evenings, when they had been sitting together over a manuscript, that Prudence's love for him, if that was what it was, had suddenly flared up. Perhaps 'flared' was too violent a word, but Prudence thought of it afterwards as having been like that. She remembered herself standing by the window, looking out on to an early spring evening with the sky a rather clear blue just before the darkness came, not really seeing anything or thinking about very much; perhaps an odd detail here and there had impressed itself upon her mind — she liked to think that it had — the twitter of starlings, a lighted window in another building — and then suddenly it had come to her *Oh, my love* . . . rushing in like that. (p. 37.)

To emphasise that romance in fiction and romance in life are never quite the same, Pym has Catherine Oliphant, a short story writer in *Less Than Angels*, question a scene she has just written. A lover in a novel may quote lines from Tennyson — *'Dear as remembered kisses after death'* — with 'an anguished expression' on his face to 'a girl standing with a rose in her hand', but it is unlikely that a lover who exists outside the pages of fiction would. (pp. 27–8.) Catherine must decide that it is time fiction reflected more accurately life as women experience it, for we learn in *A Glass of Blessings* that she has rewritten the story. The 'women under the drier at the hairdresser's', (p. 28) whom Catherine imagines reading the story, learn instead of 'a young man and girl holding hands in a Greek restaurant, watched by the man's former mistress'. (*Glass*, p. 152.) Catherine in *Less Than Angels* is the mistress-participant in just such a scene. She watches Tom, the young man whose indecision has made him quite unlike her imagined lover of 'strong character who would rule her life'. (*Angels*, p. 27.) Pym's point is clear: fiction should cease portraying an idealised version of love.

Pym's women who look for romance and excitement do not find it. Jane Clevelend acquiesces to the realities of life as a clergyman's wife. She dresses in frumpy clothes and listens to gossip, hoping to find in others' lives the passion her own lacks. But, of course, she never does. When a wife persists in looking for romance in her own life, she may come close to losing a husband. Wilmet Forsyth, a young woman of thirty-three who dresses to be noticed but who now seldom succeeds in getting her husband to comment on her appearance, finds herself attracted to Piers Longridge, who does compliment her. He is a perfect romantic subject, brilliant but unsuccessful, a handsome man with a Byronic touch. The hint is that he may drink too much. What better vehicle for a woman's desire to be needed, to do some good, and to escape from the mundaneness of her 'bleak and respectable' (*Glass*, p. 10) life. Wilmet hurries off to meet him one afternoon, feeling that she is about to have an adventure just like one in a novel. 'May has always seemed to me, as indeed it has to poets, the most romantic of all the months. There are so many days when the air really is like wine — a delicate white wine, perhaps Vouvray drunk on the bank of the Loire'. (p. 188.) She envisions herself rushing up to him and greeting him with an 'extravagant gesture, like covering his eyes with my hands'. (p. 189.) But he rejects even the lesser romantic gesture she settles on, holding her 'hands . . . outstretched, waiting to be taken in his'. Nor does he respond to her 'enthusiasm' for the lupins. Her dream is completely shattered when he takes her to his lodgings and introduces her to Keith, the young, un-educated man with whom he lives and who really does make a good 'wife', devoted to cooking and cleaning. (How better to deflate a woman's romantic projections than through giving her a male competitor.) Preoccupied with her own thoughts, Wilmet has accepted her husband's working late, and only when she and Rodney are drawn together to look for a house does she discover that he has been having an affair, too. The Woman is Prudence Bates.

As if to emphasise that she is chronicling rather than creating the lives of women and the men the women meet, know, and in some instances even love, Pym has characters in later novels meet or discuss characters from earlier novels. We learn in *The Glass of Blessings*, for instance, of Prudence having yet another 'unsatis-factory love affair' with Edward Lyall, the MP she meets on a train at the close of *Jane and Prudence*. In *No Fond Return of Love*, Dulcie Mainwaring sees Wilmet and her husband, along with Piers and Keith, the four having become friends by the end of *The Glass of Blessings*, standing in the castle of the Forbes family. Their striking appearance makes Dulcie feel they are − 'Like characters in a novel'. (p. 193.) But we know that their lives are no different from hers in spite of their appearance. That Mildred Lathbury has married Everard Bone, with whom she has dinner in *Excellent Women*, is mentioned in *Jane and Prudence* and *Less Than Angels*. What we learn of characters' later actions is predictable, for life in a Pym novel is not made up of crisis and denouements. As one character of Pym's remarks, 'There was something almost frightening and at the same time comforting about the sameness of it all'. (*Gazelle*, pp. 16−17.) Love, won or lost, effects no meta-morphosis of character.

Pym's novels dramatise the point E. M. Forster makes in *Aspects of the Novel*: 'love is neither so intense nor such an ever-present interest as novelists have led us to believe'.[5] People, unlike characters, are not nearly so 'sensitive' to love. None of the four central characters in *Quartet in Autumn* are in love, nor do they want to be. They find it difficult even to remember those 'loves' they have known − mother, father, wife. Letty does not even understand romantic love: 'Love was a mystery she had never experienced. As a young woman she had wanted to love, had felt that she ought to, but it had not come about.' (p. 54.) She has had beaus, but she has never experienced the desire to make her life a part of theirs, or theirs a part of hers.

Those who do decide to join their lives with another do so most often out of a desire for comfort and convenience, a man looking for someone to care for him and a woman looking for 'Something to Love'. This, as Pym depicts it, is what romance is all about. In *Some Tame Gazelle*, which has as its epigraph lines from Thomas Haynes Bayley: 'Some tame gazelle, or some gentle dove: / Something to love, oh, something to love!', Bishop Theodore Grote has been turned down by Belinda Bede. She prefers living with her sister, Harriet, another fifty-year-old spinster, and 'loving' Hoccleve, a man with whom she doesn't have to live. Grote is unshaken by her refusal and quickly finds another who can serve as a Bishop's wife. Harriet, like her sister Belinda, enjoys caring for a man who will never become a husband. Harriet cooks, makes jellies, darns, and knits for young curates in return for their appreciative flattery of her still carefully attended appearance.

Both Belinda and Harriet find titillation in romantic possibilities and 'dote' upon men in spite of their preference for a life without marriage. For, as Pym emphasises, women have had their image of being a female shaped by poets, novelists, and writers of popular drama, musicals, and pulp fiction. Imaginative creations have also shaped their expectations of men, love, and life. As subscribers to Boots Book-lover's Library or its lists, holders of degrees in humanities from Oxford, and viewers of television dramas and advertisements, they have had life presented to them as a love story and man and his work depicted as hardly less important than that of divine messengers. While Pym gently mocks women's naïvety and their romantic susceptibilities, she incisively exposes male pretentiousness, men's pompous acceptance of their own importance, and their vain belief in the myth they have created.

Archdeacon Henry Hoccleve serves as a good example of man as seen through the eyes of Pym. As one of the clergy, those who would explain the ways of God to man, he preaches sermons that are little more than occasions to show off his learning, which is, after all, only scraps of remembered quotations. Hoccleve, who owes his rank to the church connections and scheming determination of his wife, Agatha, chooses to have the children of the Sunday school recite for a church festival: '*In dingles deep and mountains hoar / They combated the tusky boar*'. (p. 41.) The lines provide him with an opportunity to lecture the congregation on the history on the word *dingle*. To impress his visitors, two librarians, he plans an elaborate service and sermon on Judgment Day. He is haughty, scornful, and indulgent in his manner of delivery, but the sermon's subject is only another excuse for him to recite 'a long string of quotations, joined together by a few explanations'. (pp. 109–10.) The quotations stretch from Flatman in the seventeenth century to Eliot in the twentieth, and are, of course, no more appropriate or comprehensible to his flock than is his selection of the children's recitation. Pym records that the effect of the sermon on the congregation is to spoil their dinners by making the service longer than usual and to offend their sensibilties by suggesting that they are like the great evildoers in history. Pretentious, Hoccleve 'liked the sound of his own voice'. (p. 110.) A poseur, he makes a show of meditating among the tombstones, brooding over the mortality of man, as if his thought never descends beneath the level of Young's *Night Thoughts*. Petty, he is jealous of the attention paid to Edward Plowman by the women of Plowman's congregation. Peevish, he acts out the literary cliché of being weighed down by the heavy cares of his job, though even on the day of a church festival he doesn't rise before 11 a.m.

To make sure that the reader does not miss her point that Hoccleve is no better a choice for a woman to effect some good in the world than Causabon was for Dorothea Brooke, Pym reveals Hoccleve's thoughts as he waits for the famous Theodore Grote, missionary Bishop of Mbawawa, Africa, who is, by the way, equally lacking in character or learning to justify the importance he claims. Hoccleve smiles delightedly, thinking of the gloomy guest room with no view, the lumpy mattress made up with sides-to-middle sheets, the bedside lamp that does not work, and the carefully selected books on the bedside table that do not include selections from his collection of thrillers, which he keeps locked up in his study. So much for the exalted work, cares, and character of the clergy, who are neither better nor worse than the historians, literary scholars, anthropologists, or government men portrayed by Pym.

Pym's novels, then, call the whole myth into question. In them she turns the myth back into fiction. She constantly reminds her readers that neither characters, nor love, nor destiny is as grand as it has been portrayed. Mildred Lathbury, 'mousy and rather plain' in 'shapeless overall and old fawn skirt', introduces herself in *Excellent Women* by saying, 'Let me hasten to add that I am not at all like Jane Eyre, who must have given hope to so many plain women who tell their stories in the first person . . .' (p. 7.) When a friend learns that Mildred's new neighbour is a Naval Officer, he quotes to her the famous lines: *'They that go down to the sea in ships: and occupy their business in great waters; These men see the works of the Lord: and His wonders in the deep'*. (p. 16.) But the poetry is only an idealised depiction of the reality. Mildred thinks, 'I did not like to spoil the beauty of the words by pointing out that as far as we knew Rockingham Napier had spent most of his service arranging the Admiral's social life'. And it should be added that, from what we and Mildred learn later in the novel, most important to Rocky was the arrangement of his own affairs with the Wrens. (Wilmet and her friend Rowena in *A Glass of Blessings* recall brief romantic entanglements with Rocky Napier.) So much for the sentiments about the noble life of the sailor!

Neither does Jane Cleveland find that life in the country lives up to the expectations she has of it from her reading of novels: 'I didn't think it would be like this. I thought people in the country were somehow noble, through contact with the earth and Nature . . .' (*Jane & Prudence*, p. 137.) Through such disappointments, Pym emphasises that literature has presented an idealised portrait of life. Misled by the picture of life in Victorian novels, William Caldicote supposes that the 'unfortunate gentlepeople' (*Excellent Women*, p. 68) whom Mildred Lathbury attempts to aid are wealthy aristocrats from Belgrave Square. Instead they are 'daughters of clergymen or professional people' who might be considered 'tragic cases' but certainly not in the dramatic Shakespearian mode, for, as Mildred remarks to William, they have fallen from no grand height either in rank or person.

In fact, if one thinks of life as a drama in which man struggles to some great end, then the characters in Pym's novels, men and women, are spectators rather than actors. If her characters are judged in traditional literary ways, they are a 'disappointment', as Dulcie Mainwaring puts the case against Viola, whom she befriends in *No Fond Return of Love*: 'Dulcie felt as if she had created her and that she had not come up to expectations, like a character in a book who had failed to come alive, and how many people in life, if one transferred them to fiction just as they were, would fail to do that!' (pp. 167–8.) Viola, instead of being a romantic tragic heroine of mystery and frustrated stormy passion, is 'just a rather dull woman, wanting only to be loved'. Pym has Dora observe that people, unlike characters in novels, would rather read about a 'great sorrow' or a 'great love' than experience it; in fact, even one rather minor involvement is enough for most people to decide that they will step back and enjoy life from the vantage point of watching others.

Unlike 'a well-thought out novel, where every incident had its own particular significance and was essential to the plot', (*Fond Return*, p. 89) in life the day-to-day activities of others seem like so much trivia. But then people, as opposed to characters, dwell on trivialities – another observation Pym makes through Dora. The traumas people experience are likely to be of no more import than the one Miss Lord frets over: the man behind her in the cafeteria line was served baked beans after she had been refused them. (*Fond Return*, p. 88.) If the distinguishing mark of a character, as Forster has suggested, is that he is 'tirelessly occupied with human relationships' and his life reflects little of the daily activities that people invest their lives in, Pym's characters are anti-characters.[6]

The decisions that weigh heavily on the minds of the two ageing spinsters in *Some Tame Gazelle* are what to serve for dinner or what to wear to church. Belinda wonders if she should knit a pullover for Archdeacon Hoccleve, a suitor who married another and now lives next door and for whom 'her passion had mellowed into a comfortable feeling, more like the cosiness of a winter evening by the fire than the uncertain rapture of a spring evening'. (p. 17.) (Pym has a keen ear for the literary clichés which people have appropriated to conceptualise their lives.) Standing in Miss Jenner's shop, Belinda thinks that she might make some mistake – the ribbing might have a missed stitch that his wife Agatha would discover or the sweater might be 'too small, or the neck opening too tight' – and at last decides 'the enterprise was too fraught with dangers to be attempted . . .' (pp. 83–4.)

It is not just the aged or timid spinsters whose lives are composed of trivia. The Parochial Church Council in *Jane and Prudence* is bitterly divided over the issue of the parish magazine cover. Opposed to those who want the high altar pictured are those who have selected the lychgate since the high altar might make their magazine look too much like St Stephens, which celebrates High

Mass and Confessions. Whether high church or low church services are preferable looms large in the minds of many of Pym's characters to whom the distinction, however, seems either only aesthetic or mythic — to be Popish means one has to kiss the toes of the Pope. Church affairs consist of the problems of decorating the sanctuary for harvest time — are wild flowers permissible or not? should a loaf of bread be real or made of plaster? Typically it is the mundane that captures the individual's attention. It is his church's 'unique oil-fired system . . . the only one of its kind in the West Country' about which a vicar lectures ladies visiting his church and not the church's Norman architectural heritage. (*Fond Return*, p. 184.) His comments cause Dulcie to wonder about 'the curious obsession of the clergy with paraffin, almost as if it were some kind of holy oil'.

Just as curious is the obsession of the head of a famous university research library with 'improvements'. (*Gazelle*, p. 127.) He abandons his intellectual pursuits of some twenty years to focus on the heating and plumbing systems for the Library. 'Serious' scholarship, however, seems no less trivial; it is no more than the study of some obscure poet of the late seventeenth and early eighteenth centuries who, in the eyes of most, has *not* been so 'curiously neglected by posterity' (*Fond Return*, p. 121) as Aylwin Forbes and his publisher, the Oxford University Press, suppose. Even a serious student of literature is apt to agree with Dulcie's assessment that Aylwin might be better occupied 'putting his marriage to rights than in collating variant readings in the works' of Edmund Lydden, whose poetry's most outstanding feature seems to be its *unfinished* state. (p. 122.)

Scholarly niceties mean little not only to the non-academic world; they seem to be little more than a game to those of the inner circle, the need to publish producing the unearthing of subjects whose only value is that they can be the focus of a book since they have not been treated before. As Miss Foy, librarian for a university, remarks to Viola, who has done research for Aylwin on his project: 'You were lucky to find one so obscure that not even the Americans had "done" him . . . It's quite serious, this shortage of obscure poets'. (*Fond Return*, p. 18.)

But literary scholars are not the only ones who occupy themselves with trivia. Pym seems to suggest in *Less Than Angels* that the anthropologists might be better occupied studying their own society than running off to Africa to discover the meaning of some choking sound made in a language spoken by only some five persons, a project which so fascinates Father Gemini that he helps himself to the research grant money that was to provide aid to one of the aspiring young anthropologists for fieldwork for his project. Pym derides both the insignificance of their work and the lack of nobility in their characters. Miss Esther Clovis loses her job as secretary of the Learned Society because she can't make tea:

> It is often supposed that those who live and work in academic or intellectual circles are above the petty disputes that vex the rest of us, but it does sometimes seem as if the exalted nature of their work makes it necessary for them to descend occasionally and to refresh themselves, as it were, by squabbling about trivialities. The subject of Miss Clovis's quarrel with the President was known only to a privileged few and even those knew no more than that it had something to do with the making of tea. Not that the making of tea can ever really be regarded as a petty or trivial matter and Miss Clovis did seem to have been seriously at fault. Hot water from the tap had been used, the kettle had not been quite boiling, the teapot had not been warmed . . . whatever the details, there had been words, during the course of which other things had come out, things of a darker nature. Voices had been raised and in the end Miss Clovis had felt bound to hand in her resignation. She had been very lucky to be appointed as a kind of caretaker in the new research centre, for it happened that Professor Mainwaring, in whose hands the appointment lay, disliked the President of the Learned Society. (pp. 12–13.)

While it may not be time yet for historians to 'be permitted to do research into the lives of ordinary people' (*Fond Return*, p. 18) or for anthropologists, who are almost as numerous in Pym's novels as clergymen, to stay at home to examine the rites and customs of their own society instead of chasing off to Africa to study primitive tribes, Pym clearly feels it is time for novelists to do just that. Like Henry Green, an author she mentions in *Jane and Prudence*, her artistry lies in making us care about those who require the greatest measure of human sympathy – characters neither beautiful nor heroic, neither ugly nor evil, whose greatest accomplishment is coping with life in a landscape that offers no mountains to climb nor deserts to be endured. Hers is, in fact, the landscape of the everyday, the social gestures of which she depicts in interesting, careful, and amusing detail.

In *Less Than Angels* Pym suggests that she is a kind of anthro-pologist of her own society as she records not only the scholarly rituals of vying for recognition among one's peers — festschrifts, granting and receiving of research grants, and, of course, the social and learned meetings — but also the courting rituals of catching the eye of a man — the debutante balls, the pursuit of academic subjects, and the attention of another man. Nor do con-versational manners, such as the use of first and last names escape her attention. 'It's an interesting study, when you come to consider it. The lower you are in status, the more formal the type of address used, unless you're a servant, perhaps', as one of her student anthropologists remarks. (p. 21.) Pym leaves no doubt that the world of contemporary English society is still a man's world: Mrs Foresight's 'expression as she listened to Miss Lydgate's plans for the writing up of her linguistic researches, was one of rather strained interest. Women must so often listen to men with just this expression on their faces, but Mrs Foresight was feminine enough to feel that it was a little hard that so much concentration should be called for when talking to a member of her own sex. It seemed, somehow, a waste of effort.' (p. 16.)

Pym rejects as romantic the fictional and historical idea that life is lived in pursuit of noble ends. The sermons her clergymen preach are dull, the scholarship of her anthropologists and literary historians picayune, and the work of her government officials in-significantly routine. Tom Mallow in *Less Than Angels* dies 'accidentally shot in a political riot, in which he had become in-volved more out of curiosity than passionate conviction'. (p. 231.) And, though John Akenside is an important enough figure to have someone edit his letters, he 'had a finger in nearly every European political pie at the time of his death, . . . one had never been sure what it was he actually did'. (*Gazelle*, p. 61.)

Pym mocks the pretentiousness of tragedy but proclaims the dignity of the quotidian. That those who have been ignored by fiction and by history, those who have neither jobs of importance nor loved ones who depend upon them, who are elevated by neither cause nor passions, are worthy of being attended to is the posture which informs Pym's fictional world. *Quartet in Autumn* tells the stories of four unmarried about-to-be retirees, Edwin, Norman, Letty, and Marcia. They identify with the newspaper accounts of old people, living alone, dying of hypothermia, sensing that to others their lives may be just as redundant as the lives they read about. The jobs they hold in the company are so unimportant that not only does no one know what they do but also after they retire their department is to be 'phased out' (the deputy assistant director thinks it must be 'women's work' because of its insignificance). (p. 102.) There is not even a need for them to be 'replaced by a computer'. (p. 101.)

Of the four, only Edwin has ever been married: only he 'would be spending Christmas in the traditional and accepted way in his role as father and grandfather'. (p. 83.) But Edwin is glad to escape from the 'jolly family party' (p. 92) just as he now seems glad to be without a wife: 'he had all the freedom that loneliness brings — he could go to church as often as he liked, attend meetings that went on all evening, store stuff for jumble sales in the back room and leave it there for months. He could go to the pub or the vicarage and stay there till all hours.' (p. 16.) Like Edwin, the others dread Christmas, but not because they will be lonely; for indeed they, too, prefer the 'freedom of loneliness' to the 'noise and exuberance' (p. 59) and demands of close human contact. They dread instead that others will feel the need to issue them Christmas dinner invitations out of guilt and pity, and they accept those invitations because they feel compelled to allow others, at least on that day, to act out the socially prescribed role. They are glad, however, that the next day they can look forward to their own pursuits, Letty to the Kensington sales, Marcia to 'tidying out a drawer' (p. 87), and Norman to the solitude of his bed-sitting room and thoughts of the tales his three fellow workers will tell of how they spent Christmas.

In the novel Pym makes Letty's finding a room, in which she can lead a life of independence and privacy, a moral victory; for Letty had coped. She had neither succumbed to the pressures of her friend to go to a home in the country for elderly women nor had she remained in her former lodgings with its new landlord and his many relatives and their strange intrusive customs and smells. As Letty thinks about her life and those of her friends she realises that they are filled with 'infinite possibilities for change'. (p. 218.)

Pym would even have us so adjust our concept of what we consider a noble human drama that we can conceive of Marcia Ivory, not as a social case history, but as a woman. She treats with respect Marcia's reclusiveness, her refusal to be 'helped' by the social worker whose job it is to make people belong to a group, eat proper diets, and keep a clean house. She endows with human dignity Marcia's death from malnutrition, with stores of neatly arranged tins of food in her cupboard, drawers full of meticulously wrapped new clothes along with folded bags and plastic wrappers, furniture covered with dust and a furball from Snowy, the cat who had died years before, still on the bed cover, and a shed full of cleanly-rinsed milk bottles in case of another national emergency like the last, when, as Marcia remembered, it was a case of 'No bottle, no milk'. (p. 64.) Fearful of the world, Marcia has known only her mother and the surgeon to whom she had submitted her body because he was like God, distant and pure. As with her other characters Pym insists that we measure her by her own individuality and not by some idealised concept of what a life or a person is supposed to be. Destiny, for Pym, is clearly a private matter, and her fictions ask us to take people on their own terms.

Like all significant art, Barbara Pym's is subversive. Her gentle ironies mock the romantic paradigm and her characters' acceptance of it. Life is not a love story nor an ethical problem. For Pym's characters it is frequently a drama of tea, pigeons, and gossip. Though her portrayal of life focuses on its mundaneness and on her characters' self-deceptions and self-pretensions, Pym's is not the pen of a satirist. She depicts her characters' psychic landscapes with the compassionate understanding of a humanist and celebrates their successes in being individuals despite the pressures of an impersonal society which would make them into nothing more than spinsters, clergymen, or clergymen's wives. Her focus on the nexus between the individual and his society, which she has detailed with the keen eye of an anthropologist, brings to the fore the problem of selfhood. Because her characters do not conform to the model by which our society and fictions confer value upon men and women, Pym raises the question of what it means to be human, and, in particular, what it means to be among those fiction has ignored.

NOTES

1. V. Woolf, *A Room of One's Own* (New York: Harcourt, Brace & World, 1957) p. 87.
2. Ibid., pp. 35–7.

3. The editions of B. Pym's novels used (which will hereafter be cited with abbreviated titles in the text) are as follows: *Some Tame Gazelle* (London: Jonathan Cape, 1978); *Excellent Women* (London: Jonathan Cape, 1978); *Jane and Prudence* (London: Jonathan Cape, 1953); *Less Than Angels* (London: Jonathan Cape, 1978); *A Glass of Blessings* (London: Jonathan Cape, 1979); *No Fond Return of Love* (London: Jonathan Cape, 1961); *Quartet in Autumn* (London: Macmillan, 1977) and *A Sweet Dove Died* (London: Macmillan, 1978). Pym has also published a short story, 'Across a Crowded Room', in the *New Yorker*, 16 July 1979. Published posthumously (Pym died in January of 1980), and after the completion of this essay, was *A Few Green Leaves* (London: Macmillan, 1980), which is in subject and tone similar to her previous novels.

4. K. Millett, *Sexual Politics* (New York: Avon Books, 1971) pp. 42–3.

5. E. M. Forster, *Aspects of the Novel* (1927; reprinted New York: Harcourt, Brace and Company, 1954) pp. 54–5.

6. Ibid., p. 56.

5 Cold Enclosures: the fiction of Susan Hill

Rosemary Jackson

> And then we came to that old country
> Where the ice and snow do lie,
> Where there's ice and snow,
> And the great whales blow,
> And the long night does not die.
>
> *The Cold Country*, p. 79

Susan Hill's fictional output has been substantial and has been well received by the English literary establishment. Between 1961 and 1976, she published nine novels, two short story anthologies, one collection of radio plays, and received recognition with the Somerset Maugham Award in 1971, the Whitbread Literary Award in 1972, and the Rhys Memorial Prize in 1972. Her success enabled her to be financially independent as a writer from 1963 onwards. Unlike many of her contemporaries, Susan Hill does not seem to be primarily concerned with the subject, or the subjection, of women. A female consciousness rarely forms the centre of her tales, and questions of women's social position appear merely as vague shadows hovering on the edges of her writing. Yet, in spite of this subordination of women, a close reading of Hill's work seems to vindicate a feminist approach. For her victims, her peculiar cast of artists, idiots, children, lonely and dying men and women, are all romantic figures who have given up the struggle to live in an adult, 'masculine' world. They are enclosed within their fears of engagement with a difficult, demanding actuality. They withdraw into passive, dependent situations, feeling that they do not know how to 'live'. Hill seems to pose their problems in metaphysical terms — as to whether life is worth living at all — but behind these there are considerable economic and emotional factors which have deter-mined their senses of 'failure'. As her fiction develops, a resolution slowly emerges, but it is achieved at a considerable price, and it shows that the real issues behind her work are related to problems of female survival.

I shall consider Hill's writing as a whole, and take it more or less chronologically, as it deals with these issues of detachment and desire for life. As a body of writing, it shows considerable unity: from *The Enclosure* (1961) to *The Land of Lost Content* (1976), the same preoccupations appear in it. Plots, themes, and motifs, recur with a striking similarity in different texts, as they move toward a resolu-tion of a basic desire to enter life. Perhaps the most powerful of Hill's images, and the most central, is the one which is found in her work time after time, of a cold, frozen country, of ice, snow, still water, frost, winter. A tension between apprehending ice/winter/sterility and longing for warmth/summer/fertility is constant in her fiction. It is graphically expressed in two identical dream images, found in the openings of *Strange Meeting* (1971) and *The Bird of Night* (1972). These haunting images, primarily oneiric scenes which are not readily translated from visual into verbal discourse, can be regarded as the imaginative centre of Hill's fiction. The first tells of John Hilliard's (his name coincides with Hill's) wartime dream:

> at first, he dreamed only of horses, standing beside a hawthorn hedge in winter. The dark twigs were laced over with frost. There were four or five horses, and the breath came out of their nostrils and rose to hang and freeze, whitening on the air. He heard the soft thud of hoof on hard earth and the metal bits champing. Their muzzles were like the soft backs of moles. . . . For a while, half-sleeping again, he still heard the gentle tossing of the horses's heads, saw their breath smoking, saw ice meshed with cracks across a puddle.
> Outside in the darkness, a hundred yards away, the soil became paler and drier, became sand, and the path led down to the beach. (pp. 12–13.)

The second tells of Harvey Lawson's similar memory:

> How often I must have dreamed, every night of my long life perhaps, and forgotten all of them except this one.

I was dreaming of winter. I stood in a lane beside a hawthorn hedge and the frost had laced the twigs over with delicate, brittle strands of ice, powdery snow lay balanced between. There was a puddle of water at my feet, iced over and trans-parent except in the centre, where it had been cracked by a single stone and the ice was meshed out in fine lines from a hollow core. Beside me stood two horses, and the breath came steaming out of their nostrils and froze at once upon the air, they tossed their heads and their eyes shone, I could hear the harness chinking. I had a hand on the neck of one horse, the muscle was thick and strongly fleshed, and the coat faintly sticky to my touch. The hawthorn hedge glittered. (p. 17.)

For both these dreamers, ice and snow represent their emotional isolation, whilst heat and breath indicate their desire that this coldness be counteracted by something more vital and physical. Frequently, coldness is associated with artistic control, with the act of writing, or with a quest for beauty/purity. Hill's novels and stories recount a gradual thawing of that ice landscape, in a slow renunciation of aesthetic withdrawal.

The title of Susan Hill's first novel, *The Enclosure*, indicates its concern with imprisonment and detachment. Its heroine, Virginia, uses novel writing to control experience. It gives her a sense of superiority over others, of (in-)difference. But her hyper-sensitivity is exposed as egotism. She regards others as less troubled, less perceiving than herself. Her son Philip turns Catholic, and Virginia 'wondered how anyone could be so obviously content and undisturbed', (p. 32) 'she was amazed again at the complacency with which he regarded life'. (p. 34.) Her husband, Guy Stirling, she holds as less sensitive than she is, 'He bluffed himself, as always, into believing that everything was really quite normal'. (p. 114.) The narrator permits no ambiguity in our response to this woman writer: she is a monster of egotism, and all her suffering constitutes a necessary penance for her selfishness. She is described as an 'emotional adolescent', insensitive to Guy's depths of feeling. 'Man, to her, was animal. She could never believe that Guy could experience a woman's subtlety of emotion . . . did not realise that almost physical pain her coldness gave him'. (p. 137.) She is locked in an 'innate selfishness, which she projected so often on to other people and saw in them', (p. 125) being 'a woman whose understanding of men scarcely penetrated the surface, in spite of the influence of passionate love'. (p. 174.) Moral judgements of Virginia, for not giving to others, are plentiful. It is 'her own fault' that her life sinks into 'futility and hollowness', and 'Any observer might have remarked, with justice, that it served her right . . . Virgina never tried to realise the fact that she was unhappy was basically her fault . . . she would not recognise her own selfishness'. (pp. 171, 173.)

Virginia's eventual success as a writer, with a room of her own, is presented not only as a rather Pyrrhic victory, but as an absolute failure in human terms. She has been unable to respond to Guy's patient devotion, and unable to be a 'real' woman − her preg-nancy is 'unreal' to her, and her child, a daughter, is stillborn. Virginia ends in the same enclosure in which she began, with a curious sense of hollowness, of wanting something more. 'She seemed to be living in an enclosure which she hated with an agonis-ing intensity, but out of which she would not let herself escape.' (p. 147.) 'The enclosure was still intact.' (p. 159.) Unlike similar metaphors of imprisonment in Anais Nin's *Under a Glass Bell* (1944), Sylvia Plath's *The Bell Jar* (1963), or Anna Kavan's *Ice* (1967), Susan Hill's image in *The Enclosure* does not relate detach-ment from experience to specifically female anxieties. It allows for neither understanding nor pity. She does not consider the ideo-logical implications of her explicit and implicit judgements about Virginia. She presents the issue as being beyond gender. In fact, her condemnation of a woman for giving priority to her work barely disguises a deep unease, verging on guilt, about her own position as a writer. Female freedom or independence is made synonymous with selfishness. We are left, simply, to condemn a solitary woman writer in the provinces, despising her for her cold-ness, and longing for the warmth, colour, passion, and energy, which have retreated with the man, Guy, into a distant metropolis.

Idealisation/idolisation of the male as the locus of energy is intensified in *Do Me a Favour* (1963). A successful writer, Monica Bristow, suspends her career for the sake of Dan Lindsay, a dashingly Byronic type, with dark features, high cheekbones, thick-set jaw, rakish alcoholic behaviour, aristocratic roots and all. Frequent lapses into Lawrentian prose indicate disturbingly masochistic features on the part of the woman writer. Monica wants to be brutalised, as if this will awaken her out of her work into real life. 'She wanted him to make love to her as harshly as he could, without compassion or being gentle − there was merely what she supposed was an animal yearning for him'. (p. 92.) The further their romantic affair proceeds, the further she sinks into this mine, 'The deeper she penetrated, she began to see into the darkness and to know'. (p. 131.) A classic romance plot nicely contains this knowledge in a cosy marriage, an unexpected pregnancy, and a 'placid contentment'. Monica accommodates herself completely to Dan's larger-than-life, egotistical existence. She experiences a 'complete loss of purpose for anything but this' (p. 174), and 'She wanted to build round her a big, noisy, stable family, with Dan in the centre . . . It was essentially a feminine dream . . . she loved him — she would have done anything he wanted'. (pp. 172–3.) 'Dan's company was all she wanted.' (p. 217.) For all their generational differences, the women in the novel uphold identical values. Monica goes a little further than her elders along a path towards a career, but happily recedes into a marital enclosure. She vindicates the words of the old Mrs Christoff, who tells her: 'Your career is important. You write well. But marriage and children is a greater career in the end — for a woman . . . children are a greater gift than knowledge.' (p. 39.) Monica — and Susan Hill — defend a similarly Victorian notion of women's role. Whereas *The Enclosure* had given Virginia an ending of despair for her devotion to work, *Do me a Favour* gives Monica the joys of self-sacrifice, in her choice of heart, instead of art.

By retreating into domestic security, Monica blinds herself to the unpalatable 'terrible truths' which hang outside. These truths are perceived only too clearly by Peter Goosens, a tragic, doomed figure who is the first in a long series of similarly depressed protagonists in Hill's work. Peter is constricted by the 'hell' of London and the horrors of his marriage. Everything exists, for him, over an edge of violence. He is drawn towards death. 'He pulled the blade over his skin slowly, with a tense, terrifying desire to use it on himself or her [his wife] with violence.' (p. 122.) 'In the end, there was no cure for what he had to live with.' (p. 125.) Just as in Virginia Woolf's *Mrs Dalloway* (1925), where death instincts are channelled into the suicidal figure of Septimus Smith, who impales himself by falling onto sharp railings, so, in *Do Me a Favour*, destructive instincts are concentrated into Peter, who throws himself into the Thames from Waterloo Bridge. 'The river below was running high, but not rough, and it looked filthy — it just went on and on . . . [he swung] up on to the railing.' (p. 185.) It is

the first of many deaths by drowning in Hill's fiction. When
Monica watches an insect crawling over a picture of a sea storm,
she reintroduces this motif of drowning, but refuses to accept that
sense of futility which it evokes.

> She sat still, and suddenly noticed a small insect − an ant or tiny
> winter fly − on the opposite wall. It was crawling, very slowly,
> hardly moving . . . [it] made its way across the glazed canvas.
> She saw it go up the side of a grey rock, over the edge and down
> again, getting caught in a rush of foam that broke over it, and
> going down again, into the sea, across the sea to the other edge
> of the picture, a tiny black speck, moving, it seemed, without
> any legs, just moving aimlessly across the picture. Perhaps it did
> have an aim. (pp. 218−9.)

The conjecture in this 'perhaps' is translated into a certainty, in
Monica's world, by confining herself to recognised aims for a
woman, of producing children and protecting her husband. This
plot sets the pattern for Hill's subsequent fiction. Images of futility
and death are produced by a finite number of natural objects −
moths, crows, peacocks, flies, insects, corpses, bones, birds of
prey, 'owls, ravens, hedgehogs, snakes − augurs of death and mis-
chance', (*Strange Meeting*, p. 19) and they darken Hill's world,
drawing her most vulnerable subjects towards suicide. Opposed to
them, and set comparatively lightly in the balance, are less convincing pictures of community, of family life and love, and a
promise of summer.

In *Gentleman and Ladies* (1968) and *A Change for the Better*
(1969) humane values are sustained with difficulty against a dark
awareness that everything returns to ashes and dust. The title of
the first indicates an imbalance in Hill's writing between the
importance attached to male and female characters. Apart from a
local vicar and two bird-like doctors, the only man in the novel is
Hubert Gaily, a ponderous middle-aged figure, slow but innocent
in his child-like existence with his mother. He is the centre of a
female universe. He hangs on to domestic routine in a defence
against a grotesque reality, living in fear of change. 'Maybe it was
only to be expected, a sudden change that tilted your world side-
ways, slipped the ground from under you a shade.' (pp. 38−9.)
Outside little enclaves of love and caring established by Hubert,
his friend Florence Ames (whose name recalls Dickens's innocent

Florence in *Dombey and Son* and Amy in *Little Dorrit*), and
Dorothy Shottery, lies a bleak world of the dead, dying and indifferent. There is very little plot. The novel opens with the funeral of
Faith Lavender, an old spinster, and closes with that of her sister,
Isabel. The third, Kathleen, suffers a stroke and paralysis, which
make her infantile. The three Lavender sisters are a Chekhovian
trio, slowly dying in an English countryside, surrounded by
similarly empty female lives. Pictures of these female friends
accumulate into a stark tableau of suffering, which is something of
a *danse macabre*. Every woman is locked in her sense of isolation,
resenting her lack of freedom, but too trapped by hostile circumstance to act. Isabel merely laments her wasted years. At twenty-
eight, 'She had looked out of her bedroom window upon an unjust
world, upon undeserved sadness, upon concatenation of ill-luck,
upon at least equal odds of sickness, spinsterhood and narrow
horizons'. (p. 20.) Alida Thorne, a sixty-one-year-old acquaintance, has her mother put away into a nursing home in a final bid
for self-fulfilment, but is portrayed as a bitter, selfish woman. Her
mother, Eleanor, is 'carted away like a splitting and discarded
mattress beside someone's dustbin' (p. 125) into a world where the
only possible movement is into death or dementia, where 'Each
day passed, that was all'. None of them is 'free from the threat'
(p. 137) of immanent decay. They all live in fear. 'The thoughts of
madness and senility frightened her', (p. 61) 'there are no words to
convey the fear, the blank fear'. (p. 113.) Even Hubert ponders
'death and dying. You had to think of it, now and then.' Rather
like Elizabeth Gaskell's *Cranford* a century earlier, *Gentleman and
Ladies* accumulates portraits of female gentility which barely
cover an apprehension of futility. Grotesque similes are all to do
with the traps of women's lives. 'The sunlight showed up a dead fly
on its back beneath the window. Isabel started. She did not like to
be reminded of dead things, even flies, by the stiff, still bits of leg.'
(p. 21.) Gaily remembers reading about 'a woman, crushed to
death by a car that had pinned her against a wall. She had been
walking to the shops, doing nothing, carefree, and it had killed
her.' (p. 205.) They are images simply presenting what is — their
static form makes it impossible to imagine difference.

A Change for the Better gives no sense of change at all. Various
lonely old people sit, waiting for the end, in an English seaside
resort, out of season. Major Carpenter, looking out to sea, thinks
of the deaths approaching his friend Isepp and himself, and

complains that 'We are caught like rats in a trap'. Deirdre Fount, an ageing divorcee, longs for the death of the mother who has trapped her in restrictive habits, but when her desire is realised, she sinks back into her mother's character. Her name recalls Synge's *Deirdre of the Sorrows*. Only old Mrs Carpenter determines not to be imprisoned by such defeatism.

> She is very young, she thought, not yet forty, and already she has given in, she is afraid of life, she will have nothing to look forward to in the future. Well, that shall be a warning to me . . . [I must make] some effort to live my life independently . . . *My* future is entirely up to me. (p. 222.)

Placing the one note of self-determination in the voice of an old widow, without a trace of irony or ambiguity, severely qualifies any sense of women's growth in *A Change for the Better*. Things are irredeemably stuck and static. None of the women escapes. Movement is confined to the ebb and flow of the sea, which erases all their lives, and to Deirdre's son, James, who rejects her and leaves to make a life of his own. It is clear, in these early novels, that Susan Hill has little faith in women's strength. She effects a virtual polarisation of 'female' and 'male' qualities: characters in whom the first predominate cannot compete on equal terms and they sink back, defeated, into actual death or into analogous states of death-in-life. *I'm the King of the Castle* (1970) is a carefully structured narrative along these lines of conflict between 'female' and 'male', resulting in the acquiescence of the 'female' part, which is reluctant to assert itself on 'male' terms.

Central to *I'm the King of the Castle* is a classic drama of rivalry for a family/kinship structure. Eleven-year-old Charles Kingshaw comes with his widowed mother, Helena, to stay at the Warings, a Gothic mansion owned by Joseph Hooper, whose wife, Ellen, has been dead for six years. Helena gradually replaces Ellen in the father's affections. But in the traditional family structure of father-mother-child which results, there is no room for both Charles and Edmund, Hooper's eleven-year-old son. One of the boys has to be excluded. The narrative built around this drama is a well-sustained, tense account of Charles Kingshaw's increasing sense of persecution and alienation. Unable to fight, and unwilling to abuse his integrity by happily giving in to the Hoopers as his mother does, Kingshaw moves away from the Warings to the woods outside, eventually drowning himself in an enclosed pool. Here, he is safe. 'He liked the smell, and the sense of being completely hidden. Everything around him seemed innocent.' (p. 70.) But its innocence, its immunity to adult corruption, is at the cost of ceasing to be alive. Kingshaw's suicide indicates a despairing conviction on Hill's part, that moral innocence is incompatible with survival in an adult world whose rules are patriarchal. Kingshaw refuses to accept Hooper's masculine values. He does not enjoy hunting and killing, he hates war games, he plays with dolls as opposed to toy armies, he chooses not to employ his power to hurt others. He says, 'I can *do* anything. He knew that he would not.' (p. 154.) It is this choice which determines his necessary death in a world dominated by the Hoopers and what they represent. 'He was only good at plodding along by himself, not at competing', (p. 195) and 'he knew that he was the loser.' 'He might as well give up, as he always gave up in the end . . . he knew that there was no more hope for him . . . It was pointless.' (p. 181.) 'He was not cowardly. Just realistic, hopeless. He did not give in to people, he only went, from the beginning, with the assurance that he would be beaten. It meant that there was no surprise, and no disappointment about anything . . . He knew that there was no hope, really.' (p. 53.) This defeatism is of the same kind which kills Peter Goosens in *Do Me a Favour* and darkens the scenes of *Gentleman and Ladies* and *A Change for the Better*. Innocence, childhood, truth, beauty, goodness, are assumed to be incompatible with entrance into adulthood. But behind Hill's humanistic vision there lie some telling sexual differences which reveal this negativity to be a rejection, and fear, of patriarchy.

Kingshaw and Hooper do not compete on equal terms. Kingshaw represents the 'feminine' and Hooper the 'masculine'. Kingshaw owns nothing and is therefore seen as being nothing, as a mere cipher. Hooper (his name suggests, hoop, ring, trap) is his father's son, a little man of property, with a tradition of economic strength and material security behind him. He taunts Kingshaw, that 'Anybody who hasn't got a father is useless'. (p. 113.) This judgement is quickly internalised. Kingshaw thinks, 'It was his father's fault really, because his dying had been the start of it all, the not having enough money, and living in other people's houses . . . He wished she [his mother] was dead, instead of his father'. (p. 114.) Both boys perceive that their drama is a reflection of what is happening between Mr Hooper and Mrs Kingshaw.

Hooper sees it as reinforcing his power, and he says condescend-ingly, 'Look, it's all right, Kingshaw, it's only what ladies do. If she hasn't got a husband, she's got to find one', (p. 117) but Kingshaw is nauseated by his mother's surrender, 'He wanted to shake her . . . He was sick with shame at her'. (p. 130.) The two levels of plot, adult and child couples, parallel one another, and make it possible to read Kingshaw's drowning as a violent image of his mother's emotional suicide in the marriage in which she loses her identity. Unable to be a 'man', yet unwilling to play the losing role of 'woman', Kingshaw is left with no alternative but death. His isolation cannot be preserved indefinitely in the real world. 'He liked being alone, because he was used to it, he was safe with him-self. Other people were unpredictable.' (p. 46.) It is guaranteed only in a fatal, watery enclosure. 'This was his place. It was where he wanted to be . . . when the water had reached up to his thighs, he lay down slowly and put his face full into it and breathed in a long, careful breath.' (pp. 221–2.) He can accept neither his own nor his mother's sexuality. After seeing a calf born, he wants to erase the 'terrible truths' of birth, and of sexuality, but he realises that innocence has been lost. 'You could never return to the time of not-knowing.' (p. 38.) In retreat from such knowledge and from the difficult sexual politics of an adult world, Kingshaw (just before adolescence) sinks into an almost intra-uterine state, in a pool of death in which impossible growth is no longer demanded.

Such withdrawal into perfect states of death, or of death-in-life, is thematically central to the tales collected in *The Albatross and Other Stories* (1971). They are similarly hopeless about the pos-sibilities of sustaining innocence, or joy, or security, in an adult world. The title story concentrates goodness in characters who are killed or estranged from ordinary life. Ted Flint, the sole figure of strength, is killed in a violent seastorm. Dafty Duncan, the retarded consciousness at the centre of the tale, is cut off from normality. He experiences the world as a relentlessly cold place, and external scenes are literally and metaphorically ice-bound, in landscapes which come to predominate in Susan Hill's imaginative world. 'The air shone with frost . . . It was cold enough, now, to freeze the sea.' (p. 79.) 'The gutters were all frozen over, icicles hanging in a clear smooth stream down from the backyard tap . . . Outside, nothing moved, it was as though the world had been bound by ice and frost and only he was free and alive. . . Out on the path, beside the sea wall, the cold was like a solid block through which he had to pass. He thought the skin of his face would peel off.' (pp. 84–5.) This ice landscape is an objectification of Duncan's estrangement from life: his mind is 'numbed', 'blocked off', he is not engaged with things. He tries to 'clear out the frozen feeling, understand what he must do'. (p. 66.) A slow thaw sets in only when Duncan has killed his mother: violence against her life-denying restraints and indifference erupts in Duncan's manic action of tipping her in her wheelchair, into the sea, then setting fire to their home. But he is not released by this violence. He immediately hides in a barn where 'He felt safe, dark. So this was where he had wanted to be, then. This place', (p. 87) and later he is removed to an actual prison. No one with any vitality is left to enjoy the thaw which moves through the natural world in the tale's ending. Other stories in *The Albatross* are equally hopeless. Solitary figures make pathetic attempts to release themselves from years of frustrating isolation, but they all end in ludicrous failure. Miss Parson, the sixty-nine-year-old spinster in 'Cockles and Mussels', dies from food poisoning after a timid excursion into the night life of a seedy seaside resort. 'I have lived too sheltered a life, she thought, I have never known enough about the truth of things, about what really goes on' (p. 124) but her lonely Saturday night out is 'a little too aimless, too trivial to count as life.' (p. 133.) Like the heroines of Jean Rhys, these isolated females are trapped in their own futility. A solitary woman in 'Friends of Miss Reece' (whose name is homonymous with that of Rhys) can do or say nothing, as she lies dying of cancer. Isolation is presented as a tragic, but apparently inevitable, condition of female maturity.

Even in 'Somerville', where the isolate is a selfish old man, a sense of inevitability militates against a critical perspective which would read withdrawal as cowardly or wrong. Somerville sees no-one, exists from day to day, caring only for himself and one hedgehog, a version of himself. He is unable to respond with compassion when a young local girl visits him, and is repulsed by her talk of birth – she is unmarried, pregnant – and death – her grandmother is dying of cancer. He cannot face these physical truths. 'He felt tainted by the mess of other people's lives.' (p. 167.) He seeks to distance illness, pain, sexuality, emotional demands, into a vague realm of unpleasantness which need not infect him.

Somerville thought, do not tell me this, it has nothing to do with me, I want to hear nothing of your grandmother. I have thought of all that, gone through all those questions and solved them, years ago, the problems of living and dying. It is sealed and packed away, that knowledge. I will not listen to you. It is nothing to me. (p. 153.)

His enclosure is an aesthetic one. Like Virginia, in *The Enclosure*, Somerville has withdrawn into a perfect isolation as a way of anaesthetising himself against painful experience. He is a portrait of the artist, 'a spare, rational, ascetic man, a believer in the symmetry and clarity of life, obsessed by the beauty of the knowledge that the world contained five regular solids, no more and no less, a romantic'. (p. 141.) He cannot face change. He does not open his mail. He lives in a romantic universe, in nostalgic love for Barton, a dead friend from his youth, reading and re-reading Barton's last letter, which had described the land of ice and snow in which they were stuck. '"You don't care about anything here", Barton had written, "except the bloody cold, and keeping yourself moving, on your feet, keeping on . . . I can tell you, I know what hell is and it isn't hot, it's cold, it's this frozen, bloody country"'. (p. 139.) Somerville chooses to stay in this infernal landscape, rather than move into somewhere less known or less fixed.

John Hilliard in *Strange Meeting* (1971) is a younger version of Somerville. He, too, is a lonely figure. 'He had . . . the odd sense of completeness, of holding everything within himself, of detachment.' (p. 32.) He is cut off from ordinary existence. 'It was like being under water or some mild anaesthetic, everything around Hilliard and within him was remote, people parted and moved and reformed in bright, regular patterns, like fragments in a kaleidoscope.' (p. 34.) Like Somerville, he idealises a young male friend, Barton.

David Barton is the most romantic of Hill's male idols. He is everything she most values in terms of humanist ideals. He has all that lesser mortals lack, 'some quality − gaiety, composure, and sensitivity' which make of him 'a good man'. Subjected to horrific scenes in the French trenches during the First World War, Barton hangs on to his humanism by reading Henry James and Sir Thomas Browne, and by playing Schubert, Mozart, Brahms on a portable gramophone, whilst shells explode around him. His idealism is ravaged by his meeting with death, as he comes to 'know' truths which had previously been distant and had left his innocence intact. He sees corpses piled together, 'bloated and black, unburied for weeks' (p. 74) and perceives a new emptiness, a nausea, in things. There is 'Something old and bad and dead, a smell, a feeling you get as you walk across the street. It is not simply the bodies lying all about us, and the fact that the guns are firing, it is something else, something . . .', (p. 83) something which makes him feel old, as if 'he had seen and heard all that he ever needed to see, all the fear that there could be'. (p. 85.) His face is transformed from being childish into one which 'knows'. Literature and music cease to signify in the face of this knowledge of inhumanity and death. Barton tears to shreds his volumes of Thomas Browne, ashamed of their pretence of order or beauty. Life, he thinks, is 'wicked and pitiless, it's all one Godawful mess, and how can I let that man, that great man, lull me into a kind of acquiescence? Be romantic about it? Is that right?' (p. 124.)

This questioning of art and its humanistic values is gradually silenced in *Strange Meeting*. Barton's lost illusions are re-discovered by Hilliard, who takes upon himself Barton's life after the latter's disappearance in battle. Hilliard finds in Barton's perfect family the security he had always desired, 'to have a family, to whom you were so close, about whom you could talk so lovingly, people you missed every day, and admitted to missing'. (p. 56.) 'It was as though he had been standing in a dark street looking into a lighted room and been invited in'. (p. 100.) Hilliard purchases from Harrods the collected works of Sir Thomas Browne, and some Henry James and E. M. Forster, as he assumes Barton's role as a guardian of moral value. The horrors of war seem to be redeemed by this inheritance. Hilliard re-surfaces from a shell hole, with 'death, all around him', (p. 167) in which he has dreamt of swimming with his sister, Beth. In the dream, she transforms into Barton who tells him that everything is all right. Against the nightmare offensives of *Strange Meeting*, this imagery of sea, water, and redemptive drowning, suggests another safe, romanticised and childish condition, which is far removed from the military, 'masculine' world at the novel's centre, and cannot be reconciled with it. Hilliard's own emotional detachment, expressed in that crucial opening dream of ice and snow, which I quoted at the beginning, is resolved, as he moves toward Barton's human warmth and love. But Barton is significantly absent by the end. That intangible 'something' which he represented survives only in nostalgic recollection, at one remove. Through this nostalgia, a romantic idealism is preserved intact, despite the novel's constant betrayal of the vulnerability, and inviability, of such ideals.

This kind of ambivalence towards romantic difference, at its most extreme in Susan Hill's loving portraits of artist figures who are doomed to non-existence, is dramatically presented in the divided narrative of *The Bird of Night* (1972). In many ways, this novel echoes Thomas Mann's *Dr Faustus* (1947), in which a pedantic scholar, Serenus Zeitblom, recounts the tragic death-in-life of a great composer, Adrian Leverkühn. Susan Hill's much simpler version of romantic possession is occasionally embarrassing at the side of Mann's original, but it relies upon a similar structure. An English Egyptologist, Harvey Lawson, mediates the doomed life of a great poet, Francis Croft. Like Leverkühn, Francis is seen as mad, but a genius. He suffers all the pains of romantic agony, his suffering being the price of his art. He is unable to participate in ordinary living. He calls himself 'the bird of night', the owl who 'does not praise the light'. 'He believed in good, and, most especially, in evil, in God, but more personally, in the Devil.' (p. 21.) When the text shifts into the artist's deranged consciousness, it tries to give an experience of madness from within, in an elliptical idiom taken from the Bible, Blake, and English literature.

> 'He casts forth his ice like morsels; who can stand before his cold?'
> I shall soon go away to live in a wood for the wood likes to have night-owls, that it may have matter for wonder, and if it is winter with you in your North country, look carefully at the six-cornered snowflake, and give thanks for that. I send you greetings and goodwill, for I cannot love you. (p. 38.)

Art and ordinary life, or simple caring, are assumed to be incompatible. Francis, like his predecessors Kingshaw in *King of the Castle* and Dafty Duncan in *The Albatross*, is a childish, immature figure. He is surrounded by Harvey's mystification of the artist, as if he were of a superior sensibility, and by definition outside normal categorisation. 'No tight, careful little structure will contain the man', Harvey claims, 'His work overflows . . . He was a man of violent feelings, a man of beliefs and passions, he was a poet with a vision, he had everything, everything to say.' (p. 11.) Like his hero in Coleridge's *Ancient Mariner*, Francis inhabits a metaphorical landscape of ice and snow, which images his closure within a romantic egotism. His dark vision imposes periodic bouts of madness which are intolerable, and drives him to repeated suicide attempts, culminating in a successful one as he sacrifices himself by letting his blood in the local church. Harvey's awe-full devotion to Francis permits no ironical perspective on a dedication to romanticism, even though its ending is death. *The Bird of Night* continues that tragic polarity which is found throughout Hill's fiction, in positing an either/or choice between art/life, romanticism/actuality. The first is beautiful, but cold, inhuman, whilst the second is messy and limited, but alive. Yeats posed the problems of romantic withdrawal in similarly absolute terms in his poem 'The Choice':

> The intellect of man is forced to choose
> Perfection of the life, or of the work,
> And if it take the second must refuse
> A heavenly mansion, raging in the dark.[1]

By articulating difficulties in these extreme terms, Hill makes it impossible to envisage art as a force for life. Her artists are all estranged, damned figures, 'raging in the dark', and denying all that is human and warm.

Nearly all of Susan Hill's writing presents problems in such a manner that no positive resolution seems possible: a passive acknowledgement of tragic inevitability is the dominant mood. The stories in *A Bit of Singing and Dancing* (1973) are in this vein: they are bleak pictures of ordinary people confronting lost illusions, with nothing to put in the place of their romantic expectations. In the title story, Esme Fanshaw, in her fifties, is liberated by her mother's death and a small inheritance. She feels anything is possible. 'She thought, this is how life should be, I should be daring, I should allow myself to be constantly surprised. Each day I should be ready for some new encounter.' (p. 107.) But her mother is replaced by a man, Amos Curry, a door-to-door salesman and street entertainer. He enters her house as a paying guest, and a dull awareness at lost opportunities seeps into the story, despite its surface perkiness. 'Now, all the plans she had made . . . were necessarily curtailed, and for the moment she felt depressed, as though the old life were going to continue.' (p. 113.) Esme, like Deirdre Fount in *A Change for the Better*, and Hill's other aging female victims, is seen with a shrug of the shoulders which arouses pathos rather than anger. The reader is numbed into a similar disbelief in the possibility of change. The same

collection contains many hopeless cases, trapped in hotels, boarding houses, empty mansions, old people's homes, geriatric wards,
sterile marriages. 'How soon can I leave?' is a sad tale of two lonely
women, Miss Bartlett and Miss Roscommon, the first always
rebelling against the other's claustrophobic affection, and longing
for autonomy. Miss Bartlett keeps resolving to start a new life,
aware that her role has been unremittingly passive: 'she had never
chosen, only drifted through her life from this to that, waking
every morning to the expectation of some monstrous good fortune
dropped in her lap'. (p. 60.) She dares to make a stand, and leaves
Miss Roscommon's house for her own, only to find it physically
crumbling around her. Aware that she is too weak to realise her
desire for freedom, Miss Bartlett returns to her friend's enclosure,
to find her a corpse on the living room floor. For Hill's unfulfilled
ladies, there is neither leaving nor returning, only a constant,
static, dissatisfaction.

This misery is explicitly related to women's oppression within patriarchal society in some scenes of *A Bit of Singing and Dancing*. In
'The Peacock', fifty-four-year-old Daisy Buckingham looks back on
her empty married life. She remembers how she had learnt to silence
her own anger at being restrained, and had been taught shame at
her sporadic outbreaks of violence when she desired freedom.

> She had felt frustration and anger and misery welling up within
> her like a boil, she had thought, I am only thirty four years old, I
> am still young. I have surely hope and fulfilment before me, why
> should I be in this place, why should I be still tied to my father,
> how can I bear it? (p. 127.)

Marriage had appeared to be her only means of survival within a
social structure which castigates unmarried women as failures.
Within a month of her father's death, Daisy meets and weds
Humphrey, 'a man she had married for fear that there might
prove to be no alternative'. (p. 137.) Daisy does not comprehend
the nature of her discontent, but there are strong intimations of its
origins in a male-dominated family structure. She protests too
much that Humphrey is not the cause of her misery:

> She tried to pin down what she wanted, what was really wrong.
> It was not Humphrey, it could not be Humphrey, for he had
> come as the answer to her prayer, he was a good man and he had
> taken her out of the old life . . . it had not, in the end, been

excitement that she had longed for, she had been very content to settle for something else, for the status of a wife, for security from the shame of spinsterhood . . . (p. 129.)

Daisy's unhappy life is symbolically portrayed in a telling episode when she is accidentally trapped in a summerhouse, and finds herself locked in with a male peacock. She hates the bird as a creature of bad fortune, and wants to escape. 'She wanted to scream, to claw and hammer at the closed door. Oh help me.' (p. 138.) She is impotent. She is a mere absence. 'I have never known myself, never tested myself, I have never truly lived.' (p. 139.) She is unable to release herself from the locked house, anymore than she can escape from her marriage. Her promises of self-fulfilment sink into mere daydreams. Unlike many contemporary depictions of elderly women daring to assert themselves, such as Angus Wilson's *Late Call* (1963), Susan Hill's tales of eleventh-hour bids for female freedom are always pathetic failures. Another story in this volume, 'Missy', narrates the frustrated attempt of old Mrs Ebbs to escape from a geriatric ward. 'She had a right to choose . . . All her life, she had let others decide, father and husband, she had been as helpless as she was now, in this bed.' (p. 150.) She walks out into the night, convinced 'she was entirely free', (p. 154) but is incarcerated again. In 'The Custodian', an old man who assumes a female role towards a young boy, mothering him, caring for him, is rejected by the boy's father. He is abandoned, as a weak, housebound figure, no longer necessary. The hopelessness here, despite its male protagonist, is related to the inertia and impotence which are generated by a passive female condition. The mother figure is left, isolated, to wait for death. Having survived ice and snow, in the hope that 'ahead . . . lay only light and warmth and greenness', (p. 84) s/he meets with no reward for playing a woman's role. 'Happiness did not go on.' These tales are so relentless in depicting the futility of women's aspirations towards fulfilment, that they might appear parodic, were it not for the tragic, pathetic manner in which they are told.

Humour, in fact, apart from occasional streaks of black comedy, is always a long way away from Hill's fiction, nowhere more so than in her solemn tale of grieving, *In the Springtime of the Year* (1974). Structurally and thematically, this is much simpler than her previous novels. Its biblically-named characters, Ruth, Ben, and Jo, point to the novel's religious quality: it is a parable of finding meaning in life. Ben is killed whilst felling an elm tree, trapped underneath it in a crucifixion posture. Ruth, his young widow, and other local characters, seek to come to terms with this apparently meaningless death. Time after time, Ruth experiences mere futility. 'There was no point . . . For there is only this world and the misery of it . . . the whole world should never have been.' (p. 42.) Ratheman, a curate whose young daughter dies, loses his Christian faith in a similar sense of nihilism. '"There was no meaning to it . . . there is only cruelty, there is no purpose in any of it. It means *nothing*."' (p. 151.) It is only through a religious conviction of the soul's immortality that Ruth learns to accept Ben's death. His end comes to seem right and necessary in a natural cycle. 'Birth and death and resurrection, and one tunnel led into the next.' (p. 122.) An old labourer, Potter, who was with Ben's corpse, has a parallel experience of transfiguration. Ben's death, like Christ's, redeems them. Potter says 'I couldn't doubt the truth after that . . . It was death and − and life. I'd never doubt that now.' (p. 133.) Through these spiritual awakenings, Ruth ceases to be a stranger in the world. She moves from winter − again ice landscapes dominate much of the novel − to spring, with a symbolic scene of resurrection on Easter Day. She is able to stand, simply, on the earth, and to accept a cyclical changing of seasons, since death and birth merge into one.

> The first ice and a hard frost came . . . Her breath smoked on the steel-cold night air, and the grass and the vegetable tops were coated with a thin frost, like powdered sugar . . . There was winter. There would be spring. (p. 169.)

Lying behind the Christian, and at times Lawrentian, metaphysics of *In the Springtime of the Year*, there are some hints of Ruth's growth towards independence as a woman. Ben's death releases her to be herself. 'She . . . did not know how she might live for the rest of her life. But Ben was dead, and laid in his grave, and she would move on, from one day to the next.' (p. 169.) She is not a radical female figure. But she does come to realise that her passivity had been related to her conditioned dependence upon a father or male protector. 'Until now she had brought about no real developments in her life by any exercise of her own will; things had happened to her, and she had accepted that . . . She was afraid of taking any initiative with time and circumstance, people and places. She had never done so, because her father had been there, and Ben.' (p. 141.) Ben, like Prince Charming, had seemed to awaken her, 'She had been a chrysalis muffled in an opaque, papery shroud and it was Ben who had awakened her', (p. 137) but her subsequent awakening to herself is much more difficult. Ruth learns that it is not enough to 'simply wait' for outside influences. She moves out of her lonely cottage to assist Ratheman's family and to help Ben's unmarried pregnant sister, Alice. In social terms, women's position does not seem to have advanced far beyond Elizabeth Gaskell's *Ruth* (1853), which recounts the desertion of an unsupported pregnant woman. But in terms of the development of Hill's fiction, Ruth is a step forwards. Like Sylvia Plath's Esther, in *The Bell Jar*, who listens to her body pulsing life, 'that old heartbeat, I am, I am',[2] Ruth gradually discovers her own life, independently of male protection. 'She took a deep breath, held it within herself, let it go softly, she thought, I am myself.' (p. 154.)

Throughout Susan Hill's novels and stories, the same themes and motifs have recurred and have led gradually towards a resolution of the problem of withdrawal from adult experience — a problem she presents as related to detachment as an artist and retreat as a woman. *In the Springtime of the Year*, with its ending of minor triumph, lets the woman move towards self-discovery and re-entry into community life. But feminist issues are conflated with metaphysical ones, as Ruth learns the value of her own life through an apprehension of grace and love. This is typical of a confusion in Hill's presentation of women. On the one hand she presents their problems as actual and socially determined. Her victims are trapped in oppressive social structures, and their frustration stems from unhappy marriages, loneliness, alienation as spinsters, and ostracisation as artists. On the other hand, their 'real' selves are presented in relation to eternal rather than historical time, and they are seen to be suffering from the fact of being mortal. They are caught, with her male victims, 'like rats in a trap', their immanent deaths threatening them with a sense of futility, of never having actually 'lived'. Her women, and her 'female' men, are locked in hopeless situations, ignorant of their desire for freedom until they have lost the youth/energy/courage/power necessary to realise that desire. They end in fantasies of what-might-have-been, or in actual defeat by death. Susan Hill's posing of metaphysical questions, the priority she gives to ageing characters facing their own extinction, means that basic feminist issues are elided. Because of this, any optimism is the result of 'grace', of religious faith, and *not* the result of a conviction that human beings have the power to control their own destinies. One form of passivity has been exchanged for another. Her women, and men, are no more 'free' at the end of her work than they were in *The Enclosure*.

In the radio plays collected in *The Cold Country*, Susan Hill's central preoccupations are dramatised in a clear, distilled form: they reveal the illusory nature of any resolution to the problem of enclosure, at least in the terms she has stated it. *The End of Summer* (1971) introduces her familiar notion of the impossibility of sustaining happiness and childlike innocence. Tom and Sally, young lovers, are isolated on an island, surrounded by a flooding river. Water, rain, owls, cats, cocks, ravens, foxes, bats, monsters are constant motifs, reminders of distress. They haunt Sally with their implications of death. Tom tells her she has an 'over-developed sense of fate, of doom, of disaster . . . it's very neurotic', (p. 21) but Sally cannot resist it. She is terrified of approaching winter, of ice, and rather than witness its slow petrifaction, she drowns herself in the flood. There is no final resurrection: the play ends with the sound of endless rain. *Lizard in the Grass* (1971) revolves round Jane, an orphan in a convent boarding school, isolated in her visions of death by drowning. She has a long imaginary dialogue with John, a spirit who keeps her company like a medieval *memento mori* figure, whispering 'It is generall / To be mortall . . . No man may him hide / From Death, hollow-eyed', (pp. 69–70) until all we hear is the sea and the tolling of a single funeral bell. *The Cold Country* (1972) is, perhaps, Susan Hill's bleakest piece, uncompromising in its icebound landscape. It is set in a region of ice and snow, with four men stranded in a tent in uncharted territory, in the middle of a blizzard. One of them, Jo, ventures outside and is frozen to death. Of the others, Barney is killed with an ice-axe, his murderer, Chip, leaves the tent to go to his own death, and only Ossie remains, to await his inevitable end as 'wind and blizzard take over'. In their extreme situation, the four men keep asking what life means. 'Why don't we all go outside and lie down face first in the snow and die? Why are we bothering at all? Have you asked yourselves that?' (p. 75.) They discover only that 'there is no answer. Not now. Not for us.' (p. 100.) 'The world is a bleak place. You look for a bolt hole, that's all.' Their long day's journey into night promises no escape, except into the ultimate enclosure of death.

Literary allusions echo throughout *The Cold Country*, as they do in all of Hill's writing. The folk refrain, used as an epigraph to this essay, is central in setting the mood, as is the traditional mourning lyric, the Lyke-Wake Dirge. Another central literary motif is Hans Andersen's fairy tale, *The Snow Queen*. Barney remembers his mother reading it to him. The Snow Queen had no heart, she was pure, cold reason, made entirely of ice, 'her eyes gleamed like two bright stars but there was no rest or repose in them'. (p. 85.) She inhabited a palace whose halls were 'all alike, vast, empty, icily cold and dazzlingly white. No sounds of mirth ever resounded through these dreary spaces. No cheerful scene refreshed the sight.' (p. 85.) The Snow Queen stands as an allegorical figure behind all the many sequences of ice, snow, frost, and winter in Hill's fiction, embodying in her cold body all those aspects of death-in-life which had militated against 'ordinary' engagement with the world from *The Enclosure* onwards: aesthetic detachment, narrow rationality, asceticism, inhumanity, indifference, egotism, idealism, quests for perfection. It is no accident that this figure is a female spectre, presented as abusing her power. A movement away from her cold, palatial enclosure, her Tennysonian Palace of Art, is made to coincide, in Hill's fiction, with a renunciation, not only of art, but also of female autonomy.

Strip Jack Naked (1974) finally moves away from the sterility of that cold country, at least in its desire. Its heartless centre, James, is a consummation of Hill's idealistic characters. Like Hamm in Beckett's *Endgame*, James sits in his wheelchair, withdrawn from life. His first words are, 'Grey, grey and grey. Why does the sun never shine now'? (p. 137.) He has left behind a world of colour and change. His enclosure is 'bleak', 'austere', permitting 'nothing superfluous', allowing nothing to get out of control. It permits neither dancing, nor laughter, nor music, nor alteration. Randal, his brother-in-law, calls it 'a burial place', as if it were a removal to 'the womb, or the cradle'. James claims to have seen everything, to have reached the truth in his ascetic purity. But Randal reminds him that his perfect life is sustained at the cost of not really living.

What has it done for you, this precious three years locked away in this house? This . . . 'purging', this inner voyage of discovery, this sack-cloth and ashes game? It's driven you mad. (p. 148.)

In fact, James has withdrawn into his monastic existence in order to avoid the pain of his child's death and his wife's subsequent suffering. Jane, his wife, endured a mental breakdown after the child's death (by drowning), and through her suffering has moved on, into life. 'I feel different', she tells him, 'Clean. As if I'd been put into cold storage and then brought out again and . . . very slowly thawed. Restored. Ice-maiden . . . I used to be that. Heartless. But now it *beats*.' (p. 154.) She insists that his negativity, his defeatism, is wrong. The enclosure is of his own choosing.

> Diana: I don't understand why you are *here*. Why you like it.
> James: Does it seem to you that I *like* it?
> Diana: Then go. You are perfectly free.
> James: Not so.
> Diana: There are no locks. (p. 156.)

Gradually, James moves away from his self-imposed condition of death-in-life. Shadows shift from black into violet, his grey surroundings begin to be coloured. He realises that it is stasis which is cowardly. 'Death is easy, Randal. Dying is easy. Sitting still among the shadows is easy . . . But . . . to live . . . That is the hardest thing of all. And I must do it. I must.' (p. 169.) It recalls a central quotation from *Strange Meeting*, where Barton had marked out Thomas Browne's words, 'It is a brave act of valour to condemn death but where life is more terrible, it is then the truest valour to live'. James's resolution to 'get up and walk', to find colour and change, puts an end to those various retreats into aestheticism, despair, suicide, death, or mere vacuous endurance, which had, until then, and *In The Springtime of the Year*, characterised Hill's timorous protagonists.

Not surprisingly, in terms of the opposition that Hill constructed between 'art' and 'life', the resolution of that feeling of being enclosed in an inhuman aestheticism involves her in a complete repudiation of fiction. Randal reminds James in *Strip Jack Naked* that outside his perfect grey world, everything is chaotic. 'Life is disorganised and messy . . . Outside the door of this room. There are loose ends, questions, various answers and sometimes . . . no answers. A series of choices, awkward events . . . accidents. Distress.' (p. 142.) In the name of engagement with these external contingencies, a cold country of art is renounced altogether. Susan Hill abandoned fiction in the late 1960s in a gesture towards a less etiolated, less enclosed, activity — and a more respectable female role — maternity. In doing so, she made explicit certain assumptions which had been present throughout her writing. Instead of clarifying or confronting difficult ideological issues, about the role of the artist within contemporary culture, and the problem of women's oppression within patriarchy, Susan Hill's work evades them. Her art is trapped within a tradition of humanism — and its essentially realistic mode (made slightly expressionistic by grotesque images and a filtering of experience through non-adult minds). Her women are trapped in their ignorance of the political roots of their misery. Attempts to resolve these questions on an apolitical, metaphysical level prove both unsatisfactory and, as Hill's fiction illustrates, impossible. It is no accident that Susan Hill's work has been so well received by a liberal literary tradition, for it ends by silencing its own timorous interrogation of some of the fatal and crippling effects of a patriarchal, 'male' culture and retreats into a familiar 'female' enclosure of defeatism.

Hill's images of the female role within patriarchal culture are unequivocally bleak ones of wasted lives. She silences women's utterance of quiet anguish in a familiar and traditional manner. Woman's 'voice [is] stilled', her 'body [made] mute, always foreign to the social order' — for in Kristeva's words, 'in the entire history of patrilineal or class-stratified societies, it is the lot of the feminine to assume the role of *waste* . . . .'.[3]

NOTES

All the texts cited are published by Penguin, London except for the following editions: *The Enclosure* (London: Hutchinson, 1961); *Do Me A Favour* (London: Hutchinson, 1963); *Gentleman and Ladies* (London: Hamish Hamilton, 1968); *A Change for the Better* (London: Hamish Hamilton, 1969); *The Cold Country and Other plays for radio* (London: BBC, 1975).

1. W. B. Yeats, *Collected Poems* (London: Macmillan, 1950) p. 278.
2. S. Plath, *The Bell Jar* (London: Faber, 1963) p. 167.
3. J. Kristeva, *About Chinese Women* (1974), translated by Anita Barrows (London: Marion Boyars, 1977) p. 14.

6 The Clinical World of P. D. James

Bernard Benstock

The prominence (and even pre-eminence) of women authors of detective fiction is neither unusual nor particularly significant, but the emergence of an accomplished writer of any subgenre is worth attention. As the Golden Age of Mystery Writing, that halcyon period between the two world wars, has long since vanished, publishers and reviewers have been lavish in passing down the mantles of the royalty of that era (whether Dorothy L. Sayers', or Agatha Christie's, or even Ngaio Marsh's) to members of the newer generation. The renaissance of excellent and original crime fiction during the last two decades in England should eventually tarnish the significance of that artificial Golden Age, and among this new generation (Nicholas Freeling, Ruth Rendell, Colin Dexter, Peter Lovesey) P. D. James may well reign supreme. Her seven novels to date (*Cover Her Face, A Mind to Murder, Unnatural Causes, Shroud for a Nightingale, An Unsuitable Job for a Woman, The Black Tower,* and *Death of an Expert Witness,* published between 1962 and 1977) present a body of superior fiction that, as good detective stories invariably do, extends beyond the limitations of the subgenre of crime fiction. The assumption that a wide gulf inevitably exists between all 'serious' writing and the writing of detective novels has long been open to question: inept writing is equally bad in every fictional format, and good crime fiction ranks with some of the best fiction, usually because it transcends the basic requirements of the format.

The distinctive qualifications that Phyllis Dorothy White (née James) brought to the writing of crime novels pertain to her actual

vocational career as a principal administrative assistant for the
North West Metropolitan Regional Hospital Board in London,
and later as a Civil Servant with the Department of Home Affairs
(in the Criminal Department). Few detective writers have had even
a modicum of practical experience in the offices and laboratories
of police bureaus, much less in the dens of iniquity they describe
(Dashiell Hammett has been held in awe for actually having been a
Pinkerton detective and Janwillem van de Wetering was in fact an
Amsterdam police sergeant). The necessity of supporting a family,
in which her war veteran husband survived for a while as a mental
patient, provided P. D. James with a clinical environment on
which she capitalised for many of her novels, realistic settings from
which she derived unusual and even grotesque possibilities, transforming the most literal and ordinary materials into the amalgam
of imaginative art. The recent reaction against that most traditional ambiance of the Golden Age mystery, the isolated English
country manor house whose genteel decorum is violently disturbed
by an unexpected murder, has caused many detective writers to
attempt to set their scenes in areas of plausible reality: few have
succeeded as convincingly and dramatically as P. D. James.

Not that she has been totally immune to the remote and bizarre
locale, and even her hospitals and nursing homes and forensic
laboratories have their ancillary 'attachments' nearby. An asylum
for the incurably crippled located on the Dorset coast (but without any actual view of the sea) has its mysterious black tower
down the coast road; a forensic lab in the wild Fen country its
deconsecrated private chapel, designed by a disciple of Christopher Wren; a country house just outside Cambridge its
primitive, unused cottage with a deep, dangerous well where a
child had once accidentally drowned; a nursing school its
ominous garden shed. James has never yet duplicated her scenes of
crime, ranging from a single London location, a psychiatric clinic
on a fashionable London square (not without its murky back
alley), to various compass points fanning out into the reaches
beyond the Home Counties. Perhaps the most conventional was
the setting for her first novel, *Cover Her Face*: an Elizabethan
manor house in an Essex village, but with its back garden walls,
nearby stables, and convenient ladder to be moved against a back
window. From the first, P. D. James was able to make even the
most ordinary seem somewhat sinister, and it is not without
significance that this Essex community contains a refuge for

unwed mothers, and that the son of the manor house is a doctor in a London hospital.

The efficacy of a Sense of Place has become progressively more important for P. D. James. The village and town settings of the first two novels are almost prosaic compared to the later variations on the atmospherically unusual; only the beauty of Cambridge in *An Unsuitable Job for a Woman* relieves the gloom of the succeeding works, yet even here there are strong contrasts to the tranquil scene on the quad, the elegant house in which the Tillings live, and the seductively lulling boat trip on the River Cam. A purposeful ambiguity hovers over Sir Ronald Callender's estate-turned-laboratory:

> The house was obviously Georgian, not perhaps the best Georgian but solidly built, agreeably proportioned and with the look of all good domestic architecture of having grown naturally out of its site. The mellow brick, festooned with wisteria, gleamed richly in the evening sun so that the green of the creeper glowed and the whole house looked suddenly as artificial and unsubstantial as a film set. It was essentially a family house, a welcoming house. But now a heavy silence lay over it and the rows of elegantly proportioned windows were empty eyes.

This constant undercutting of the potentially positive description delineates an essential quality in James's attitude toward the world she describes. There are several caustic descriptions of ugly dwellings, of the smug bourgeois and the insipid poor, but the subtle undermining of the manor house highlights an important 'Jamesian' technique. Binary oppositions are less apparent in a second description, in *An Unsuitable Job*, of a house called 'Summertrees', despite the promising introduction:

> It was a large Victorian edifice of red brick, set well back, with a wide turfed verge between the open wooden gate leading to the drive and the road. Cordelia wondered why anyone should have wanted to build such an intimidatingly ugly house or, having decided to do so, would have set down a suburban monstrosity in the middle of the countryside. Perhaps it had replaced an earlier more agreeable house . . . The garden suited the house; it was formal to the point of artificiality and too well kept. Even the rock plants burgeoned like morbid excrescences.

Marked ambiguity is enhanced in Cordelia Gray's description of the 'suicide' cottage behind Summertrees, a cottage that she takes residence in during the case and comes to feel at home in:

> It was, she thought, a curious place, heavy with atmosphere and showing two distinct faces to the world like facets of a human personality; the north, with its dead thorn-barred windows, its encroaching weeds, and its forbidding hedge of privet, was a numinous stage for horror and tragedy. Yet the rear, where he had lived and worked, had cleared and dug the garden and tied up the few flowers, had weeded the path, and opened the windows to the sun, was as peaceful as a sanctuary.

These three dwellings, experienced by Cordelia in quick succession, bracket the range of possibilities in the relatively stark environment postulated by P. D. James. Only those places in which someone has devoted time and effort, a measure of love and attention, an indication of an individual personality or the shared love of a pair of occupants, have a human resonance and an element of beauty. The destructive defeat caused by poverty, the aesthetic indifference emanating from bourgeois complacency, or the callous indifference coming from narrow ambition can turn any residence into a demeaning hovel or an architectural horror, reflecting relentlessly the lives within.

Cordelia's quiet supposition ('Perhaps it had replaced an earlier more agreeable house') pinpoints an endemic pattern in the settings of all of P. D. James' novels. Almost every important building that serves as the central stage of her tragic dramas has been converted from something else, and each is either in the process or in potential danger of being reconverted or abandoned or torn down in turn. The Steen Clinic *(A Mind to Murder)* was originally founded and endowed by Hyman Stein ('the sons all changed their name to Steen . . . and the clinic was given the anglicised name'), taken over by the government 'following the 1946 Act', and threatened with drastic changes; after the murder is solved, there is 'a rumour that the Regional Board may close the clinic and move everyone to a hospital out-patient department'. In *Shroud for a Nightingale* a government inspector arrives at the nursing school both at the beginning and at the end of the novel. Her first impression is of 'an immense Victorian edifice of red brick, castellated and ornate to the point of fancy, and crowned with four immense

turrets . . . An immense conservatory was grafted onto the right
side of the house, looking, thought Miss Beale, more appropriate
to Kew Gardens than to what had obviously once been a private
residence.' Her conclusion that 'as a nurse training school Nightingale House was obviously quite impossible' is corroborated when
she returns to resume the inspection that had been interrupted by
murder. A 'new temporary school' of 'low, functional, cleanlook-
ing lines' stands in stark contrast to the remains of Nightingale
House, 'clumsily cut in two by a giant's cleaver, a living thing
wantonly mutilated, with its shame and its nakedness exposed to
every gaze'. Miss Beale concludes that 'it was a horrible house; an
evil house. It should have been pulled down fifty years ago. And it
had never been in the least suitable as a nurse training school.'

The most grotesque horror of a house appears in James' most
Gothic book, *The Black Tower*, a family home in Dorset converted
by its owner into an asylum for the incurably crippled. Commander Adam Dalgleish views it on first sight as critically as
Cordelia and Miss Beale had glimpsed Garforth House in Cam-
bridgeshire and Nightingale House in Hampshire:

> It was a powerfully-built, square, stone house dating, he
> guessed, from the first half of the eighteenth century. But the
> owner had been unlucky in his architect. The house was an
> aberration, unworthy of the name Georgian.

Like Nightingale House, Toynton Grange has an appendage
grafted on,

> a one-storey stone extension to provide ten individual patients'
> bedrooms on the ground floor and a clinical room and addi-
> tional bedrooms on the floor above. This extension had been
> joined to the old stables which ran at right angles to it providing
> a sheltered patio for the patients' wheelchairs. The stables
> themselves had been adapted to provide garages, a workshop
> and a patients' activity room.

Like the Steen Clinic it is slated to be taken from the private sector
into public domain, undergoing still another transformation.

The Hoggatt Forensic Science Laboratory made its transformation more smoothly, passing from the single authority of its
founder:

Colonel Hoggatt started it in Chevisham Manor when he was Chief Constable in 1860, then left the manor house to his force when he died. Forensic science was in its infancy then . . . We're the only lab with its founder's name. That's why the Home Office has agreed that the new Laboratory will still be called Hoggatt's.

There are numerous such indications in James' novels that the old order has indeed changed, and is now in a new flux of changing still again, with a certain loss of continuity on some occasions and a greater degree of depersonalisation as well. Brenda Pridmore's enthusiastic explanation of the Hoggatt 'continuity' is a rare instance, and at times internally contradicted in *Death of An Expert Witness,* and the persisting portrait of the colonel that Brenda cites in the laboratory lobby is countermanded by the new director's choice of a painting prominent in his office, Stanley Spencer's image of the Virgin's Assumption from Cookham, purposefully selected to discomfit his staff. Howarth's predecessor had apparently represented an older order himself: 'Old Doc Mac was one of the really great forensic scientists — but there's no denying that he'd let the reins slip a bit in recent years. Howarth has already increased the work turnover by ten per cent.' Dalgleish approves of the architecture of the manor, but reacts to the ways in which lovely old rooms have been compartmentalised (something he also noticed in Nightingale House). And lurking on the periphery is the dangerous maze of the incomplete new structure, in which Brenda gets trapped and terrified on her short cut home.

The only institutional building to survive unchanged of all of James' scenes of crime is Sir Ronald Callender's scientific think-tank at Garforth House, which had undergone no great disruption from manor house to institution. 'The stable block has been converted into laboratories', Cordelia learns from Miss Leaming. 'Most of the east side is now glass. It was a skilful job by a Swedish architect, functional but attractive.' The transition here is as painless as anywhere, although Cordelia is disconcerted by certain human transformations, the scientists having to dress for dinner, and even the lab assistant, the frighteningly morose Chris Lunn, dresses in the unsuitable role. With the murder-execution of Sir Ronald, the revealed infanticide, the institution is left without its director, a disruption of its continuity that is not without its dire significance.

The two novels that are not centred in institutional environments,

Cover Her Face and *Unnatural Causes*, none the less reflect elements of the symbolic edifice so manifold in the other five books. In *Unnatural Causes* where the action is focused in a handful of cottages along the Suffolk coastal cliffs (James' two coastal novels are her most Gothic), each dwelling is an exemplum of the personalities of its resident, from the genteel warmth and comfort of Dalgleish's aunt's house to the aloof position of the great retired novelist R. B. Sinclair. The cottages are perched precariously, defying the elements and gravity, and the storm which culminates at the climatic moments of the novel devastates the home of the murderess and sends her to her death, almost claiming the life of Adam Dalgleish as well. In *Cover Her Face*, tentative and probative as most introductory detective novels are, and least characteristic of the matured product, the only institution as such is the nearby St Mary's Refuge for Girls, which provides the murder victim of the story and one of the suspects, its Warden. Martingale, the Maxie home in which the murder takes place, is until that event a comfortable and pleasant place. After the arrest of Mrs Maxie, when Dalgleish inadvertently passes through the village, St Mary's Refuge looks 'empty with only a lone pram at the front door steps to hint at the life inside. The village itself was deserted, somnolent in its tea-time five o'clock calm.' But more important is Martingale: 'It was dustier than he remembered, and somehow more bare but his trained eye saw that there was no real change, only the naked look of a room from which the small personal change of living has been tidied away'. Masterful in her description of menacing environments and edifices undergoing drastic upheaval, P. D. James is also skilful in pregnant understatement.

These 'Jamesian' variants on the Fall of the House of Usher may have larger ramifications for the condition of contemporary Britain, but the author is careful to avoid resounding statements and is refreshingly free from moralising (unlike Agatha Christie and even Nicholas Freeling, severe critics in mystery fiction of the 'contemporary scene'). None the less, the world she describes is one of either fine traditions fading out or obsolete traditions still well dug in, of ugly buildings that are retained and of beautiful buildings that are cannibalised. Stables that once housed fine horses have either been sold off *(Cover Her Face)* or converted to garages *(The Black Tower)* or laboratories *(Unsuitable Job)*. Renovations, even when they do suggest an element of progress, are inefficacious,

as in the London address of one of the shadier suspects in
Unnatural Causes:

> The cobbled entrance was uninviting, ill-lit and smelt strongly
> of urine. Dalgleish, unobserved since the place was obviously
> deserted, passed under the archway into a wide yard lit only by a
> solitary and unshaded bulb over one of a double row of garages.
> The premises had apparently once been the headquarters of a
> driving school and a few tattered notices still clung to the garage
> doors. But they were dedicated now to a nobler purpose, the
> improvement of London's chronic housing shortage. More
> accurately, they were being converted into dark, under-sized
> and over-priced cottages soon, no doubt, to be advertised as
> 'bijou town residences' to tenants or owners prepared to tolerate
> any expense or inconvenience for the status of a London address
> and the taste for contemporary chi-chi.

By contrast, Adam Dalgleish lives high above London, in a flat at
Queenshithe overlooking the Thames, which readers have not yet
had an opportunity of visiting.

It is invariably in the constitution of a mystery writer's detective
that the particular emphasis is focused; in the fashioning of a
Wimsey or Poirot, a Maigret or Marlowe, the author displays the
specific strengths in handling the genre and the pointed thrust of a
strong viewpoint. Dalgleish is no exception, and P. D. James has
shown both care and restraint in the creation. In giving dimension
to her detective-hero she has resisted the traditional tendency to
assign to him a set of idiosyncrasies (a monocle and penchant for
incunabula; moustache wax and a reliance on grey cells; or the
habit of staying with the same drink until a case is solved). Instead
she has chosen to make Adam Dalgleish enigmatic and even
ambiguous: no one particularly likes him, except his creator and
presumably her readers, and those who have to work under his
supervision usually harbour active dislike for his cold and reticent
personality. The assumption that fictional detectives are well-
developed and fully fleshed-out characters (after all, they
reappear in so many books and have so many opportunities to
reveal the intricacies of their inner selves) is obviously an erroneous
one: a handful of surface characteristics persists book after book,
and although we get to know them over a long haul, we rarely get
to know them any better. Rarely do they 'age', much less 'mature'

(although some get married and raise families); we spot them instantly by superficies and mannerism: excessive corpulence, epicurean excesses, and the tending of orchids at 11 a.m. spells Nero Wolfe, regardless of any inner turmoils he may be experiencing. Interestingly enough, Adam Dalgleish is almost unrecognisable *except* for his inner feelings. From the second book on, each volume refers to the death of his wife and newborn son at the instance of the child's birth, and Dalgleish's alternate career as a publishing poet, and these factors delineate his ambiguous attitudes toward his profession, his determined attitudes toward crime and evil, and his uncomfortable attitudes toward the people with whom he comes into contact. Chronological time ticks relentlessly away and Dalgleish ascends from Detective Chief-Inspector *(Cover Her Face)* to Superintendent *(A Mind to Murder)* to Chief Superintendent *(Shroud for a Nightingale)* to Commander *(Black Tower)* − a whirlwind career when one remembers the decades it took for Maigret to receive his well-deserved promotions; but we live in an accelerated age in which a flesh-and-blood Adam Dalgleish must be quickly brought into line with the wooden but world-famous James Bond.

First impressions are relatively insignificant. A tendency to endow police heroes with overpowering good looks (Marsh's Roderick Allen is constantly noted as very handsome, and Creasy's Roger West has even assimilated the nickname 'Handsome') obviates the necessity of complex description and the disparities of human characteristics. Dalgleish has his share of such good looks and his interest in handsome women, but most often they find in each other barriers of personality that immediately endanger any enduring relationship. British practitioners have been less punctilious in adhering to the admonition not to mix the detective genre with the romantic, and saddle the lone wolf sleuth with an encumbering love relationship (one that cannot be pushed out the door at the end of the book), much less the ongoing responsibility of a spouse. With the second Dalgleish novel, in which the memory of the dead wife and son is introduced, a romantic attachment is tenuously established with Deborah Riscoe, the aloof divorcée who had been a suspect in the first novel − which ended with an almost inadvertent return visit to her after her mother had been convicted. *A Mind to Murder* has at its opening the accidental meeting of Adam and Deborah at his publisher's party, but before he can ask her to have dinner with him, a murder across the square at the Steen Clinic deflects him from his primary purpose. His reluctance to undertake the case, and his feelings of illness at the end of the first evening on it, underscore his complex character, and Dalgleish is hardly at his best in solving the murder of Enid Bolam. (Dalgleish takes time out to light a candle in a Catholic church on the fourteenth anniversary of his wife's death.) It is a morbidly self-tortured Dalgleish who elects to call Deborah for dinner once the murder is solved, and *Unnatural Causes* begins with the information that they have been having a serious and passionate affair, and that he is escaping to the sanctuary of his aunt's house both to recover from an arduous murder investigation and indecision about Deborah Riscoe. The murder he encounters there (which he eventually solves, although the responsibility is not his) becomes a determining factor in his decision to ask her to marry him − the case becomes inextricably related to the personal relationship − but Deborah takes the decision out of his hands by refusing to 'loiter about on the periphery of his life waiting for him to make up his mind'. Thereafter Dalgleish is condemned to his lonely vocation, a condition that had long been predetermined by his own state of mind in the earlier novels.

An interesting intrusion in the Dalgleish canon is the appearance of Cordelia Gray as a private sleuth in *An Unsuitable Job for a Woman*, not without precedent since Christie added Miss Marple to her stable of detectives, but more coincidental with Sayers deploying Harriet Vane: first as the accused rescued by Wimsey *(Strong Poison)*, then as an amateur investigator on her own, with a Wimsey, now in love with her, solving the case *(Have His Carcase)*, again on her own until Wimsey arrives to successfully ask her to marry him *(Gaudy Night)*, and finally as her husband's collaborator in detection *(Busman's Honeymoon)*. Engaged in her own new profession as a private investigator, Cordelia knows Dalgleish only by reputation, but it remains with her as a weighty knowledge. She quotes his edicts and advice to herself throughout the investigation, having heard the Dalgleish code from her partner, once a CID man who worked for and apparently venerated his mentor, although Dalgleish had had him dismissed from the force. Cordelia's unorthodox handling of the events and her illegal tampering with its resolution bring her suddenly under Dalgleish's scrutiny. In a *deus ex machina* virtuoso performance he unearths all the salient facts and puts them in place without leaving his armchair, but Cordelia stands her ground and

Dalgleish becomes her exonerator and accomplice. In confronting Dalgleish she undergoes an exceedingly trying experience, but it is apparent that she is indeed impressed:

> He sounded gentle and kind, which was cunning since she knew that he was dangerous and cruel, and she had to keep reminding herself of how he had treated Bernie. At some moments during the interrogation she had actually wondered whether he could be Adam Dalgleish the poet.

The temptation of a Wimsey–Vane sort of romance must have lingered on for a while in the minds of P. D. James' readers, especially at the opening and closing instances of the next novel. Dalgleish is once again at the centre of the stage and in an unusually uncomfortable frame of mind. *The Black Tower* begins with Dalgleish in hospital (recovering from an illness he had assumed was to have been fatal) and ends with him in hospital (recovering from a near-fatal encounter with a murderer). In the first instance he had unexpectedly received a personally picked bouquet of flowers from Cordelia, and was obviously pleased and intrigued; in the second we learn that under sedation 'he's been quoting King Lear. Something about Cordelia anyway. And he's fretting because he hasn't said thank you for the flowers.' The possibilities are certainly there, yet in *Death of an Expert Witness* there is no further allusion to Cordelia Gray.

Dalgleish in Danger is a far more common condition than Dalgleish in Love, and P. D. James has undoubtedly found it preferable to activate her detective narratives with a spate of murderous attacks on Adam Dalgleish. Such aspects of brutality are standard fare in the hard-boiled school of (most American and Continental) crime fiction, where private investigators eventually accumulate more scar tissue than punch-drunk pugilists. Such mayhem committed on Scotland Yard operatives in the genteel variant of *roman policier* is relatively rare, outside the work of John Creasy. Despite the scores of Maigret novels available, one would be hard-pressed to find a handful of instances in which the Inspector's life is in danger — as far back as the early encounter with the 'enigmatic Lett' for an instance in which he was actually wounded, his pride more injured than his shoulder. Lord Peter Wimsey received a similar wound in *Clouds of Witness*, but shrugged it off as barely worth his attention, practically an accident. By comparison, Adam Dalgleish finds himself exposed to three vicious attacks with homicidal intent, undergoing trials by torture despite his safe official position that would ordinarily make him immune from attack: hanging on a roof ledge during a gale attempting to rescue a crippled woman, he has his hands maliciously hacked by her leg braces before she is tumbled into the torrential flood; at the edge of a cliff he is shot and grappling for his life before help arrives; walking through the dark hospital grounds he is murderously cleaved with a golf club before being rescued. In the last case he stubbornly and stoically refuses medical assistance for fear that he will be too sedated to trap the criminal, allowing his wound to be sutured without anaesthetic: 'The pain was an abomination, made bearable only by anger and by obstinate determination not to betray weakness. He set his features into a rigid mask. But it was infuriating to feel the involuntary tears seeping under his eyelids.' In P. D. James' 'normal' world, acts of gratuitous violence are hardly uncommon, and despite his aloof demeanour Dalgleish takes upon his flesh many of the brunts of the world's madness.

Diagnosing the trouble with Dalgleish is no easy matter. The first words that he utters (in the first book) are memorable ones and ominously characteristic: asked if he wants to interview the suspects, Dalgleish replies, 'No, I'll see the body first. The living will keep.' Both pragmatic and austere, the response serves as an apt introduction to Adam Dalgleish, and his behaviour in *Cover Her Face* remains rather unremarkable until the coda section in which he visits Deborah Riscoe after her mother's conviction for manslaughter:

> Despite their apparent easy companionship Dalgleish was morbidly sensitive to every word. He longed to say something of comfort or reassurance but rejected each of the half formulated sentences before they reached his lips. 'I'm sorry I had to do it'. Only he wasn't sorry and she was intelligent and honest enough to know it. He had never yet apologised for his job and wouldn't insult her by pretending to now.

In essence he impresses the reader in being so professional and committed that even his strong reservoirs of compassion take second place, which makes him appear to be haughty and unresponsive. In condoning Cordelia Gray's humane deception,

Dalgleish on one hand concedes the inability after the events to prove what he knows actually happened, while on the other he somewhat enjoys confounding ministerial interference. When the assistant commissioner assumes that Dalgleish is 'becoming more philosophical', he counters: 'only less obsessive, or perhaps merely older'.

Dalgleish was probably never really young: James begins his career *nel mezzo del' cammin* quite intentionally (*her* world is no place for an inexperienced, enthusiastic police officer). The son of an Anglican clergyman he had apparently had a 'solitary and lonely boyhood', and he reacts to the news that his assistant had been a Boy Scout patrol leader by remembering that his youth had 'been devoid of these tribal delights', maliciously conjecturing that Masterson might well have become something quite different from a policeman: 'Given a different heritage, a different twist of fate and he may have easily been a leader in a street gang, his essential ambition and ruthlessness channelled into less conformist paths'. Dalgleish is not only alone but a confirmed loner, accepting the premise that all survivors are by definition suspects until logically eliminated from contention. In involving himself with Deborah he knows that his 'solitary life would be threatened. He knew this with complete certainty and the knowledge frightened him. Ever since the death of his wife in childbirth he had insulated himself carefully against pain; sex little more than an exercise in skill; a love affair merely an emotional pavanne, formalised, danced according to the rules, committing no one to nothing.'

His professed *nadalismo* remains intact throughout, colouring his relationships with others. Since suspects forfeit all claims to his personal rapport (notice that several of the actual murderers pay particular court to Dalgleish: Mary Taylor in *Shroud* and Julius Court in *Black Tower* are 'worthy adversaries' who treat him as a social equal), it is primarily with his professional associates that relations are often strained. There is no indication of this in the initial volume, where he interacts with both the local super-intendent and his own assistant without tensions. Whenever the Yard is called in, there are awkward situations to be overcome with the local police: but in these cases Dalgleish is both correct and cordial. In the two instances in which he is *not* the officer in charge, but merely an off-duty visitor, the contacts prove ticklish. In *The Black Tower* he is accepted by Superintendent Daniel with tolerance (and professional respect), but in *Unnatural Causes* the atmosphere between him and Inspector Reckless is tense and often threatening, and it is apparent that Dalgleish takes secret pleasure in outdistancing him in solving the murder. But with his superiors and subordinates the antagonisms (politely muted) are persistent: when Dalgleish reports to the Assistant Commissioner on Cordelia Gray's activities, we learn that 'the two men disliked each other but only one of them knew this and he was the one to whom it didn't matter'. In two instances (*Shroud* and *Expert Witness*) we hear often from Dalgleish's assistants, Masterson and Massingham, and it is apparent what each of them *knows* but cannot say.

One may speculate in vain as to what Dalgleish has done to offend the two detectives: most likely nothing other than maintain his distance and remain inaccessible to them. Massingham can begrudgingly allow that Dalgleish's treatment of suspects often earns him their respect: 'He made no specious promises, never bullied the weak or indulged the sentimental. And yet they seem to like him, thought Massingham. God knows why. At times he's cold enough to be barely human.' (Dalgleish, in turn, wonders why this son of a peer chose police work, but never asks because he respects the man's privacy — and is not at all sure 'that he wanted to hear the answer'.) As with the Assistant Commissioner, the antagonism is mutual, and when they concluded the case 'Dalgleish wished never to see Massingham again. But he would see him again and, in time, without even caring or remembering. He never wanted to work with him again; but he knew that he would.'

Masterson also harbours his resentment against his superior and 'disliked him heartily'. None the less he is able to suspect 'that the antipathy was mutual, but this didn't particularly worry him. Dalgleish wasn't a man to prejudice a subordinate's career because he disliked him.' The plebian Masterson is far more outspoken (within his own thoughts) than the peer's heir, and reacts to Dalgleish's suggestion that a policeman who cannot temper relentlessness with kindness may be enjoying his work sadistically:

This from Dalgleish! Dalgleish who was so uncaring about his subordinates' private life as to seem unaware that they had any; whose caustic wit could be as devastating as another man's bludgeon. Kindness! And how kind exactly was he himself? How many of his notable successes had been won with kindness? He would never be brutal, of course. He was too proud, too fastidious, too controlled, too bloody inhuman in fact for anything so understandable as a little down-to-earth brutality.

Masterson's own earthiness is never in question, yet it takes a strange path in coping with his suppressed hostility toward Dalgleish. With ulterior intentions he offers one of the student nurses a lift into London, and seduces her in a dark, secluded spot along the road; later he realises the significance of that 'quick lay': 'It had struck him at the very moment of entering Julia Pardoe that his act, in its anger and exaltation, was in some way directed against Dalgleish. But it never occurred to him to ask why.'

The enigmatic Dalgleish defies categorisation. In essence he exists primarily in counterpoint to the murders he investigates, which he regards as only the surface manifestations of a whirlpool of evils in the world around him. Relentless and remorseless he pursues his vocation, suspicious of those he interviews to an extent beyond their positions as suspects in the particular crime. In the first book he avers that 'while he was in charge of this case none of his suspects need think that they could retreat into private worlds of detachment or cynicism from the horror of what had laid on the bed upstairs', and in the last book he notes that 'murder was always solved at a cost, sometimes to himself, more often to others'. The cost to himself becomes prohibitive in *The Black Tower*, and his temporary residence at death's door (no result of a murder investigation but from misdiagnosed illness) determines his decision to pack it all in: 'Judges' Rules, rigor mortis, interrogation, the contemplation of decomposing flesh and smashed bone, the whole bloody business of manhunting, he was finished with it'. Yet the five murders in the novel are relatively bloodless (two are barely more than painlessly dispatching frail moribunds), although Dalgleish himself is the eventual object of prolonged violence, and something in the process of solving the crimes — almost despite himself — causes him to abandon his decision to quit. During the course of the somewhat half-hearted search for a possible murderer Dalgleish admits, 'The truth is . . . that I don't know what, if anything, I'm investigating, and I only spasmodically care. I haven't the stomach to do the job properly or the will and courage to leave it alone.' There is no doubt that his presence and persistence engenders further killing; the local police, content with natural and accidental causes, were perhaps wise to 'leave it alone'.

In the interim between *The Black Tower* and *Death of an Expert Witness* Dalgleish acquiesced to resuming his profession, and there is no further talk of changing direction. Not only are we to assume that his job is a necessary one, but also that it is of vital necessity to Dalgleish. His apparent method of sublimating this distaste for what he encounters (encounters in himself) is in his poetry:

> he had worked eighteen hours a day for a month until the case was solved. And his next book of poems had contained that extraordinary one about a murdered child which no-one at the Yard, even those who professed to understand it, had had the temerity even to mention to its author.

Even the possibility of counterbalance in love and marriage to Deborah Riscoe was in the process of being eliminated in *Unnatural Causes*, as the intensive concentration on detection continued to make increasing demands on him. His private life was kept in abeyance; his public obligations were becoming a total commitment; and his private world was only occasionally allowed in his writing of poetry. The importance then of that outlet from his frustrations and substitution for love cannot be under-estimated, and its relationship to detection reveals itself in odd juxtapositioning:

> But the strain of the case was still with him and it would take more than the winds of a Suffolk autumn to clean his mind of some images. No reasonable woman could have expected him to propose in the middle of this investigation and Deborah had not done so. That he had found time and energy to finish his second book of verse a few days before the arrest was something which neither of them had mentioned. He had been appalled to recognise that even the exercise of a minor talent could be made the excuse for selfishness and inertia.

It would be inaccurate to think of Dalgleish as a detective who is also a poet, or both a working detective and a practising poet: Dalgleish is a poet *because* he is a detective.

If the strongest element in detective fiction is ambiance (and few serious readers of the genre would bother to maintain that it is in the ingenious puzzle), then its greatest weakness is characterisation.

Successful character presentation would soon obviate the possibility of assuming until the denouement that all seven or eight suspects are equally likely to be guilty; to really *know* an individual in a detective novel is to know his most basic aspects of personality, and a practising murderer would be difficult to disguise as just another integer in a drawingroom. P. D. James takes remarkable chances in allowing her people (the guilty as well as the innocent) to carry portions of the narrative in interior monologue without either fudging on their most vital concerns or giving themselves away. Agatha Christie's Dr Shepherd narrates all of *The Murder of Roger Ackroyd* without tipping his hand until Hercule Poirot unmasks him at the end, but the reader eventually learns that the doctor is *writing* his transcript for the eyes of others. James allows many of her characters to act independently of the narrative, on occasion usurping Dalgleish's investigative function and refining the detective's activities out of existence, without ever compromising honest characterisation, lessening the developing enigma, or revealing more than is concealed. Her people are moulded in accord with Maigret's jaundiced vision that everyone is capable of murder when the unique combination of circumstances present themselves, and she can allow for full character development without fear of overexposure for the murderer. And part of her success in this area derives from the equal role played by women: twice as many female murderers as male; not a single male murderer in the first four novels.

P. D. James's talent is well within the English tradition of characterisation by idiosyncrasy and eccentricity, nor does she shy away from the grotesque. Each of her novels is memorable for a series of bizarre persons (some in major capacities but many merely in walk-on roles), yet what is most remarkable is that each novel posits an internally consistent gestalt of characters. *Cover Her Face* offers a particularly decent family and their guests, so much so that the reader is tempted to accept the traditional, class-conscious explanation (which is never correct) that the murder must have been committed by a passing tramp. What the Maxie family stands for seems eminently worth preserving, and Mrs Maxie herself the most solid element in the family. Yet once her moribund husband finally breathes his last and that responsibility is lifted from her, she can confess to Sally Jupp's murder (albeit unintentional) — without cheating Dalgleish of his deduction. The faithful family retainers prove over zealous in their dedication, and when Stephen Maxie is accused of withholding evidence that would have cleared Derek Pullen immediately, he is callous enough to reply: 'I didn't lose any sleep over him. He had no right on our property and I told him so.' The sinister Mr Proctor contributes the almost obligatory grisly touch when he absolves himself from guilt as the right-handed strangler:

> He gave a sudden convulsive movement, there was a click and a moment of sheer unbelievable comedy as his artificial right hand fell with a thud on the desk in front of Dalgleish. They gazed at it fascinated while it lay like some obscene relic, its rubber fingers curved in impotent supplication.

The hinge of interesting character reversal in *Cover Her Face* does not suddenly swing toward any of the actual suspects, but to the victim herself. Sally Jupp was lovely and cheerful, self-reliant and hard-working, and presumably admirable in refusing to reveal the name of her child's father. Vindication arrives with the husband whose identity had to remain secret, but it is tainted by the revelation of her perverse pride in keeping the secret, her disdain for others, her heartless toying with Stephen Maxie. When she is eventually catalogued by an objective observer as 'pretty, intelligent, ambitious, sly and insecure', it becomes apparent that the relevant disclosure in the novel ironically concerns the corpse that 'had lain on the bed upstairs'. Whereas the average mystery yarn gravitates centripetally, thinning out as it moves from the initial complexity toward oversimplification and the tying up of loose ends, James' narratives move centrifugally into greater complexity and density.

The first novel involved two unrelated events accidentally disguising an unintentional killing as premeditated murder; *A Mind to Murder* combines two unrelated crimes, the blackmail more heinous than the slaying. A sombre, somewhat defeated Dalgleish comes close to failure through overconfidence, following the pungent trail of the fresh herring to trap a blackmailer, but unaware of just how intertwined the threads of the lives involved actually are. It is in the monolithic structure of the Steen Clinic community that knots are tied so closely, and within the desperate interdependencies the weakness of that structure gives way to blackmail and murder. The administrative and nursing staff dote on the doctors, jealously guarding their favourites, who are themselves weak and self-divided professionally, and therefore

personally. The clinic administrator is theatrical and hollow; Dr
Steiner is nervous and insecure; Dr Bagueley easygoing and put-
upon, victim of a neurotic wife. In this situation the egomaniacal
porter Peter Nagle can run roughshod, conscripting a fauning
Jennifer Priddy into his conspiracy and neutralising a sick, ageing
fellow porter. The Steen is a decaying society in which weak and
ineffectual authority creates a vacuum that the conscienceless
Nagle (modelled on Pinkie in *Brighton Rock*) quickly fills, and
when authority becomes unresponsive and unapproachable, even
the meek cousin can rise up in murderous wrath. Nor does
Dalgleish's uncovering of the two culprits manage to bring stability
to the Steen (Nagle's conviction will be for a minor offence, and
Miss Bolam will be judged incompetent to stand trial): and the
clinic will itself be taken over and changed drastically.

The 'community' represented in *Unnatural Causes* is a *laissez-
faire/laissez-vivre* arrangement of generally literary people, each
essentially living in privacy from each other, but socially inter-
locked either in vague companionship or for security when in
danger. When the storm breaks they congregate at the cottage of
Dalgleish's aunt (except for the distanced and reclusive Sinclair),
and Dalgleish muses that perhaps

> they could neither bear their own company nor feel at ease with
> each other. This at least was neutral ground, offering the
> comforting illusion of normality, the age-old protection of light
> and a warm fire against the darkness and enmity of the night. It
> certainly wasn't a time for the nervous or imaginative to be alone.

Malevolent Nature in Suffolk mirrors the malevolent and mal-
content natures of those residents of the 'art colony': from the
superficial and mercenary writer of romantic trash to the arch
drama critic and effeminate journal editor ('They're a spiteful lot,
queers', remarks Inspector Reckless with equal spite; 'Not violent
on the whole. But spiteful'); plus a surly Cambridge under-
graduate visiting her aunt and the severely crippled and
disgruntled typist who emerges as the murderess. In this atmosphere Adam Dalgleish takes refuge after his trying experience on a
murder case, but it is to his saintly Aunt Jane (who has her parallel
in *The Black Tower* in Father Baddeley) that Dalgleish retreats,
only to have the community descend upon him with the murder of
the detective novelist to solve. The urban counterpart to this rural

enclave is far more invidious: a Soho nightclub owned by an exonerated (but guilty) murderer, his hustlers, henchmen, and hangers-on. Although pathetic and hideous Sylvia Kedge is revealed as a multiple murderess after her attack on Dalgleish, several elements of the narcissistic colony redeem themselves under pressure: the effete Justin Bryce proves himself a man of action and the disdainful Oliver Latham even more heroic in rescuing Dalgleish. None the less, a pall hangs over the grim novel which James reactivates to advantage in successive volumes.

Shroud for a Nightingale, in turn, is particularly claustrophobic in its community relations; most of the book transpires in the hospital grounds, and mostly in Nightingale Hall. Here we encounter a tight society of diverse women (nurses and nursing students), with implied bitchiness, a lack of privacy, sexual frustrations and neuterisations. The students are undergoing their rites of passage, while the adult nurses (all vaguely in their forties) experience trials by fire when first one, then another student is killed. Some of the young people are basically good and kind, but many are weak-spirited and weak-willed (Dakers), cold and impersonal (Fallon), mean-spirited (Pearce), rich enough to be relieved of their studies (Harper), or sexually vindictive (Pardoe). The women essentially reflect the characteristics of their juniors, but the developing enigma concerns the search for the one that had been a Nazi nurse who escaped conviction as a war criminal because she was then too young. Their names invite speculation: Mavis Gearing (sex-starved and timid); Hilda Rolfe (lesbian and angry); Ethel Brumfrett (haughty and unimaginative). Yet it is the beautiful, serene, efficient Mary Taylor who is unmasked as Irmgard Grobel, and although her 'devoted' companion Brumfrett committed the murders in order to protect her and maintain her hold over her, Brumfrett eventually becomes her victim. Nor are the murders necessarily the most heinous aspects of the plot, although the method used to dispatch Pearce is unusually gruesome. The emotional blackmail employed by both Pearce and Brumfrett repels Dalgleish, since it enjoys 'its secret knowledge under the cloak of generosity, kindness, complicity or moral superiority'; both the Pardoe—Rolfe and Pardoe—Masterson sexual partnerships are vicious and destructive; Masterson himself is easily dislikeable, and the grotesque woman who 'blackmails' him into being her dancing partner is wildly repugnant, 'an extraordinary apparition, painted like the caricature of a stage whore'.

Minor roles are played by an arrogant doctor intent on exacting large fees, a struggling young writer who sustains himself through complete selfishness, and an eminent pathologist, 'an expert in death who obviously enjoyed his work' — 'Dalgleish despised him as a ghoul'. Dalgleish as a character is more complex in *Shroud* than heretofore, least like a poet, cold and unfeeling, yet capable, at the end, of a *beau geste*, destroying the confession note after Mary Taylor's suicide. The Sins of the Past loom large throughout the novel (reminiscent of the plots of Ross Macdonald's later work): the war trial, the suicide of a spendthrift actor, and the ghost of a hanged girl that haunts Nightingale Hall. The kindness and bravery of the halfwitted servant girl who saves Dalgleish's life offer one of the few elements that relieve the totality of horror plaguing P. D. James' *Shroud*.

James' scalpel seems more exploratory than incisive in *An Unsuitable Job for a Woman*, but this may only be an illusion brought on by the relatively sunny environment of her Cambridge setting, and the brooding Adam Dalgleish temporarily supplanted by a sanguine Cordelia Gray. The dredging up of the hidden past, the Ross Macdonald approach, now becomes a dominant motif, symbolised by the ominous well in which a four-year-old had once drowned and from which Cordelia tortuously extricates herself in miraculously foiling a murderous intent. The grim facts eventually revealed include: that illegitimate child that drowned, the hanged youth who learned at twenty-one the true identity of his mother and was killed by his father, the body desecrated by his father and cleansed by his real mother. The garish painting and transvestment of Mark Callender, a doctored murder made to look like an accidental strangulation during sexual experiment, is the most horrifying, but not the sole grisly event in the book. Cordelia's discovery of Bernie Pryde's bloody suicide; the rotting food left at the scene of the crime that she isolates and preserves as evidence; her attempt to interview the vegetating doctor in a state of advanced senility; the revelation of the sexual liaison between Elizabeth Leaming and Chris Lunn; and Lunn's sudden death in a head-on collision — these add heady touches to *An Unsuitable Job for a Woman*.

Nobility of character is a rare commodity in James' novels. One is certainly expected to assume that Cordelia (like Dalgleish) has it, but among those in *An Unsuitable Job* it is the murdered youth who is by far the strongest contender, while Cordelia's dead father — a bohemian Communist poet — and the Sister Perpetua at her convent school are also in contention. Falling a good deal below are the cynical but unmalicious friends of Mark Callender, the Trillings and others who find the body and attempt to disguise the sexual-deviance evidence. The Cambridge Set in general gets poor marks from Cordelia:

> She had never in her life attended one of those innocuous if boring gatherings for the routine consumption of gossip, gin and canapés but, like her father who had never attended one either, she found no difficulty in believing that they were hot beds of snobbery, spite and sexual innuendo.

It is the ambiguity of her sexual morality that taints Elizabeth Leaming who, as Sir Ronald's mistress, had given birth to the son that his wife could not have, in order to assure that Sir Ronald got his father-in-law's money; never succeeded in having either her motherhood acknowledged or her relationship with her lover legalised; doubled as the lab assistant's mistress as well; and eventually executed Sir Ronald when she learned of his murder of their son. Coldly correct and punitive she none the less emerges as a sympathetic person, and Cordelia risks everything in covering up her act of retaliation, especially when one considers Sir Ronald's conscienceless monomania. A product of upward mobility he is totally without scruples in his determination to ensure the success of his scientific laboratory, a latterday variant on the 'mad scientist' with his devotedly evil 'servant', Chris Lunn.

Illicit sexual liaisons and misalliances, never far from the surface in any P. D. James thriller, erupt in *The Black Tower* as companions to the plague of impending and surprising deaths. The three homosexual couplings seem more healthy and benign than the two extramarital heterosexual combinations, but sex is never a happy arrangement, as the various mis-marriages testify. (Witness Dr Hewson, discontent with both his wife and mistress, since he has a penchant instead for fifteen-year-old girls.) With the death of old Father Baddeley, an ineffectual Good Angel even when he was alive and presumably serving the spiritual needs of Toynton Grange, nothing relieves or redeems the gloomy atmosphere of pettiness, poison pen letters, spiteful animosities, self-delusions, parasitical relationships, human exploitation — not to mention the siege of homicides. The assorted cripples are pathetic and often unpleasant, but the nature of the deaths indicates that, at least, none of them is a murderer: that would have to be someone ambulatory, either one of the staff or one of those peripheral to the Grange. The possibilities are extensive since the dramatis personae include a secret reader of pornography, a sexually frustrated alcoholic, a sexually ambiguous male nurse, a gossipy shoplifter, a disgraced doctor, an overly masculine woman, a nurse who had once caused the death of a geriatric patient, and an ex-convict handyman built like ape-necked Sweeney. The skeleton-in-the-cupboard in this case is the Victorian ancestor who 'walled himself up inside the tower and starved himself to death' — his descendant, with a phobia of fire, almost dies in the tower when the murderer starts a small conflagration on the ground level while he is upstairs perusing his pornographic novels. That the staff are cloaked in brown monkish habits adds to the spooky anonymity with which the killer can wander freely through the house and grounds, but it is when the 'survivors' are dressed for the pilgrimage to Lourdes that James unleashes her most caustic comic touch:

> The pathetically depleted party had a bizarre air of slightly spurious joviality. Dalgleish's first impression from their varied garb was that they proposed to pursue quite different and unrelated activities. Henry Carwardine, in a belted tweed coat and deerstalker hat, looked like an Edwardian gentleman on his way to the grouse moors. Philby, incongruously formal in a dark suit with high collar and black tie, was an undertaker's man loading a hearse. Ursula Hollis had dressed like a Pakistani immigrant in full fig whose only concession to the English climate was an ill-cut jacket in mock fur. Jennie Pegram, wearing a long blue headscarf, had apparently made an attempt to impersonate Saint Bernadette. Helen Rainer, dressed as she had been at the inquest, was a prison matron in charge of a group of unpredictable delinquents.

The Dalgleish of *Black Tower* is a rather depressed and undecided convalescent, far less removed and authoritarian than ever before. His role as a poet is underplayed; that of a widower remote. Only his 'belief' in the dead Father Baddeley, who many years prior had been his father's assistant curate, sustains him in an investigation in which he has neither an official function nor a clear directive, although the audacity and flair of his adversary, Julius Court, keeps Dalgleish up to the mark. His professional expertise is sharpened by an egalitarian cynicism that tells him that 'every death benefited someone, enfranchised someone, lifted a burden from someone's shoulders, whether of responsibility, the pain of vicarious suffering or the tyranny of love. Every death was a suspicious death if one only looked at motive, just as every death, at the last, was a natural death.' The Dalgleish of *Death of an Expert Witness*, by comparison, is far less involved and less intro-spective, almost returning full circle to the first adventure. Despite Massingham's antagonism and accusations of coldness, his person-ality is de-emphasised, and it is primarily as a professional performing a professional function that he is presented. There is no conflict with the local police, no physical danger to him during the investigation, and no great emphasis on his inner anxieties, although the dangers to the four-year-old William in the closing sections of the book apparently awaken moments of anxiety.

The overwhelming question of *cui bono*, however, is as omnipresent in *Death of an Expert Witness*. Motives for murder abound: a newly appointed director having to deal with a dis-appointed staff member passed over for the job; a beautiful and talented woman whose husband had died tragically, whose in-volvement with her half-brother is somewhat suspect, and whose string of love affairs has begun to look chronic; a disinherited cousin whose happiness in her lesbian marriage depends on find-ing money to buy the cottage that they are living in; an insecure employee badgered by aggressive authority and terrified of losing his job; a corrupt policeman whose wife has left him because he won't take a job working for her father; a doctor whose former wife is threatening to win custody of his children. Yet most of those involved are above suspicion: *Expert Witness* in many ways is more than a piece of detective fiction – its complex of characters dominate the action and their interaction as vulnerable humans emotionally involved with each other exists beyond the framework of the murderous events. So much more pathetic then is the denouement of the novel, the shattered lives left over after the two corpses are buried and the murderer incarcerated: the woman whose lesbian lover has been killed; the aged father whose son is dead; the woman whose lover has been arrested; and most dis-tressed, the children of the arrested murderer. As in the first book, the 'murderer' is a better person than the victim, but in this case the aggrandising influence of evil takes a giant stride forward – the second murder dooms Dr Kerrison, who admits, 'I forfeited so many rights when I killed Stella Mawson, even the right to feel pain'.

In *Expert Witness*, as throughout the sabbatical of P. D. James novels, architectural structures encapsulate significant patterns. Stella and Angela (their relationship possibly star-crossed) had attempted in vain to transform Sprogg Cottage to Lavender Cottage, but it is the Wren chapel – actually designed by a disciple – that mirrors periodic transitions. Old Hoggatt 'was almost entirely without aesthetic taste . . . He used it as a chemical store once it was deconsecrated'; recently it had been used for a concert by a string quartette, which then disbanded; then for Domenica's sexual assignations; and finally for Stella's murder. Such careful attention to the minutia of detail characterises James' handling of 'clues' that illumine greater mysteries than the solving of homicides: and future investigators will find themselves examining and analysing various *clous*. For particular notice: contented companionate living arrangements between two middle-aged women; dank hallways that smell of cabbage, urine, and furniture polish; slovenly housekeeping and tinned, processed and artificial foods; artificial flowers, but even worse, hothouse roses, 'etiolated scentless blooms'; ancillary characters with reverberating names (Alice Liddell, Moriarty, Freeling, Philby). And since the mantle of Dorothy L. Sayers has been made readily available to P. D. James, it would be profitable to trace the figure in the carpet which delineates James' indebtedness to Sayers: parallels between *Unnatural Death* and *Unnatural Causes*; storm sequences in *Unnatural Causes* and *The Nine Tailors*; the university settings of *An Unsuitable Job for a Woman* and *Gaudy Night*; East Anglican family names in *Death of an Expert Witness* and *The Nine Tailors*; the mountain-climbing experience of the murderers in *Death of an Expert Witness* and *Whose Body?* Rarely since Sayers has a writer of thrillers diagnosed existing society with such microscopic precision, dissected human character with such relentlessness, and examined so many minute cells and tissues of dead, dying, and diseased organisms.

NOTES

The citations in the text are to the following editions of James' books: *Cover Her Face* (London: Hamish Hamilton, 1962); *A Mind to Murder* (London: Hamish

Hamilton, 1963); *Unnatural Causes* (London: Hamish Hamilton, 1967); *Shroud for a Nightingale* (London: Faber and Faber, 1971); *An Unsuitable Job for a Woman* (London: Faber and Faber, 1972); *The Black Tower* (London: Faber and Faber, 1975); *Death of an Expert Witness* (London: Faber and Faber, 1977).

7   Women and Children First: the novels of Margaret Drabble

Gail Cunningham

Margaret Drabble's novels to date run from *A Summer Bird-Cage* (1963) to *The Ice Age* (1977): from the bright, bouncy era of swinging sixties' privileged youth to the shivery, depressed days of the mid-seventies and their attendant middle-aged disillusions. In the progression of her novels, each of which is very precisely identified with the time of its composition, we see the glittering world of intellectual and artistic attainment being replaced by a dangerous and declining Britain with bombs and gunfire in the streets; the Oxford of *A Summer Bird-Cage*, with its golden sunshine and gowned students, is represented symptomatically in *The Ice Age* by a classics don, in a damp and chilly country cottage, grumbling tediously about the decline in educational standards and writing arid verse nobody reads. The range of characters and settings has matured and expanded with the author's skill while remaining recognisably consistent. But cast and scene have grown older and tarnished, have moved with the times: the summer of the first title has weathered into the ice of the latest.

The apparent literary—critical neatness of this contrast is one which would probably appeal to Margaret Drabble herself, for her work is in every respect highly literary. It would not quite be true to say that all her novels are written about intelligent arts graduate women, but it is *perpetually* clear that all are written by one. Margaret Drabble's double first in English from Newnham

College, Cambridge could obviously have fitted her for a career as a literary critic, and she has produced successful work in this discipline. But the brilliant English scholar and sensitive critic is ever present too in her novels. Four out of the current eight have quotations, literary or religious, as titles, and all are permeated with references and tributes to other writers, particularly to nineteenth-century and Edwardian novelists. *A Summer Bird-Cage*, with its neatly-wrought comparisons and contrasts of marriage types, inevitably recalls *Pride and Prejudice*; *Jerusalem the Golden*, as she says herself, is 'almost as much a tribute to Bennett'[1] as her biography of him; *The Millstone* (1965), about a guiltily virginal intellectual whose one sexual encounter produces an illegitimate child, makes a neat inversion of Hawthorne's *The Scarlet Letter* ('but the A stood for Abstinence, not for Adultery') (p. 18); and *The Waterfall*, in which the heroine falls in love with her cousin Lucy's husband, deliberately invokes *The Mill on the Floss* ('those fictitious heroines, how they haunt me', says Jane, 'Maggie Tulliver had a cousin called Lucy, as I have . . .') (p. 153.) Nor are the literary influences apparent simply in the larger structures of the novels, for smaller references to characters' reading or scholarship are frequently used to define or reinforce thematic meaning. In *The Garrick Year* (1964), for example, Emma Evans' progression from self-consciously isolated and often angry spectator to committed participant is signalled by her rejection of the 'list of facts . . . dates of events preceding the Sicilian Vespers', which she reads while mechanically feeding the baby, in favour of material more specifically concerned with the individual and the human — 'Wordsworth, and Hume, and Victorian novels'. And at the end of *The Ice Age* Anthony Keating, having failed in turn as academic, entertainer and property speculator, finds himself in the middle of an East European military coup contemplating with astonishment the bizarre moral codes by which he appears to be acting and reading examples of similar peculiarity, ancient and modern, in Sophocles and John le Carré: to complete the literary-moral map, he ends up, with triumphant neatness, pondering Boethius in a Walachian jail.

It should not be concluded from this, though, that Margaret Drabble's novels are either over-scholarly or intellectually pretentious. On the contrary, her consciousness of working in the honourable tradition of the Victorian novelist anchors her more firmly than many modern writers to the common concerns of life, to love, marriage, the family. Like the Victorian novelist, too, she constantly insists in her work that moral problems, investigated within a meticulously charted social framework, are to be treated seriously. Family background, the interaction of parent and child, of husband and wife, or of lovers, provide the basic material of her novels and are treated, moreover, without the more fantastical instances of violence, madness or sexual perversity so often associated with modern fiction. Although her characters are usually raised by intellect, wealth or talent above the average or the typical, their enforced contact with the possibly mundane but more commonplace patterns of domestic life provides the fruitful friction which the novels examine. Repeatedly, we find her characters enunciating such insights. In *The Garrick Year* eccentric, beautiful Emma sees her marriage to the 'flashy, commercial' Welsh actor David Evans as 'a good gamble . . . each thinking that the other possessed the wildness to which we wished to chain ourselves forever, . . . each thinking that we had committed ourselves to unfamiliarity'. (p. 26.) But when her fury at an unplanned pregnancy is transformed by the birth of her daughter into 'delighted and amazed relief' at her maternal devotion she confesses that it is 'a common story' but is 'proud of its commonness'. (p. 27.) Rosamund Stacey in *The Millstone* also finds that pregnancy brings an awareness of the facts and feelings of maternity, conventional, even clichéd, for most women, but very remote from her isolated scholarly life: 'I am sure that my discoveries were common discoveries; if they were not, they would not be worth recording'. (p. 68.) And in *Jerusalem the Golden* Clara, painfully cutting loose from her drab and repressive Northern background and searching for 'an emotional situation of unparalleled density and complexity', 'a spirit of confusion' (p. 22) finds it, paradoxically, in a close-knit family group. 'Babies, mothers and fathers had hitherto been for her the very symbols of dull simplicity. She saw that she had been wrong about them, and possibly therefore about other relations of life.' (p. 22.)

Clara's revelation, her sudden understanding that the most ordinary concerns can provide the density and complexity she seeks and can illuminate, moreover, the 'other relations of life', is typical of Margaret Drabble's novels. It is a specifically female kind of insight, and indeed with the possible exception of *The Ice Age* all the novels stick very closely to the woman's experience. Margaret Drabble herself sees nothing restrictive or unnatural in novels being identified with the sex of the author, finding more surprising the claim made by some writers that no difference can be discerned between the products of male and female novelists.[2] This does not, of course, necessarily imply that her own novels take a starkly feminist stance. Indeed, one of the most notable features of her work from this point of view is that while a great many of her heroines seem tailor-made for feminist exempla, being intelligent, independent and successful, the actual espousal of the feminist cause is often pushed back into an earlier generation. Frances Wingate's mother in *The Realms of Gold* is a gynaecologist, 'ardently caught up in population control and abortion law reform' and 'speaking frequently of the need to emancipate woman from the chores of domesticity and child-rearing' (p. 83); in *The Waterfall* Jane, the morning after her muddled and solitary childbirth, remembers how her mother and aunt 'had had a conspiratorial pregnancy, having coolly resolved to share the troubles and the discussions and the inactivity' and reflects 'on the amazing apparent control with which her mother's generation had planned their lives and their families' (p. 14); and Rosamund in *The Millstone* describes her mother as 'a great feminist. She brought me up to be equal. She made there be no questions, no difference.' (p. 29.) This is a conscious device of the author's, a desire 'to give credit where credit is due' to the feminist tradition, and to counter the facile assumption she finds particularly among Americans that the woman's movement is something which sprang from nowhere in the mid-sixties.[3] But the implications in her fiction are more complex. Often we find her pointing out that the most apparently emancipated behaviour is part of a tradition. When Sarah in *A Summer Bird-Cage* watches her rich and beautiful sister Louise calling for her lover at the theatre, as many a Victorian gentleman called for his chorus girl, she feels 'a glow of admiration' for this role reversal. Yet further reflection suggests that far from being glibly modern

> there was almost something classic in her position, something more deeply rooted in the shapes of life than the eternal triangle of a woman's magazine . . . Louise herself realized that she was part of an unbroken line, rather than a freak. And she drew real pleasure from that concept. (p. 180.)

Similarly, in *The Millstone*, Rosamund's position as unmarried mother and career woman, superficially a paradigm of modern feminism, is linked firmly with its nineteenth-century parallels: 'I'm one of those Bernard Shaw women who wants children but no husband', she says, with only a hint of defensive bravado. (p. 106.) Nor is it merely a question of recognising historical or literary lineages. The clarity of the feminist issues faced by the earlier generation in Margaret Drabble's novels becomes blurred for the contemporary woman: the straightforward questions have to a large extent been answered, and in showing that those answers are not necessarily of much help she pushes the woman question a stage beyond that of the formal campaigner. Sarah's observation of Louise, and her experience of friends' marriages both conventional and bohemian, lead her to the conclusion that her own life is 'a truly unprecedented mess'. Frances Wingate, apparently secure with both career and lover, finds herself inexplicably uneasy:

> Something rebelled in her, something began to make trouble: she found herself saying things like, 'it simply isn't in me to spend the rest of my life ruining my career for a man who will never marry me'. *(The Realms of Gold*, p. 79.)

And this confusion of clichés, one conventional (demanding marriage) the other progressive (the fear of ruining her career) muddles her thinking to the extent of causing a break with her lover which temporarily wrecks her happiness.

For the typical Margaret Drabble heroine, then, the forms of modern feminism are acknowledged and, often, consciously embraced, but the complexities of life are repeatedly shown to demand the painful forging of a more personal, individual morality. 'One can't have art without morality', says Jane Grey in *The Waterfall*, (p. 232) enunciating, presumably, the conviction of the author. Reviewing the circumstances of her life in terms which she describes as 'hysterical . . . maybe' — 'renunciation, salvation, damnation' — Jane justifies herself on the grounds that 'life is a serious matter, and it is not merely hysteria that acknowledges this fact: for men as well as women have been known to acknowledge it'. (p. 52.) In a novel whose plot, as we have seen, recalls *The Mill on the Floss*, the moral terminology also reminiscent of George Eliot is clearly appropriate. But this emphasis on the seriousness of life and its concomitant moral problems, the necessity insisted on so repeatedly by George Eliot for characters to create their own moral convictions, is typical of all Margaret Drabble's novels. Rose Vassiliou in *The Needle's Eye*, rejecting finally the temptation of easy capitulation to her ex-husband's perverse demands and determining to continue her agonised struggle to live by her own somewhat eccentric principles feels 'beneath the terror, on some level rarely visited, exultant, full of exultation, because, after all, in the human spirit there was depth, there was power, there was a force that would not, could not accept any indulgence or any letting off'. (p. 199.) It is a moment, one of many in Margaret Drabble's later novels, which in its attempt to convey the scope of spiritual struggle within a realistically observed, almost commonplace, human situation, clearly reflects the influence of the Victorian psychological novel, and of George Eliot in particular.

The earlier works – from *A Summer Bird-Cage* to *Jerusalem the Golden* – are less ambitious in moral and spiritual range, but correspondingly more specific about the day to day dichotomies in woman between ambition and restriction. Shy, scholarly Clara, in *Jerusalem the Golden*, attaining admiration and popularity by her unexpected adolescent burgeoning, 'drew the appropriate moral – the possession of big breasts, like the possession of a tendency to acquire good examination results, implies power'. (p. 46.) And this conflict between, as it were, brains and breasts, between professional aspiration and social expectation, is one suffered in some degree by all the early heroines. Interestingly, this most fundamental aspect of the modern woman's movement appears at its strongest in those of Margaret Drabble's novels which were written before any great resurgence of feminism had begun in Britain: these women are experiencing the conflicts at first hand, not through the medium of an already existing movement with its conventions and clichés. Sarah, in *A Summer Bird-Cage*, is shown

> thinking how unfair it was, to be born with so little defence, like a soft snail without a shell. Men are all right, they are defined and enclosed, but we in order to live must be open and raw to all comers. What happens otherwise is worse than what happens normally, the embroidery and the children and the sagging mind. I felt doomed to defeat. I felt all women were doomed . . . I can get very bitter about this subject with very little encouragement. (pp. 28–9.)

In *The Millstone*, Rosamund reflects on the irony of conceiving a child from her first and only sexual encounter, seeing it, characteristically, as some sort of retribution for her unwomanly state as frigid intellectual:

> My friends had babies. There was no reason why I shouldn't have one either, it would serve me right, I thought, for having been born a woman in the first place. I couldn't pretend that I wasn't a woman, could I, however much I might try from day to day to avoid the issue? I might as well pay, mightn't I, if other people had to pay? I tried to feel bitter about it all, as I usually did . . . (p. 16.)

And *The Garrick Year* explores most thoroughly of all the tensions between domestic responsibility and wider ambition. Emma Evans, deprived of her chance to become the first woman television news-reader, and removed from her glamorous London life to the countrified provincial town of Hereford for her actor husband's season at the Garrick theatre, finds herself thrust angrily back into the role of bored housewife. *The Garrick Year* opens symbolically with a marital row whose violence shakes plaster from the walls and produces a 'marriage bed, pushed into the middle of the room, stranded there far from the harbour of the walls, and filled with grit'. (p. 19.) Once removed to Hereford, and observing with stony detachment the theatrical antics of her husband and colleagues, Emma weans her small son from the breast – 'I thought with relief of that sterile bottle' – restores her figure to its spiky thinness, and frees herself to do, in effect, nothing. (p. 55.) 'What was wrong with me, I wondered, what had happened to me that I, who had seemed cut out for some extremity or other, should be here now bending over a washing machine to pick out a button or two and some bits of soggy wet cotton?' (p. 108.) These images of grit, dryness and sterility are continued in the contrast between Emma's barely-consummated affair with the theatre's director and her husband's cheerfully irresponsible adultery with the nubile young actress Sophy Brent, who 'was on the side of all the flowering greenery . . . built for liaison and fruition'. (p. 146.) The melting of Emma's dry reserve comes first through her un-characteristic flood of grief over a series of domestic accidents which leave her 'damp with milk and blood and tears' – emblems, clearly, of womanhood – and then through her rescue of her daughter Flora from near-drowning in the River Wye. Flora's accident brings husband and wife together in a spontaneous moment of unity, and the year which opened with the grit in the marriage bed mellows into natural images of parental respons-ibility — 'that rocky landscape that I had foreseen had now become a waters' edge with ducks and mud' — and a harmonious family outing in the country marred only by the sudden startling sight of a snake. (p. 153.)

> But 'Oh well, so what', is all one can say, the Garden of Eden was crawling with them too, and David and I had managed to lie amongst them for one whole pleasant afternoon. One just has to keep on and to pretend, for the sake of the children, not to notice. Otherwise one might just as well stay at home. (p. 172.)

A qualified and ambiguous conclusion, perhaps — neither an Ibsen-like slamming of the door on domesticity, nor a facile resurgence of family feeling — but it is a convincing resolve of the experiences related in the novel, and a realistic pointer to the future.

That Emma's relaxation and acquiescence should be brought about largely through the accident to her daughter is indicative of another general characteristic of the novels. Margaret Drabble seems to offer two main kinds of thematic focus, one through literary references, as we have already noted, and the other through children: they reflect, in fact, the two extremes of the typical Margaret Drabble heroine, the brains and breasts dichotomy. Jane Grey spells this out most explicitly:

> The strange confidence with which I found myself able to handle a baby could, perhaps, have given me an identity, could have rescued me from inertia: I could have turned myself into one of those mother women who ignore their husbands and live through their children. But with me, this did not happen; my ability to kiss and care for and feed and amuse a small child merely reinforced my sense of division — I felt split between the anxious intelligent woman and the healthy and efficient mother. (*The Waterfall*, pp. 103–4.)

Hers is the common daily conflict experienced by many an educated mother. But children in Margaret Drabble's novels are also given a moral and emotional role of wider significance.

Decisive moments, of action or understanding, are frequently expressed through incidents involving children or babies. Rose Vassiliou sets out on her course of moral experiment, identifying herself to a censorious society as 'the girl who had given all her money away to the poor, or something ridiculous like that', (*The Needle's Eye*, p. 22) when she sees a newspaper photograph of an African child, victim of 'a very little civil war', sitting naked beside its mother's corpse, 'its face lost, its eyes sagging blank with nothingness'. (p. 115.) And the comparison of values between Rose, living in surroundings made dingy and squalid by her voluntary renunciation of inherited wealth, and Simon Camish, who has struggled up from his working-class background to a life of loveless affluence, is pointed most acutely by a neat pairing of incidents involving children. Rose relates to Simon a crucial moment from her past, when she observed a deformed boy and his mother bidding goodbye outside a hospital, 'and she had kissed him so tenderly, and he had run off, waving, smiling, radiant, illumined, his mother waving with a tender pride . . . and Rose had remembered that sudden change of countenance, that sudden transformation of what she had understood to be a grim relation, and could never think of it without a lifting of the spirit'. (p. 246.) The next day Simon, with the memory of this story fresh in his mind, queues in his local greengrocer's listening to a father giving a typical shopping list for the area ('cucumber, melon, French beans, have you any Cos lettuce, it must be Cos') and realises with a shock of embarrassment and pain that the prattling son at the man's side is a mental defective out on a rare visit from his institution. At the back of these cameos, clearly, is Wordsworth's 'The Idiot Boy', a poem frequently invoked by Margaret Drabble in such contexts. And the incidents emphasise also the wider application of the contrast between Rose's family of cheerfully resilient children, scruffy but content, and Simon's home, to which he can return to discover his son miserably picking at a scratch meal supervised by the *au pair*, and be made to feel that 'there was something hopelessly wrong with a life where a child sat in a kitchen eating a fried egg in terror, watched by a hostile alien, while adults in the drawing-room gulped down alcohol and displayed their unlovely hypocrisies'. (p. 187.) Similar examples can be found in almost all the novels: Alison Murray's daughters in *The Ice Age*, one hopelessly retarded by cerebral palsy, the other a sullen and jealous adolescent, tearing their mother in two by their conflicting demands on her emotions; Jane Grey's son in *The Waterfall*, howling with misery day after day as she leaves him, for his own good, at nursery school; the various styles of maternity which Sarah, in her quest for an appropriate role in a shifting social climate, witnesses in *A Summer Bird-Cage*; and Rosamund's baby daughter in *The Millstone*, who, as we shall see, becomes the focus for the novel's moral resolve. Children do, after all, form a major part of most women's lives, and can thus be used naturalistically to point thematic significance; and they also, interestingly, seem to allow the author a full expression of profound emotional response where in other contexts she is more inclined to employ oblique hints or intelligent exposition.

A general survey of Margaret Drabble's themes and preoccupations suggests what is in fact the case, that her novels have a high level of consistency, are all cast in a similar mould. But it is impossible to do justice to the extent of her achievement, to the deeply-satisfying skill with which she integrates theme and structure, and presents character within a deftly detailed social framework, without analysing some of the novels in detail. Any of her works could be selected for the purpose: she has so far had no obvious failures. But one from the earlier period, and one more recent production, can at once reveal the nature of her basic talent, and illustrate the extent of her range and development.

The Millstone, as well as being perhaps the best of the early novels, displays with great clarity the way in which the various common characteristics so far noted can be fused together in a single theme. Rosamund Stacey is the product of parents with 'an extraordinary blend of socialist principle and middle class scruple' who have instilled in their daughter a mix of feminist theories and puritan morals. (p. 27.) The effect of this is neatly conveyed in the novel's opening, as Rosamund recalls her first attempt at sexual intrigue when she and her boyfriend Hamish slink off from Cambridge to spend a night together in an hotel. Asked to sign the register, and having agreed to use the man's name, Rosamund nevertheless writes 'as large as can be, in my huge childish hand' her own surname. The resulting embarrassment and annoyance lead her to the telling conclusion that 'I was stopping the machinery, because I had accidentally told the truth' (p. 6); and her inability to conform happily to the mores of a buddingly permissive society, the Freudian slip which derives from her parents' combination of integrity and repression, seals the pattern of her sexual experience from then on. Despite repeated attempts, she never actually sleeps with Hamish, and subsequently contrives an appearance of sophisticated liberation while keeping all her relationships with men strictly platonic. It is her protracted virginity, and the puritan ideals of self-reliant individualism derived from her parents, which are as much the millstone round her neck as her subsequently conceived illegitimate child. Her parents, she says, 'had drummed the idea of self-reliance into me so thoroughly that I believed dependence to be a fatal sin'. (p. 9.) And the moral and psychological state this produces, an obsessively scrupulous, almost impersonal, attitude towards the formal obligations of personal relationships coexisting with the wildest distortions of truth in the image of herself she projects to others, is neatly linked to the intellectual work which is to maintain her independence. She is writing a thesis on the imagery of Elizabethan verse, a work of originality and scholarly exactness which will eventually ensure her a comfortable university career but which is as she confesses 'wholly uncreative'. Her research displays all the sustained effort, discipline of intellect and avoidance of laxness that her parents' outlook would commend, but, reflecting her own character, is applied to poems dealing with love, beauty and sexuality within a framework so formal and highly wrought as to negate, almost, the human application of their subject.

The circumstances of her one sexual experience are made similarly fitting. It is a casual acquaintance, the unassertive, unaggressive and effeminate George, rather than either of her two conventionally virile men friends, who is responsible for her initiation. The homosexual and the virgin meet sexually on more or less equal terms, make tentative and largely uncommitted advances to each other, and achieve a rather unsatisfactory intercourse. Rosamund remains physically unmoved but, typically, remembers her manners: 'I managed to smile bravely, in order not to give offence, despite considerable pain'. (p. 30.) This belated deflowering enables her to remove from her bosom the scarlet letter which, as she has already observed, 'stood for Abstinence, not for Adultery', but her one act of conforming to the modern morality she attempts to admire brings with it the old-fashioned retribution of pregnancy. 'Being at heart a Victorian, I paid the Victorian penalty.' (p. 18.)

Creativity of an unexpected kind is thus forced upon her. Rosamund's realisation that she must have conceived comes to her while at work on her thesis in the British Museum Reading Room, and the images of Elizabethan sonnets are abruptly blotted out by those of illegitimate pregnancies: 'gin, psychiatrists, hospitals, accidents, village maidens drowned in duck ponds, tears, pain, humiliations. Nothing at that stage resembling a baby'. (p. 34.) But after her amateurish attempt at inducing an abortion with alcohol and hot baths ends merely in tipsy euphoria it becomes clear that the baby is going to be real, and the painful process of confronting the actualities of life begins. Shackled to her parents' ideals of independence and self-denial, and to the guilt with which they compensate for their middle-class privilege, Rosamund enters the tangled world of the National Health Service as an 'initiation into reality'. In the doctor's waiting room she finds, among her fellow patients, 'representatives of a population whose existence I had hardly noticed' (p. 37); at the ante-natal clinic she is 'reduced almost to tears by the variety of human misery that presented itself'. (p. 57.) The abstracts of her parents' socialism – poverty, oppression, disease, overwork – are translated graphically into facts, and facts of which she forms a part. Inexorably, Rosamund is drawn into the dreary relish of the expectant mothers' story-swapping at the clinic:

> The degrading truth was that there was no topic more fascinat-ing to us in that condition; and indeed few topics anywhere, it seems. Birth, pain, fear, and hope, these were the subjects that drew us together in gloomy care, and so strong was the bond that even I, doubly, trebly outcast by my unmarried status, my education, and my class, even I was drawn in from time to time, and compelled to proffer some anecdote of my own. (p. 60.)

It is not merely a question of the straightforward eye-opening of a middle-class Cambridge graduate to an unknown world. The morality which lies behind the status is, more significantly, under scrutiny. Right at the beginning of her pregnancy Rosamund gets an intimation of what is in store for her. 'I felt threatened. I felt my independence threatened: I did not see how I was going to get by on my own.' (p. 39.) The values instilled in Rosamund by her up-bringing have produced a self-reliance based on isolation, on an inability or a refusal to relate to the realities of other people. She understands, excuses, and forgives – as her parents, classically, had forgiven the char-lady for stealing the silver – but as an

intelligently detached observer, not a participant. Now, responsible in the directest possible way for another's life, she has to learn
to assert, to judge, and most important of all, to receive help:

> I saw that from now on I . . . was going to have to ask for help,
> and from strangers too: I who could not even ask for love or
> friendship . . . I could feel that my own personal morality was
> threatened: I was going to have to do things that I couldn't do.
> Not things that were wrong, nothing as dramatic as that, but
> things that were against the grain of my nature. (p. 72.)

Having been 'born with the notion that one ought to do something, preferably something unpleasant, for others' Rosamund
now finds that this somewhat mechanically self-denying dictum is
to have a more deeply personal and emotional application, and
becomes aware, too, that the unpleasant things done to her can no
longer be meekly accepted as the legitimate coinage paid back for
her own privileges: 'I still crinʒed politely and smiled when doors
slammed in my face, but I felt resentment in my heart'. (p. 80.)

The need to receive help graciously seems to be completed with
suspect ease by her novelist friend Lydia's request to share
Rosamund's flat in return for baby-sitting duties. Lydia is a
genuine representative of the society in which Rosamund's disguises enable her to move. Artistic, promiscuous and cheerfully
unscrupulous about demanding favours, Lydia upsets Rosamund's carefully calculated balance of mutual debt by using the
flat's artistically congenial facilities to tap out a novel about a
scholarly unmarried mother who uses academic research as an
escape from reality. Rosamund's annoyance when she discovers
and secretly reads the typescript enables Margaret Drabble deftly
to confront the question of her own heroine's academicism, and to
counter Lydia's essentially trite point about ivory tower escapism
with a justification of scholarship as a skill worthy of respect in its
own right. It is significant too that Lydia picks as the subject of her
Rosamund-figure's research the medieval poet Henryson, a writer
whose works cannot illuminate the heroine's character in the way
that Elizabethan verse reflects Rosamund's. Lydia's novel is an
inferior work on the same subject as Margaret Drabble's, and
eventually suffers an appropriate fate in being torn up and
chewed by the baby. In this clash between life and art, life
triumphs resoundingly: but the two need not be so baldly opposed.

A discussion of Hardy's *Life's Little Ironies*, which Rosamund maintains 'had rather a profound attitude to life' and Lydia rejects as 'so mechanical. Not real' leads Rosamund to attempt a serious analysis of her feelings about the 'meaning' of her pregnancy:

> I had a vague and complicated sense that this pregnancy had been sent to me in order to reveal to me a scheme of things totally different from the scheme which I inhabited, totally removed from academic enthusiasms, social consciousness, etiolated undefined emotional connections, and the exercise of free will: up to this point in my life I had always had the illusion at least of choice, and now for the first time I seemed to become aware of the operation of forces not totally explicable, and not therefore necessarily blinder, smaller, less kind or more ignorant than myself. (p. 67.)

This is not simply a relapse into the sort of flabby irrationality displayed by her sister, who holds the view that 'you don't decide to have children. They decide to be born', but more a Hardyesque awareness of the significant accident, the revealing irony. Her pregnancy makes her face facts which are, curiously she thinks, 'precisely the same facts that my admirable parents had always so firmly presented to our childish eyes: facts of inequality, of limitation, of separation, of the impossible, heart-breaking uneven hardship of the human lot'. (p. 68.)

At first it seems that this knowledge is to be assimilated without too much emotional strain. Rosamund has a remarkably easy childbirth, produces an extraordinarily beautiful baby daughter, Octavia, and compromises her independence afterwards only to the extent of accepting free help from Lydia, and paid help two days a week from 'an amiable fat lady' while she goes to the library to work. True, she is introduced, for the first time in her life, to love, the love she feels for the baby, and the miraculous, uncritical devotion that Octavia gives in return. But in the Hardyesque terms to which the novel has already alerted us, she is obviously getting off too lightly. Only when Octavia contracts a common autumnal cold and Rosamund, after much characteristic havering and guilty soul-searching, screws up her courage to ask the doctor to do his job and come to see the child, does the full pattern begin to emerge. Octavia is discovered to have a potentially fatal heart defect, demanding immediate and extremely risky operation. The night before the baby's admittance to hospital, Rosamund lies awake in an agony of anxiety and unfocused guilt. In Rosamund's extremity of emotion, Margaret Drabble is able to fuse the two sides of her nature, the academic and the maternal. Suddenly, her Elizabethan poetic imagery shifts from the library to the heart:

> Towards morning, I began to think that my sin lay in my love for her . . . Ben Jonson said of his dead child, my sin was too much hope of thee, loved boy. We too easily take what the poets write as figures of speech, as pretty images, as strings of *bons mots*. Sometimes perhaps they speak the truth. (p. 127.)

But the final crisis comes after the operation. Octavia recovers, but Rosamund's overwhelming relief is quickly tempered by the discovery that she is not to be allowed to see the baby during its two weeks' convalescence. In her resulting confrontation with the hospital authorities, all her self-effacing dislike of fuss, her dread of inconveniencing others — qualities which, in their negative aspect of escapist selfishness, are largely the cause of her situation — have to be put aside:

> This time I felt that I would not be the only one to lose; somewhere Octavia was lying around waiting for me. It was no longer a question of what I wanted: this time there was someone else involved. Life would never be a simple question of self-denial again. (p. 132.)

When her efforts at polite insistence are met merely by the smug intransigence of a starchy Sister, all Rosamund's reserves finally break down in a fit of screaming hysterics. '"I don't care", I yelled, finding words for my inarticulate passion, "I don't care, I don't care, I don't care about anyone, I don't care, I don't care, I don't care".' (p. 133.) The apparent paradox — devotion to her daughter leading to the hysterical proclamation that she doesn't care — in fact enforces the point that the impersonal, empty caring imposed by her parents' self-denying doctrines is at last dispelled by the demands of a just personal cause. And even in the middle of her hysteria, Rosamund becomes conscious that the moment is one of psychological resolve, as intellectual understanding and deep feeling fuse into a whole personality:

> Inside my head it was red and black and very hot, I remember, and I remember also the clearness of my consciousness and the

ferocity of my emotion, and myself enduring them, myself
neither one nor the other, but enduring them, and not breaking
in two. (p. 134.)

Although the novel does not end here, this is its climax. It is an
extraordinarily moving scene, and one moreover which, in its
fusion of thematic strands with extremities of emotion both felt
and analysed, brings out the major strengths of Margaret
Drabble's writing.

The Millstone confronts squarely the question of privilege, a
question which underlies all the early novels. A common accusation against Margaret Drabble's fiction is that it remains
essentially middle class, is too clearly reflective of the author's own
background and manifest advantages. Through Rosamund's conflicts with her parents' quiet, almost inhuman, philanthropy,
extended with equal dispassion to the natives of Africa and India
as to their daughter, she contrives to persuade the reader that in
this context her heroine's 'growing selfishness' is also 'probably
maturity'. The theme is tackled in broader spiritual terms in *The
Needle's Eye*, a long, difficult and ambitious work, after which, as
she says, she became 'bored with the issue'[4] and moved on to *The
Realms of Gold*. Here we find the unusual spectacle of a woman at
the top of her profession, successful in love and motherhood, made
wealthy by her own endeavours and for the most part supremely
confident in herself. But the novel, while undoubtedly encourag-
ing in its convincing evocation of a modern woman's achievement,
is far from being a simple exercise in optimism. Where *The
Millstone* defined and followed its themes with economical clarity
within a tightly controlled framework, *The Realms of Gold*
achieves a rich complexity, a widening of perspective and a
historical and intellectual sweep which recalls the mature work of
George Eliot.

Something of the care with which this complexity is planned and
the skill of its thematic integration can be gathered from the
wealth of implication packed into the title alone. Keats' sonnet 'On
First Looking into Chapman's Homer', from which the realms of
gold is a quotation, links literary and aesthetic pleasures with the
wonder of geographical discovery, employs images of water and
rock, and evokes in the reader suggestions of the Homeric tradition
– human, archaeological, historical and legendary. All these
aspects of the sonnet are central to the novel. It deals with a family

spanning five generations and broadening out from its centre, Frances Wingate, to numerous relations of varying degrees of remoteness. The golden realms discovered by some of its members are attained through success in significantly different fields. Frances is an archaeologist who has dug a whole unknown city, Tizouk, from the arid Saharan sands; her cousin David is a geologist, realising a childhood ambition of 'changing the world charts of mineral distribution'; and her lover Karel Schmidt, a Polish Jew miraculously rescued in infancy from the Nazi invasion, is an agricultural historian, deeply devoted to the lush English countryside. Their subjects are all concerned to some degree with man's relationship to the earth, a theme pursued both through its intellectual applications and its more immediate bearings on family structures. At the beginning of the novel Frances recalls how her tutor had instructed her to 'learn to see life as a cycle, not as a meaningless succession of mutually exclusive absolute states', an injunction which she follows in academic and, eventually, in personal terms. (p. 12.) The generation cycle of the Ollerenshaw family, to which both Frances and David belong, is explored through the varying fortunes of its members, and is continually linked to the wider cycles of life investigated through the intellectual disciplines of archaeology, geology and history.

At the beginning of the novel Frances is seen alone in the best bedroom of a rather grand European hotel − a luxury earned by her status as star lecturer at an important conference − contemplating a captive octopus in a tank and attempting to stave off the familiar symptoms of encroaching depression. The biologically programmed life-cycle of the octopus provokes disquieting reflections: he, 'intelligent creature that he was, could survive in a perspex box. Though why he bothered, who could say. And the female of the species died, invariably, after giving birth.' (p. 12.) And Frances, a victim of the family streak of depressiveness which has driven her sister Alice to an early suicide and brother Hugh to advanced alcoholism, latches on to the image of the octopus' life as a focus for her own despair:

What were women supposed to do, in their middle years, biologically speaking? Have more babies, she supposed. The idea appalled her. Unlike the octopus, she seemed resolved on a course of defying nature. Maybe that was why she felt so bad? (p. 13.)

Frances' defiance of nature, despite intermittent bouts of depression, is made successful by continued hard work, professional success and, ultimately, the reacceptance of Karel's once rejected love. David Ollerenshaw, like the male octopus, creates for himself a perspex box of solitude from which he is able to devote himself, with few qualms, to the inhuman, inorganic passion for rocks and minerals. For Janet Bird, though, another Ollerenshaw cousin, denied access to the realms of gold through lack of intellect and ambition, the biological trap seems permanently closed. Married to a complacent, small-minded bully, isolated with a small baby on a dreary modern estate in the flat Midlands town of Tockley from which all the Ollerenshaws originate, she nurses her misery almost as a proof of existence. Possible avenues of help merely reinforce it, merely restate, as it were, the facts of female octopus life:

> Vicars and doctors were all the same, they told one it was natural to suffer from headaches and misery at puberty, to dread marriage, to feel ill and get cystitis when newly married, to dread pregnancy and feel ill and cry a lot when pregnant, to cry a lot with post-natal depression. It was all so natural. (p. 132.)

Reading a church noticeboard proclaiming 'I will lift up mine eyes unto the hills: from whence cometh my help', she reflects cynically that 'there were of course no hills round here, and therefore n help', though later, going into the garden to empty tea-leaves a' looking up at the beauty of the evening sky, she gets a brief flickeɪ of spiritual comfort. (p. 132.) 'The amazing splendour of the shapes and colours held her there, the tea pot in her hand. I will lift up mine eyes, she thought to herself. I should lift them up more often.' (p. 155.)

A link between Frances and Janet, apparently so different in character and fortune, is forged initially through recollections of their wedding preparations. 'There is some tribal insanity that comes over women as they approach marriage: society offers pyrex dishes and silver teaspoons as bribes, as bargains, as anaesthesia against self-sacrifice.' (p. 130.) Later they are to be brought together in more profound family rituals, but in the meantime the contemporary force of historical and anthropological perspectives is several times suggested. Janet's boring, pretentious dinner-party, for example, is presented as a frozen historical tableau, a living museum piece with all its precise illustrations of late-twentieth-century taste and custom. The point could be a trite one, a sociologist's cliché, were it not for the more subtle interpretative intertwining of past and present which increasingly emerges. Revisiting Tockley in search of some undefined feeling for family roots, Frances experiences various shocks in her observations of rural labours. Women and children gathering stones in a bare field evoke images of medieval toil and exploitation, revealed as inappropriate when she realises they are enthusiastically clearing the ground for a new school playing-field. The 'golden worlds' of the past, often pursued by archaeologists and historians, are an illusion, and the attempt to restate ancient customs in terms of ritual is a cruel distortion of fact:

> We unearth horrors, and justify them. Child sacrifice we label benevolent birth control, a dull and endless struggle against nature we label communion with the earth. We see an Eskimo child drag a dead sea-gull along a bleak beach by a piece of seal-gut, and we praise its diverse customary joys. (p. 124.)

The immediate comforts of modern life in Frances' hotel room — 'a tumbler of brandy at her elbow, a portable typewriter in front of her, a choice of two single beds . . . and a handy nylon jersey' — are in their very triviality reassuring and even exhilarating. (p. 124.)

Frances' return to Tockley, to the place of her own childhood and of generations of her ancestors, is a crux of the novel. The flat landscape, with its notorious 'Midlands sickness' which, as she recalls, drove the poet John Clare mad and perhaps accounts for her own family's depressions, is balanced also by its extraordinary fertility. As so often in Margaret Drabble's novels, the pervasive imagery is of water and stone, the creative and the arid. In childhood Frances had spent hours gazing into the drainage ditches in her grandparents' market garden, seeing in the immense variety of water creatures 'a whole unnecessary and teeming world of creation'. The newts especially fascinate her, 'survivors from a world of pre-history, born before the Romans arrived, before the bits of bronze age pot sank in the swamp, remembering in their tiny bones the great bones of the stenosaurus, a symbol of God's undying contract with the earth'. (pp. 107–8.) Her childish 'apprehension of a real answer' to the question of what it is all for — 'God had done it all for fun, for joy, for excitement in creation, for variety, for delight' — seems to be confirmed in later life when moments of intense happiness come through sudden stumblings across similar scenes of natural profusion. (p. 107.) Frances and Karel, at the first height of their love, discover a muddy drainpipe mysteriously filled with hundreds of comically-shaped, pointlessly honking frogs, 'and every time she thought of them, in later years, she felt such pleasure and amusement deep within her, a deep source of it'. (p. 25.) Similarly, her times of depression, of pain or loneliness, are described in images of water, mud, sand and rock. In her bouts of despair 'she honestly couldn't tell whether it was the depth of her being that she fell towards . . . or whether it was some squalid muddy intersecting gutter or canal, from which she would struggle wisely back to dry land'. (p. 14.) Leaving Karel, she sees that 'a future without him stretched like the desert, dry and hot'. (p. 81.) Stranded on a foreign railway station, racked with the prosaic but acute pain of toothache, she feels 'the effort of comprehension was beyond her. In the middle of nowhere, high up, a solitary lunatic, in her dry crater.' (p. 59.) It seems, then, an act of wilful perversity for Frances to direct her archaeological researches to the uncongenial heat and dust of the Sahara; and her return to Tockley, not surprisingly, becomes a return to harmony and love. The same kind of imagery is applied to other characters too. David Ollerenshaw, the one figure in the novel able to survive alone, appropriately finds intellectual and personal fulfilment through his sight of rock and water combining creativity in the Scottish islands:

> The landscape seemed alive, as though seething in the act of its own creation, for round every island the waves broke white and fell and glittered, in a perpetual swell and heave. The Isles of the Blest, he said to himself. Uninhabited, ancient. Out they stretched forever, to the North and West, to the ultimate reaches of man's desiring, where man was lost and nothing, at the edges of the world. For what did man desire, but those edges? (p. 55.)

For David, who 'had never had . . . the slightest sense of man as a necessary part of creation', this is a satisfying vision. For Hugh's family, though, the images are more sinister. His wife Natasha has created a model of twentieth-century affluent rusticity in her country cottage — 'She took no short cuts, she chopped with a hand chopper, she ground with a hand grinder, she made real stock, real bread, real marmalade, she preserved fruit'. (pp. 189–90.) Her decor is charmingly tasteful, but, significantly, in the colours of a volcano — 'everything was brown and red and black' — a point driven home when her alcoholic husband Hugh and depressive son Stephen embark on a discussion of Empedocles on Etna. She has, unwittingly, created an environment perfectly reflective of the latent violence and unpredictability of her family.

The diverse strands of the novel are brought together in two matching crises. David and Frances, summoned separately to a high-level conference in the new African nation of Adra, seem set for a professional clash over an area of the country as important for its archaeological sites as for its tin deposits. An interesting intellectual dispute seems impending — past versus present, knowledge versus wealth. But all this is abruptly cancelled by a family crisis: Great Aunt Constance Ollerenshaw is discovered, to the delighted outrage of the press, several months dead in her derelict cottage, having died of starvation in solitary squalor. The prostration of Frances' parents — from adverse publicity rather than grief — leaves her to take charge of the funeral and to sort through the remaining pitiful possessions. As Frances approaches the cottage to sift its contents with an archaeologist's professionalism and a relation's emotional involvement, the scene appears set for a moment of profound resolve:

> A terrible purity marked the scene . . . She walked up to the front door, through the swathes of grass, her feet wet with mud and dew: Oh so different, so beautifully different from the parched red sand of Adra, from the glaring altitudes of rocky, weathered Tizouk. England. A bird sang in a tree. (p. 303.)

Frances and Karel are at last reunited; David and Janet join them in evenings of family conviviality; and the funeral takes place in a country churchyard amid images of eighteenth-century pastoralism and the cathartic harmony of established ritual. But this is not the final resolve, for it is then discovered that Stephen, missing for several weeks, has become the most dramatic victim of the Ollerenshaw depression, and has killed himself and his baby daughter in a remote wood. The oldest and youngest members of

the family die at the same time: the purifying ritual extended to
Great Aunt Constance, whom nobody cared for or liked, is
negated by the tragic and meaningless death of Stephen and his
baby, cremated in a grimy London crematorium to the accom-
paniment of piped music. The abandonment of the old by Adran
nomads, the child sacrifice of the ancient Phoenicians, analysed,
explained and justified by modern academics, are rendered
starkly actual in the Ollerenshaw family. 'Death and love,' reflects
Frances at the cremation of Stephen and the baby, 'how dreadfully
they contradict all culture, all process, all human effort.' (p. 352.)
Yet recovery is possible: at the end of the novel Frances and Karel
settle down together in Great Aunt Constance's cottage, constructing a rambling, chaotic, slightly prosaic but ultimately satisfactory
family life, rebuilding continuity in immediate modern terms.
The progression of their experience is summed up in the wedding
present sent to them by David: 'A lump of pale yellow silica glass,
that he had picked up himself in the desert: scooped, pitted,
smoothly irregular, carved and weathered by the desert wind,
apparently translucent but finally opaque'. (p. 358.)

The Realms of Gold shows a development over *The Millstone* in
terms of range and complexity, in its more ambitious deployment
of imagery and symbolism, and through its greater profundity of
psychological exploration. But the most admirable qualities of
Margaret Drabble's writing are as apparent in her first novel as in
her last: the controlling intelligence, the deft handling of theme
and structure, the ability to create genuine and original illumination from the ordinary concerns of life, remain consistent. Too
often in modern fiction extremity is taken for profundity, perverse
innovation for significance, muddle and obfuscation for complexity of meaning. Margaret Drabble, with a quiet, almost
modest style, a constant clarity of presentation, and a keen eye for
social detail, continues to produce novels which place her among
the most intelligent and artistically satisfying of contemporary
writers.

NOTES

Citations in the text refer to the following editions of Drabble's books: *The
Millstone* (1965; Harmondsworth: Penguin, 1968); *The Waterfall* (1969;
Harmondsworth: Penguin, 1971); *The Garrick Year* (1964; Harmondsworth:

Penguin, 1966); *Jerusalem the Golden* (1967; Harmondsworth: Penguin, 1969); *The Realms of Gold* (1975; Harmondsworth: Penguin, 1977); *A Summer Bird-Cage* (1963; Harmondsworth: Penguin, 1967); *The Needle's Eye* (1972; Harmondsworth: Penguin, 1973). All editions were originally published by Weidenfeld & Nicolson, London.

1. M. Drabble, *Arnold Bennett* (London. Omega, 1975) p. 48.
2. Statement to author, September, 1979.
3. Statement to author.
4. Statement to author.

8 Muriel Spark:
the novelist as dandy

William McBrien

When one tries to think what the appeal *au fond* is of Muriel Spark's fiction, style, rather than theme, suggests itself. Spontaneously as we say of someone in life 'she has style', we say with immediacy the same of a distinctive writer, rare though the encounter may be. Muriel Spark is that rarity among writers today whose work enchants us first and finally by its style. That she is a woman may delay us in recognising her style as the manifestation, mostly an incidence among males until the mid-twentieth century, called *dandyism*.

Mrs Spark has herself suggested the link to dandyism in her statement that the writers 'I have read deeply are Proust, Newman, and Max Beerbohm'.[1] The authoritative description of the dandy remains the one Ellen Moers gave in her splendid study.[2] In it she details, from Brummell to Beerbohm, dandyism as both a social and literary phenomenon mentioning, incidentally, that the word appears to originate in Scottish ballads. Women, though, are not numbered in the ranks and we should perhaps neglect to locate Mrs Spark there, Scot that she is, had she not herself proposed the association. This despite the fact that London launched the post-war revival of dandyism with women as well as men among its exponents.

What are the qualities that Muriel Spark's work has in common with that of a dandy like Beerbohm? Here I want only to suggest several in a general way. Beerbohm had said that 'The old signs are here and the portents to warn the seer of life that we are ripe for a new epoch of artifice'.[3] And artifice, all the Leavisite and Naturalist

153

indictments of it notwithstanding, is a condition of fiction in which
Muriel Spark delights. Indeed, on which she insists. 'Fiction to me
is a kind of parable', she has written. 'You have got to make up
your mind it's not true. Some kind of truth emerges from it, but it's
not fact.'[4] Beerbohm does not discuss 'artifice' as a spiritual
strategy, but we know from observing dandyism and particularly
its manifestations in Wilde and the French Decadents that it
traditionally had spiritual impulses, among them to affront
puritans and materialists. Spark more than hints at this in
attaching the term 'parable' to fiction. It is *maquillage* that may
serve the spirit. One critic has said of Beerbohm that 'his
caricatures and his dandyism put aesthetic in place of moral
criteria'[5] and Spark seems often able to derive moral from aesthetic
measure though she has repeatedly drawn demarcations between
art and life. David Cecil points out in *Max* that 'The flippant and
sophisticated surface of his personality had always rested on simple
and moral foundations; in spite of irony and Oscar Wilde, Max
had continued to believe in fidelity and self-restraint and modest
contentment',[6] and these are virtues that Spark seems also to
celebrate.

Comedy, sometimes self-directed, is a source of balance in both
writers. As Beerbohm said, 'Only the insane take themselves quite
seriously'.[7] Spark is perhaps the wittiest novelist now on the scene
and this comes about not only because of her eye and ear for both
the merry and the macabre, her power as a parodist and gift for
mot, but because, like Dante and for essentially the same reason,
her metaphysic is comic. 'I believe', she has said, 'events are prov-
identially ordered',[8] and paradoxically perhaps this leads to an art
that is insouciant. And not too long! Like Beerbohm, Spark seems
greatly to value brevity and both are a rebuke to a society that puts
a premium on size. The author of masterful short stories, she
usually writes novels that are brief by 1980s standards. In part this
may be the result, too, of the liberation she enjoys from didactic
functions which in our time appear, perhaps understandably, to
have devolved on unbelievers. But no, exquisite style keeps the best
of her fiction quick, light, Mozartean in manner. Style, too,
explains her concern to succeed with *sprezzatura*. All evidence of
effort is edited out, so that in heeding Beerbohm's dictum, *surtout
pas de zèle*, she achieves a style of great gaiety, grace, and
nonchalance.

Like Scheherezade, Muriel Spark is a bewitching storyteller

and, however unreflectingly, the first tribute readers pay to her art is surrender to the engrossing tales she tells. Storytellers are in slight evidence as our century lengthens, and the novelist who aims to entertain, nearly extinct. Forster asserts in *Aspects of the Novel* 'all agree that the fundamental aspect of the novel is its storytelling aspect',[9] but latterly this has been honoured mostly in the breach. Spark's interest in narrative is long-standing and dates to her earliest literary efforts, many of which, like *The Fanfarlo*, were in verse. Among her models were the Scottish border ballads and the work of John Masefield about whom she wrote a booklength study.[10] Spark tells us in her introduction to *John Masefield* that first among her reasons for writing it was that she felt 'strongly attracted by John Masefield's narrative art', (p. ix) and 'It is with the narrative poems that I feel not only at ease but deeply engaged' (p. xi).

In earlier years, Muriel Spark had published, besides the book on Masefield, not only poetry but a critical study of Mary Shelley, and with Derek Stanford, of Emily Brontë. And the two edited *Tribute to Wordsworth*, a selection of Emily Brontë's poems, as well as letters of Mary Shelley, the Brontës, and Cardinal Newman.[11] Mrs Spark's first writing appeared in a trade journal for jewellers — the obvious and dandiacal pleasure she takes in verbal glitter might be linked to the delight she took in gems — though she presumably wrote government reports after her return to England in 1944 to work for Intelligence at Woburn Abbey. No doubt the familiarity and frequency with which she implicates espionage and related skullduggery in her work stems largely from her experiences and observations at that time. In 1947 she agreed to edit *Poetry Review*, the publication of The Poetry Society, but eventually drifted into advertising. Apparently Spark's success in a short story contest sponsored by *The Observer* in 1951 turned her seriously in the direction of fiction though finally it was a publisher's invitation which led her to write the first of to-date sixteen novels, *The Comforters*. She did so, as she later told Frank Kermode, despite the rather low opinion she had of the form and her inexperience with it.

I was asked to write a novel, and I didn't think much of novels — I thought it was an inferior way of writing. So I wrote a novel to work out the technique first, to sort of make it all right with myself to write a novel at all — a novel about writing a novel, about writing a novel sort of thing, you see.[12]

The Comforters, self-consciously an experiment in form and burdened by the autobiographical to a degree wide even of what one customarily contends with in first novels, nonetheless manages to be amusing while it disturbs, and wonderfully *mondaine* while insisting on the Christian verities. *Catholic chic* might be a term for the style though that risks implications that are slighting. Catholicism, to which Muriel Spark became a convert, is the measure in all her fiction. Derek Stanford describes Spark copying out Newman's words 'A Christian view of the Universe is almost necessarily a poetic one',[13] and this belief remains part of her signature in *The Comforters* and all of the novels that follow it. No less an authority in these matters than Flannery O'Connor wrote in 1964 to a priest friend who wanted advice about Catholic fiction that 'The English [Catholic novelists] are Waugh & Greene and Spark (Muriel)'.[14]

The Comforters is dedicated to Alan and Edwina Barnsley (the Catholic novelist Gabriel Fielding and his wife) and features a whodunit dimension in the plot that reappears with variations in virtually all of the later novels. Chesterton, Dorothy Sayers, and Graham Greene are three who precede Spark in linking terrestrial riddles with supernatural ones but they do so within the frame of the more traditional thriller. Part of Spark's uniqueness is the way in which she braids a strain of detective fiction not only with the theological, but with the psychological too − all of this adding urgency to the plot. Frequently she compounds detection with comedy of a highly original kind. Sometimes it is rousingly music hall, burlesque of a peculiarly English sort; or again it is eccentric behaviour or the tart phrase. *The Comforters*, for instance, with its tale of a grandmother who stashes diamonds in loaves of bread and supervises a gang of three oddly behaved men, inevitably recalls British films of the fifties like 'The Lavender Hill Mob'. Indeed Spark's narrative technique seems in several ways to be cinematic.

Caroline is the young heroine of *The Comforters*; reminiscent of the author, she has partly Jewish parentage (Spark's father was Jewish), writes literary criticism, and is a convert to Catholicism. According to Derek Stanford, Spark was at the time 'recovering from a nervous disorder in which certain symptoms of hallucination featured',[15] and Caroline in the novel hears voices. (Several critics have pointed up the parallels between Spark's hallucinatory experiences and the literary capital she made of them, and those of

Evelyn Waugh as they emerged in *The Ordeal of Gilbert Pinfold*.
The experiences of Virginia Woolf in this regard may also be
comparable.) Caroline is suddenly aware of a typewriter clicking
and a voice repeating words she had just said to herself. It is clear
that she overhears a novelist composing a narrative of which she is
part.

> He got out of her that the clicking of the typewriter always
> preceded the voices, and sometimes accompanied their speech.
> How many voices there were, she could not say . . . 'In fact', she
> went on, wound-up and talking rapidly, 'it sounds like one
> person speaking in several tones at once.'
>   'And always using the past tense?'
>   'Yes. Mocking voices.'
>   'And you say this chorus comments on your thoughts and
> actions?'
>   'Not always', said Caroline, 'that's the strange thing. It says
> "Caroline was thinking of doing this or that" − then sometimes
> adds a remark of its own.' (p. 55.)

Spark is obviously worrying a Joycean equation in all this: are we
present to the mind of God as fictional characters are to the mind
of the novelist? '". . . it is as if a writer on another plane of
existence was writing a story about us". As soon as she had said
these words, Caroline knew she had hit on the truth.' (p. 66.) The
novelist does offer arresting *aperçus* about the nature of
imaginative writing, and here and in many of her later novels
creation in the natural order is a clue to the supernatural. But
Peter Kemp in the fullest and best study so far written on her work
is probably right to say that excessive attention has been given to
Caroline's voices in critical considerations of *The Comforters* and
to insist on our 'following the pointer in its name'. [16] He usefully
collects the novelist's references to Job and quotes a piece she published in 1955 in the *Church of England Newspaper* called 'The
Mystery of Job's Suffering' as proof of her long preoccupation with
what becomes the central theme of *The Comforters*: how alone we
are in life, and how incomprehensible and inconsolable in human
ways. Not Laurence, her lover, nor others in literary bohemia or
the Catholic Church − the two societies she depicts − can finally
comfort Caroline. On the contrary, she suffers badly from their
stupidity and malevolence. Spark's much noticed insistence on

seeing life accurately evidently encouraged her to look unblinkingly at the religious society she, as well as Caroline, found herself
a part of, and the reader is rewarded with acidulous depictions of
churchy types. Near to Grand Guignol is Georgina Hogg, working
at a Retreat House when we first meet her. 'It fairly puts you
against Catholics, a person like that', (p. 26) says Laurence's
larcenous grandmother and there is a savage humour in the tart
questions Caroline puts to Mrs Hogg:

> 'I mean, when you say, "Our Lady said", do you mean she spoke
> audibly to you?'

> 'Oh no. But that's how Our Lady always speak to me. I ask a
> question and she answers.' (p. 32.)

When Caroline persists, Mrs Hogg tells her that 'The words come
to me — but of course you won't know much about that. You have
to be experienced in the spiritual life.' (p. 32.) Caroline's self-
description that follows mentions qualities that characterise Mrs
Spark's artistry in *The Comforters* and since, 'angular, sharp,
inquiring . . . grisly about the truth . . . well-dressed'. (p. 32–3.)
Decidedly dandy, in fact. It is persistence, a quality she gives to
Laurence in the story, that leads her to look at horrors in and out
of the Church and to agree with Caroline's homosexual uncle,
Ernest, that 'the True Church was awful, though unfortunately,
one couldn't deny, true'. (p. 89.) The novel is not underivative and
Ernest, incidentally, can sometimes talk like his Wildean
namesake: 'I am myself very detached from money . . . that is why
I need so much of it'. (p. 148.) Compton-Burnett is also an echo
here as well as in the literary surnames Muriel Spark finds in this
novel and in later ones for certain characters: Mervyn Hogarth, for
instance, — a diabolist in a Bond Street suit.

The plot of *The Comforters* is prolix: will Caroline escape her
voices as well as La Hogg and make a life with Laurence? Will
Louisa Jepp and her gang be found out? These are only two among
the story lines in the novel. It cannot be said that Spark succeeds in
unifying them or the several themes she pursues here. But the
faults rise from an embarrassment of riches. When Baron Stock
(shades of Proust and Isherwood), a literary dabbler in Black
Magic, comes to visit Caroline in hospital, she tells him that

> 'The Typing Ghost has not recorded any lively details about this

hospital ward. The reason is that the author doesn't know how to describe a hospital ward. This interlude in my life is not part of the book in consequence'. (p. 182.)

Just below we hear that

> The other patients bored and irritated her. She longed to be able to suffer her physical discomforts in peace. When she experienced pain, what made it intolerable was the abrasive presence of the seven other women in the beds, their chatter and complaints, and the crowing and clucking of the administering nurses. (pp. 182–3.)

Mrs Spark's next novel but one, *Memento Mori*, reports clearly on women in a hospital ward and their nurses, though they are all old women. Here she decides to edit them out and prepares to compose the more tautly told novels that followed *The Comforters*.

Robinson is the second novel that Spark published and as the allusion to Defoe suggests, it is about castaways. Again Spark addresses in it the problem of human isolation and loneliness. Bound by air for the Azores, the bright and independent heroine, January Marlow (literary echoes multiply) attaches herself to a male passenger – a situation that the novelist returns to more centrally in *The Driver's Seat*. The plane crashes on an island in the Atlantic which bears the name of its owner – Robinson. January and two of the men aboard survive. Three months pass before a commercial vessel appears to return them to England, and January records what meanwhile happens in a journal. The work is more poetically than novelistically imagined (Carol Ohmann's analysis of it remains the authoritative one[17]). Familiar figures and images recur: the eccentric grandmother, for instance. (Derek Stanford mentions in his book that Spark's maternal grandmother was a fabled character with advanced views, who knew both Mrs Pankhurst and Prince Kropotkin; according to him, Louisa Jepp is a fictional portrait of this grandmother. He says further that Spark's mother played and taught piano and carried a silver flask for festive drinking. She brought up her daughter to avoid housework.[18] No doubt Spark was helped to imagine the vivid, independent, sometimes flamboyant women in her novels in part by familial recollections.) January herself, with all her resemblances to the author – her husband died after six months of marriage (Spark's marriage ended early in divorce), she has one son (as has Spark), is a recent convert to Catholicism, and 'poet, critic, and general articulator of ideas' (p. 18) — is in the tradition of Caroline Rose and a type of many women protagonists in the later novels of Mrs Spark.

Though sometimes judged a weak work, and certainly an untypical one, *Robinson* nonetheless reveals bright gifts. Metaphors are original and catchy (Spark has steadily published poetry and continues to do so), the wittily dandiacal dialogue amusing, and when Robinson disappears and is presumed murdered, the narrative proceeds at the pace of a thriller. The explanation, though, of why he chose to vanish is finally unconvincing, and one of several structural weaknesses in the work. It ends with a flash forward, a cinematic not to say oracular device that Spark uses repeatedly in her novels, and glimpses of what will happen to certain of the characters and to the island itself.

Perhaps the most compelling account in the novel is that of the struggle January has, in her months on the island, to live peacefully, indeed safely, with three men and a boy. Early on in the story January recounts her impulse to worship the moon.

> I was the only woman on the island, and it is said the pagan mind runs strong in women at any time, let alone on an island, and such an island . . . I consider now how my perceptions during that whole period were touched with a pre-ancestral quality, how there was an enchantment, a primitive blood-force which probably moved us all. (p. 3.)

January's struggles with the men on the island compound the struggles she had back in England with two brothers-in-law. They are both described as disparaging to women and vehemently opposed to Marian devotion. And as Peter Kemp shows in an analysis of the differences January and Robinson have over devotion to the rosary, the male in Spark's estimation fears the material whereas feminine strength is rooted in a right appreciation of the material world. In this, as Kemp points out, Spark is affirming the attitude she praised in Proust — his use of the material as a passport to the spirit. If then, *Robinson* is a descant on Donne (Derek Stanford wrote 'I recall a poem by Muriel which started: "No man is an island / Oh no?"' [p. 127]) it is, as well, a repudiation of the Calvinism which surrounded her in her native Edinburgh and its dismissal of the material world.

'I am reading', said Flannery O'Connor in 1959, 'a very lively one [novel] called *Memento Mori* by Muriel Spark. All the characters are over 75.'[19] Paradoxically and in a way that must have cheered up the chronically-ill letter writer, this novel so occupied with the Four Last Things (Death, Judgment, Heaven and Hell) is surprisingly 'lively'. And the time, place, and action — with one exception — more conventional and familiar than in the earlier works. The novel demonstrates Spark's remarkable capacity to convey the genius of a place, and part of the pleasure she affords readers is that of conjuring up memories they may have of London, Rome, Venice, Jerusalem, South Africa, or East Side Manhattan with her evocative depictions. Again the paradox in a writer so admiring of artifice who succeeds in being as savvy a cicerone in the cities of the world as the novel can now produce. On the whole her decision to forsake the never-never land setting of *Robinson* for the very real cities of her acquaintance is one that readers approve: it is her rendering so credibly the commonplace that persuades us of the transfiguration of it she eventually reveals.

Memento Mori is, in its way, a masterpiece though remembering some words of its author to Frank Kermode, one hastens to modify 'masterpiece', not at all deprecatingly, with *minor*. 'I was writing minor novels deliberately', said Mrs Spark, 'and not major novels. An awful lot of people are telling me to write big long novels — Mrs Tolstoy, you know — and I decided it is no good filling a little glass with a pint of beer.'[20] Very much in the spirit of Beerbohm who delighted in the miniature. What Peter Kemp calls 'economy' (with implications that Spark is an artistically thrifty Scotswoman) may perhaps be more suitably appraised as her stylish penchant for brevity.

We live, of course, amid an aging population but though the physical and social sciences are growingly attentive to old people in contemporary society, the twentieth-century novel is so far only slightly so. Spark's novel offers a rare, compassionate, yet altogether unsentimental look at old people and how they confront death. Her points of departure are: Yeats and his complaint about 'this absurdity . . . decrepit age' (his use of 'absurdity' invites her to view the aged wittily); Traherne and his description of old people as 'reverent crèatures . . . Immortal Cherubims!'; and *The Penny Catechism*.

Characters hear, nearly all of them, an unidentified voice. It telephones to tell them 'Remember you must die'. Vintage Sparkle in this when mostly those who receive the advice are startled. Spark seems behind the novel to wonder why one should be surprised by what is common knowledge. The voice alters appropriately as it addresses the various respondents. Plot is sped along by our wonderment for a while about the identity of the caller, and then about the timeliness of his admonition. Will various of the characters manage to outwit, for the moment, their fate? The novel is artfully confined almost entirely to a set of upper-middle class and aged people whose past relationships are revealed as the story proceeds. (In the interview cited above, Spark has said 'When I become interested in a subject, say old age, then the world is peopled for me — just peopled with them. And it is a narrow little small world, but it's full of old people, full of whatever I'm studying.') The *raisonneur* is sometimes Charmian, formerly a popular novelist now afflicted by the fantasies that once she deliberately cultivated; sometimes Jean Taylor, once a companion to Charmian, whom the gods (or God, in Spark's view) made wise as well as old; sometimes Henry Mortimer, a retired Police Inspector whose set speech is both Socratic and Christian.

> If I had my life over again I should form the habit of nightly composing myself to thoughts of death . . . There is no other practice which so intensifies life. Death, when it approaches, ought not to take one by surprise. It should be part of the full expectancy of life. Without an ever-present sense of death life is insipid. You might as well live on the whites of egg. (p. 166.)

Charmian and Jean Taylor are both Roman Catholic and conclude with Henry Mortimer that Death is the mysterious caller.

The power to couple a sermon such as Henry delivers with high hilarity has of course literary precedents. But today it belongs almost entirely to Muriel Spark. When death, for instance, comes to the unsympathetic Dame Lettie at the hands of a nocturnal thief, the witty burden is 'don't say you weren't famously warned'. Another of the characters faces death with the unsuitable name, Tempest Sidebottome. Spark seems certainly to find Jean Taylor's realism bracing: 'Being over seventy', Jean says, 'is like being in a war. All our friends are going or gone and we survive amongst the dead and the dying as on a battlefield.' (p. 34.) In their different ways, Jean Taylor, Henry and Charmian behave beautifully in the face of death, the latter making couture part of her poise. Accepting death, they live creatively, even debonairly. No less a dandy is the novelist in the care with which she watches appropriate ends come to characters who are wise or wicked. Although one can in part agree with Peter Kemp's opinion that Spark 'is not primarily concerned with portraying character',[21] in this novel we feel perhaps for the first time that some of the characters are concerns of her affections, as well as of her intelligence, and so certain of them manage to interest our hearts as well.[22]

Stevie Smith, reviewing *The Ballad of Peckham Rye*, next of the novels to appear, wrote that 'Muriel Spark has a real genius for being gruesome and hilarious in practical circumstances, gay in city graveyards, gothic in factories'.[23] Spark seems to have turned to this tale in the manner of Virginia Woolf who found it restorative to follow her more probing novels with lighter, more fantastical books. 'Next', Spark has written, 'I wanted to give my mind a holiday and to write something light and lyrical − as near a poem as a novel could get, and in as few words as possible.'[24] The hijinks, bloody deeds, mad characters (Nelly Mahone is Peckham's Crazy Jane) and tricky talk are easily accommodated by the form and one realises the possibilities Spark has seized for the novel in her old devotion to ballads and other narrative verse. Peckham Rye, a lacklustre and working-class suburb south of the Thames, had been the site of Boadicea's suicide, and yields up to the excavations of Dougal Douglas, its comic hero, strangeness about its citizenry which the casual onlooker would never have suspected. Who is Dougal Douglas, the humpbacked sleuth whose horns have been lopped off by surgery? Stevie Smith said in the review cited, 'he is Eulenspiegel, if you like, or he is the Goethean Mephistopheles, the spirit who denies and disturbs'. He seems, this Scottish sleuth, a slapdash version of the novelist in the verbal wizardry he practices, the truths he unearths, the disturbances he engenders. His is, as well, an Eliotic voice revealing the 'Unreal City'. This novel features *Waste Land* archeology that reveals, as in the account of the midsummer night when, among assorted couplings, Mr Druce beds Merle, the ludicrousness of loveless sex. Eventually we are told, Dougal 'gathered together the scrap ends of his profligate experience − for he was a frugal man at heart − and turned them into a lot of cockeyed books, and went far in the world'. (p. 201.) This novel may be a cautionary tale for those who, in writing novels professionally, set out to invent 'a pack of

lies'[25] — one definition of fiction Spark has offered. But its
cautions are confected, as well, for common readers. And served
up with verbal panache.

In her next novel, *The Bachelors*, Spark moves north of the
Thames to Kensington while keeping to even more constricted
fictional parameters and — unlike others of her contemporaries
who re-explore familiar ground — shifting her sights to a subject
that once again is new for her. The novel is in ways a meditation
about London and 'the thirty-eight thousand five hundred streets,
and seventeen point one bachelors to a street'. (p. 241.) Some of
the landmarks are familiar, though. The medium, Patrick, who
hears voices from another world; Ronald, an epileptic, whose
affliction is in ways a terrestrial imitation of Patrick's trances; the
engrossing criminal trial and the suspense that surrounds the
safety of Patrick's pregnant and naïve fiancée whom he plans to
murder if exonerated. (As Karl Malkoff points out in his essay,
'they are, in the mode of Dostoevsky and Conrad, doubles'.[26])
Ronald is the character closest to the novelist and has, indeed,
many resemblances to his creator. 'As a Catholic I loathe all other
Catholics', (p. 83) he says, linking himself with the sentiments of
Caroline Rose; and, more importantly, Spark points out parallels
between his illness and a writer's condition. She endorses Ronald's
view that spiritualism and Catholicism are the only two religions
and rejects the former as the worship Patrick Seton practices, a
crazed kind of Calvinism that rejects material reality. 'One of the
things', Spark has said, 'which interested me particularly about
the Church was its acceptance of matter. So much of our world
rejects it.'[27]

Certainly most well-known of all Spark's novels is *The Prime of
Miss Jean Brodie*, which she published in 1961. Marcia Blaine
School, the setting, is not at all St Trinian's but it brings the latter
to mind. Derek Stanford gives the biographical background of it in
his book and says that Spark spoke of it as 'an entertainment'.
(p. 132.) Although he commends it as free of preternatural props,
the omniscient narrator practices the flash forwards and shows, in
the manner of Graham Greene in 'The Basement Room', how
children will end up. Prognostications invade the imagery. Mary,
fated to die by fire, is frightened by a bunsen burner in the school
laboratory. As has been pointed out, Edinburgh — a Calvinist city
— is an apt setting for this parable about fascism. Spark allies
herself in some respects with Sandy Stranger, the girl who betrays

Miss Brodie, enters a convent, and publishes a psychological treatise called, *The Transfiguration of the Commonplace*. Sandy, though, is not finally redeemed (her beady eyes and the manner in which she clutches at the bars of her convent enclosure convey this) and her failure seems at least in part the result of her interior resemblance in some ways to Miss Brodie. Pseudo-religion is repeatedly mocked: when Eunice embraces religion, for example, 'The phase did not last long, but while it did she was nasty and not to be trusted'. (p. 76.)

Miss Brodie is brilliantly wrought and become, in no small part through the dramatisation of the novel and its popularity as a film, legendary. With this novel Spark has the kind of popular and enduring success that only very few writers ever experience. An immensely attractive figure in certain respects whose allure we do ourselves succumb to from time to time, Jean disapproves of the Catholic Church:

> Her disapproval of the Church of Rome was based on her assertions that it was a church of superstition, and that only people who did not want to think for themselves were Roman Catholics. In some ways, her attitude was a strange one, because she was by temperament suited only to the Roman Catholic Church; possibly it could have embraced, even while it disciplined her soaring and divine spirit, it might even have normalised her. (pp. 112–13.)

Sandy thinks that Miss Brodie considers herself 'the God of Calvin, she sees the beginning and the end' (p. 161) and that 'She's [Miss Brodie] a born Fascist'. (p. 167.) The fact that Miss Brodie who, even after the Second World War, found Hitler only 'rather naughty', (p. 164) dies in the year following the armistice 'from an internal growth' (p. 72) constitutes authorial agreement with Sandy's appraisal.

However 'ridiculous' Sandy finally finds Jean Brodie to be, we are vastly entertained by her cultivation of the Set — the crème de la crème, her eccentric gestures and words (some of them again an echo of Compton-Burnett — 'For those who like that sort of thing . . . that is the sort of thing they like'. [p. 37.]) Amusing too are her battles with the bourgeoisie. Spark is in her word-wizardry everywhere active here and the pleasure one takes, for instance, in listening with her while Miss Brodie, a fan of the Duce, discourses (inaccurately as it turns out) on *ducere* as the root of *education* is matchable on almost every page of the novel. It is also a work where we can discover both the intensity and manner of Spark's response to history in her time. Her novels seem all of them to be stylishly engaged with the *zeitgeist*.

The May of Teck Club, a residence for women most of them young, located near the Albert Memorial and founded by Queen Mary before her marriage when she was Princess May of Teck, is the scene of *The Girls of Slender Means*, the novel Spark published in 1963. The events described take place between VE and VJ Days in 1945. How different are the lives of the residents from that of the Princess of Teck, though some console themselves for dreary days with fantasy and finery: Pauline pretends she dines out nightly with Jack Buchanan, and Selina has a Mainbocher gown. Dandyism of one or another sort is their strategy but it is veneer only and insufficient when the girls are caught literally in a crucible. Hopkins's *The Wreck of the Deutschland* is a text that, among others, Joanna makes use of to teach elocution, and the poem dedicated to the memory of five Franciscan nuns drowned in the Thames estuary becomes a portent in the novel of the trial by fire that besets a number of the residents in the May of Teck Club. Indeed Joanna, in many ways a martyr as she dies, reminds one of the Sister Superior whom Hopkins praised for her heroism. Nicholas, the anarchist who had idealised Selina until he watched her risk the lives of others for the Mainbocher gown, now stands instructed by the brave behaviour of Joanna and as if in response to the psalm she speaks as the flames rise — 'Except the Lord build the house: their labour is but lost that build it' — he enters the Church. Reminiscent of Celia in Eliot's *The Cocktail Party*, Nicholas dies a martyr in Haiti.

The Girls of Slender Means is then another of the examinations Spark makes of human society — always in microcosm and sharply confined in setting. Renata Adler wrote of this novel that Spark 'has created a splendid period piece, and an extraordinarily subtle parable of a larger Society which lives with the unacknowledged threat of a larger, more ominous Bomb concealed in its garden'.[28] Here she intensifies her curiosity about the relationship between individuals and history (the setting, along with the source of the climactic fire — a bomb undetonated since it fell three years before — is, of course, emblematic). And history is operative too in the slice of trendy life Spark entertainingly depicts: in this novel, set in the day of Dylan Thomas, literary types meet in Hampstead and Soho. This account comes, as is her custom, with witty observations from the narrator: 'literary men, if they like women at all, do not want literary women but girls'. (p. 95.) These secular witticisms sometimes segue into piety: 'If one is growing in grace . . . one can take realism, sex and so forth in one's stride'. (p. 132–33.) The novel is made with extraordinary perfection, both a parable (the lavatory window through which only the slim can slip to sunbathe and, in the ironic ending, to escape the fire, is a modern and metaphorical equivalent of the Scriptural 'eye of the needle'), and a glimpse into the lives of working women among whose ranks Spark remembers herself.

The Mandelbaum Gate represents a departure for Muriel Spark. Of it she wrote, 'I spent two months in Israel on "The Mandelbaum Gate". It took me a long time to write, two years. "The Prime of Miss Jean Brodie" took me eight weeks. "The Mandelbaum Gate" is much longer but it was also a great strain to write . . . It's a very important book for me, much more concrete and solidly rooted in a very detailed setting'.[29] Victoria Glendinning says in 'Talk with Muriel Spark'[30] that 'Her reading is mostly 19th-century literature' and this book, with its large canvas and complex plot, shows her affection for Victorian novels. Anthony Burgess wrote that 'Muriel Spark must have felt that she was not doing justice to her talent by exercising it only in small fictional forms. Sooner or later she had to tackle a full-length novel, *The Mandelbaum Gate*'.[31] Everything about the look of this novel is different, down to Spark's use of chapter titles. More apt than a likening of it to the Victorians is perhaps a comparison to Forster's fiction. In *The Mandelbaum Gate* the novelist is occupied with personal relationships and her theme and images often have resemblances to *A Passage to India*. Yeats is another writer whom *The Mandelbaum Gate* brings to mind. Barbara 'yearned for . . . Jerusalem, Old and New in one' (p. 181) recalling Yeats's yearning for Byzantium. For all that she admires about artifice, though, Spark does not opt to be 'out of nature'. Like Yeats's speaker she experiences the self as divided and explores the forces which divide us individually and globally. But she sets about it suavely and wittily. For example, about Jacob's success in gaining the irrevocable blessing of Isaac, she comments, 'such being the ways of the Lord in the Middle East'. (p. 21.)

Barbara Vaughan is the familiar heroine, half-Jew and Roman

Catholic, imperilled by her heritage when she passes through the Gate into Arab territory. She is awaiting news from Rome as the novel opens as to whether or not an annulment will be granted to her fiancé for an earlier marriage. He is Harry Clegg, an archaeologist. (In *Tradition and the Individual Talent* T. S. Eliot wrote that 'You can hardly make the word [tradition] agreeable to English ears without this comfortable reference to the reassuring science of archaeology'.) The plot thickens considerably as personal dramas develop against the backdrop of the trial of Eichmann, the ultimate divided self. Several commentators have underlined the 'heart of darkness' resemblance and true enough it seems that Spark's images and animadversions all address the darknesses in the self and the relationship between the wanly wicked and monsters. The novel did not please critics, some of whom considered that it foundered in allegory, and finally it seems not to have suited Spark. Writing five years after its appearance she said 'I don't like that book awfully much actually . . . I decided never again to write a long book. Keep them very short.'[32]

And more or less she has. In *The Public Image*, she shifts her scene to Rome and writes a cautionary tale about a movie actress just arrived to stardom. (One feels here as in all the novels that the heroine is for the novelist a putative self and the caution first of all self-directed.) The arrival of her novels to Italy seems, in an over-view, inevitable. Certainly Spark, who has lived there now since 1970, has a tropism towards its intensities, theatricality, and adaptability to all that is human. 'In fact, it is only a country of dramatic history, cradled in the Seven Capital Sins, that could so full-heartedly produce this popular art-form [cinema].' (p. 36.) Here, as in the depiction of Venice near the opening of *Territorial Rights* one senses in Spark an admiration for the Catholic country, resembling Auden's as he described it in 'Macao':

> Rococo images of Saint and Saviour
> Promise her gamblers fortunes when they die;
> Churches beside the brothels testify
> That faith can pardon natural behaviour.[33]

Contrary to what Auden goes on to say, though, Spark indicates she feels that something serious *can* happen in Italy. In *The Public Image*, Annabel's husband stages his own suicide (emblematically and *à la* Spark by leaping into an excavation) in an effort to

destroy her public image; and his friend, Billy O'Brien, attempts
to blackmail Annabel by publishing letters Frederick left, un-
truthfully accusing Annabel of kinky sexual practices. Along the
way Spark sharply skewers the *dolce vita* and the film world in her
rendering of them. Like the novelist, these creators of films tell lies
but have not kept the demarcations between art and reality.
Annabel is saved from yielding to their false standards by the baby
she had recently given birth to and for whom she cares more than
for herself. Though the tale sounds sentimental and awkwardly
operatic when sketched, it is saved by the irony with which events
are narrated and by the spareness of the form which, focused on
excess, proceeds in a most pared down way. Peter Kemp quotes in
connection with this novel the aesthetic Spark announced when
she came to New York to address the American Academy of Arts
and Letters, 'the only effective art of our particular time is the
satirical, the harsh and witty, the ironic and derisive'.[34] 'This', says
Kemp, 'is the rubric to which she now writes.' Her recent novel,
Territorial Rights, is in some ways sunnier, but otherwise the
evidence supports his view.

Outraged as she showed herself to be in *The Public Image* by
duplicity and 'rehearsed response' in our world, Spark gives in the
yet sparser form of *The Driver's Seat* an even grimmer view of this
world through the person of Lise who flies to a southern country,
presumably Italy, having bought for her travels wildly coloured,
garish clothes (Carlyle, a writer who interests Spark, is somewhere
behind the metaphor of clothes here and elsewhere in her novels).
She is in search of a man, not as it turns out for sex, but for death
and, resisting the sexual advances of Bill — a kind of contemporary and automated puritan with his macrobiotic diet and
scheduled orgasms — finds him in a psychopath whom she persuades to stab her. The setting and its citizenry seem abstract,
Kafka-like, artificial, impersonal; and Lise's behaviour madly apt.
Again Spark uses the flash forward artfully to catch the reader:
'She will be found tomorrow morning dead from multiple stab
wounds, her wrists bound with a silk scarf and her ankles bound
with a man's necktie, in the grounds of an empty villa, in a park of
the foreign city to which she is travelling on the flight now boarding at Gate 14'. (p. 37.) Suspense builds. 'The torment of it', Lise
says, 'not knowing exactly where and when he's going to turn up'.
(p. 85.)

There are, of course, reminiscent registers in much of this:

Memento Mori is a high echo. What many miss is the old merriment; the harsh seems altogether to have displaced the witty, though occasional wit wins through: '"I never trust the airlines from those countries where the pilots believe in the after-life. You are safer when they don't. I've been told the Scandinavian airlines are fairly reliable in that respect"'. (p. 101.) The parody of popular literature Spark encompasses in the form is apparent enough, and it may be that Kermode and Kemp are right in seeing the forms as an adaptation of the *nouveau roman*, though surely one most mischievous in intent. However grisly the tale, it is an artful orchestration of images, the dominant one suggested by the title. Spark seems here, in full agreement with the Lawrence of 'The Gods, the Gods': 'all was dreary, great robot limbs, robot breasts/robot voices, robot even the gay umbrellas'. Striking too is the resemblance between her tale and the recurrent depiction in Stevie Smith's poems of a woman who seeks out the embrace of Death, her lover. Spark said of this novel, 'I frightened myself by writing it . . . I had to go into hospital to finish it'.[35]

'How like . . . the death wish is the life urge! How urgently does an overwhelming obsession with life lead to suicide!' (p. 19) says a character in the next of Spark's novels, *Not To Disturb*, published in 1971. This is perhaps the least satisfying of her fictions, though the most 'literary'. It is *after* Webster and Shirley, as quotations point out, and modeled on neo-classical theatre with careful observance of the unities. The Brontës are also a gothic presence (the mad heir in the attic), as is Ivy Compton-Burnett, and perhaps the Shelley of *The Cenci*. Its setting and treatment of time, both structurally and thematically, remind one of the Robbe–Grillet of *La Maison de Rendez-vous*. Situating the story alongside Lac Leman brings 'The Waste Land' to mind and indeed the many speculations as to the relations between time past and time future seem Eliotic. So too does the mosaic method whereby the novelist assembles bits and pieces of the literary past to make a work that reflexively examines its relation to the tradition out of which it emerges – the relation of the *now* to the *past*. Cinematic treatment of time is also a feature Spark adopts in this novel, with its many references to cameras and filming. The novel seems to offer a parable about the decline of tradition and the import of that in a Waste Land geography. The noble Klopstocks, given over to their lonely lusts, are dead as the tale finishes and their barony the inheritance of an idiot relative, in one of the bleaker of Spark's parables.

Students of fictional form have for some time been obliged to notice the work of Muriel Spark and *Not To Disturb*, in most ways well-tempered, will repay their scrutiny. It is unquestionably recherché and represents the novelistic extremity to which she has so far travelled. Though her novels have not been notable for what Forster calls 'round characters', and usually appropriately not, she has succeeded time after time in constructing fictional worlds that are recognisable and richly human. *Not To Disturb* is still an impeccably stylish work with all the verbal magic we've come to count on in a Spark novel, but galactically cool as becomes the science fiction perhaps it is.

Probably in reaction, Spark called her next novel *The Hothouse By the East River*. For the first time she uses an American setting and convincingly renders New York City and its east side, where she lived for a period. Predictable authorial prints appear — a heroine, Elsa, who once worked for British Intelligence and suffers from hallucinations; a former espionage agent called Kiel; Princess Xavier, a New Zealand foundling, who raises silkworms on a Long Island farm, the eggs of which she warms in the folds of her breasts. '[She] might', says the narrator of the Princess, 'easily have taken a wrong safe turn, ending up as a saggy supervisor at the telephone exchange.' (p. 41.) But, as the plot develops, we discover that Elsa and her husband Paul were killed by a bomb near the end of the Second World War and are shades immured in the purgatory of an 'unreal city'. Coruscating comment is made through contrasts of Europe 1944, 'when people were normal and there was a world war on', (p. 58) with the air-conditioned, tranquillised nightmare of present-day New York. Only a dandy of Spark's dimensions could have the eye and the imagery to notice and convey what is noxious as well as nifty about 'fun city', (p. 132) though she can sometimes grow shrill. On the subject of 'problems' in the city, for instance: 'We already have the youth problem, the racist problem, the distribution problem, the political problem, the economic problem, the crime problem, the matrimonial problem, the ecological problem [she lists thirty more]'. (p. 129.) Spark raises here again questions that surfaced in *The Girls of Slender Means* about choices between fire and fire. Elsa comes via St Augustine (and Spark at least unconsciously must be led too by *Waste Land* Eliot) to collate the New York of now with ancient

Carthage. 'I came', she quotes Augustine, 'to Carthage where there bubbled around me in my ears a cauldron of unholy loves.' Joyce is here too with his motif of the dead who do not stay buried.

Though it has certain never-never land conditions, *The Hot House By the East River* is far more fleshed out than *Not To Disturb*. And, not unrelatedly, is far more engaging. Peter Kemp objects to the mix in it of the 'mandarin and garish'. (p. 152.) And true it is that the two come side by side, not perhaps inappropriately in a novel about New York. Spark has never confused the rowdy with the real despite the frequency with which she shows her preference for passion over sangfroid. The dandy is on guard against vulgarity and riot, and uses style as a control. Horror and heigh-ho go hand-in-hand in a number of Spark's novels.

Spark's invention appears to develop from *The Prime of Miss Jean Brodie* and a consciousness of Watergate. It is as if the St Trinian girls, grown now into maturity, had taken the veil without abandoning their wickedness. These nuns have 'bugged the poplar' and are 'up to the neck' (p. 2) in a scandal which 'by now . . . occupies the whole of the outside world'. (p. 5.) The Abbess, a foe of *aggorniamento*, 'sings the Latin version at the same time the congregation chants the new reformed English' (Spark is a member of the commission working on the modernisation of the English Roman Catholic liturgy), occasionally substituting Marvell's 'To His Coy Mistress' or the like. The convent is a structural equivalent of Marcia Blaine School or the May of Teck Club, and Spark, working the tradition − old in the novel − that features corrupted convents and wicked nuns, has a romp conflating the ecclesiastic with Nixon era politics. The hubristic choice the nuns make of mythology over history, mentioned recurrently, seems to constitute the sinfulness of these nuns for whom 'modern times come into a historical context, and . . . history doesn't work'. (p. 12.) 'We have entered the sphere, dear Sisters, of mythology', says the Abbess. 'My nuns love it. Who doesn't yearn to be a part of a myth at whatever the price in comfort? The monastic system is in revolt throughout the rest of the world, thanks to historical development. Here, within the ambience of mythology, we have consummate satisfaction, we have peace.' But this is Hopkins's 'poor peace' which Spark alludes to (p. 89) and allegorically she indicts the Nixon Gang and the contemporary world (as in *The Mandelbaum Gate*, heinous public evil is private failure magnified) for its effort inhumanly to transcend time. No doubt nuns are tempted by such transcendence but so, oddly enough shows the novelist, were Nixon and his Crew (the Abbess's aides are Mildred and Walburga — conventual Katzenjammer kids) about whom there was — Spark is right — something negatively nunny. Though the connection is never formally made, it is patently there in the crude language of the Abbess ('the last man I would myself elect to be laid by'; [p. 171]) key words like 'scenario'; (p. 84) polls and popularity charts that govern tactics; and electronic recording devices. The Abbess, incidentally, has substituted a course in electronics for the more conventionally clerical occupation of bookbinding, suggesting again the author's Lawrencian contempt for mechanisation. Spark is not, though, fully in sympathy with the Abbess's foe, Sister Felicity, the theft of whose thimble inadvertently turns the spotlight on the convent. Her dalliance with a Jesuit lover in the bushes, her enthusiasm about love-ins make her representative not only of a type of sixties Catholic but a parodic figure for the flower child adversary Nixon most scorned.

Beginning *in medias res*, the narrator of this mock epic backtracks in Chapter II to describe the election campaign the Abbess, whose mentor is Machiavelli, and her associates conducted. The political parallels are apparent here as well as in the unlawful entry some Jesuit novices make in an effort to discredit Felicity. Caught red-handed, they are let go by the police, but the story reaches the newspapers. The novices demand pay-offs and the Abbess meets them while trying to palm off the guilt on her aides: '"It is they [Walburga, Mildred and Winefred — Gertrude, incidentally, is a hilarious parody of Henry Kissinger: the globe trotting nun, a conspirator, yet aloof] — who have bugged the Abbey and arranged a burglary"'. (p. 99.) Then she appears on television and publicly refuses to part with doctored tapes she possesses, lamely invoking the seal of confession as her reason. In the end the Abbess, in what Spark suggests is an irreligious, because inhuman, transcendence says 'I have become an object of art, the end of which is to give pleasure'. (p. 113.)

The Takeover (1976), the first of Spark's three most recent novels, appeared to generally bleak notices. Set south of Rome in many-tiered Nemi (the archeological is again operative), where Spark has a home, it is in part an account of the balance of power between Maggie Radcliffe, a fabulously wealthy American now married to an Italian Marchese, and Hubert Mallindaine, homosexual tenant of one of three homes Maggie has acquired on the site of the Temple of Diana. Old acquaintances they'd been, and though the plot is in part an account of Maggie's efforts to oust Hubert from her property, the final scene finds them convivial and comradely. Indeed the house they battle to possess seems a symbol of the strategy each has devised as a defence against a rapidly deteriorating world. This is the Italy of our decade where communism confronts great wealth; Christianity competes with cults that are hedonistic or crackpot; forgeries are substituted for works of art; servants exchange roles with masters. In fact, this is a world less of contrasts than a blur signified (perhaps unfairly) by bisexuality and the breakdown of social roles. The lake of Nemi, best seen by Hubert from Maggie's home, is the one which 'had stirred the imagination of Sir James Frazer [Eliot's *Waste Land* mentor] at the beginning of his massive treatment of comparative religion, *The Golden Bough*'. (p. 10.)

Had he lingered, Frazer might have included an account of Father Cuthbert Plaice and his younger Jesuit confrere who speaks of 'environmental location' (p 71) and 'motionizes' (p. 103) and is exaggeratedly eager to reconcile religion with what is fashionably secular (Spark is as tart as ever in her exposure of sham within the Church), not to say the revival Hubert stages, as her self-proclaimed descendant, of the cult of Diana the moon goddess (in her survey of the seventies Spark notices the susceptibility of the young especially – the myopically left-wing Letizia in this novel is the cognate of Felicity in *The Abbess of Crewe* – to counterfeits like the Moonies). True to form, the book is serious yet soignée and far more droll than the earlier of Spark's Italian novels. Margaret Drabble only faintly praised the novel in the notice she wrote for *The New York Times Book Review* (3 October 1976), but she did say that, '*The Takeover*, despite its studied frivolity, is concerned with a very interesting subject indeed . . . on page 126 precisely [127 in the English edition], Muriel Spark . . . tell[s] us, plainly, that she is writing about money. In a couple of brilliant paragraphs, she describes the change that overtook the world in 1973, with the rise of Arab oil power and the fear of global recession.' (p. 2.) Margaret Drabble pertinently quotes part of this passage:

But it did not occur to one of those spirited and in various ways intelligent people . . . that a complete mutation of our means of nourishment had already come into being where the concept of money and property were concerned, a complete mutation not merely to be defined as a collapse of the capitalist system, or a global recession, but a sea change in the nature of reality as could not have been envisaged by Karl Marx or Sigmund Freud. Such a mutation that what were assets were to be liabilities and no armed guards could be found and fed sufficient to guard those armed guards who failed to protect the properties they guarded, whether hoarded in banks or built on confined territories . . . priceless works of art or merely hieroglyphics registered in the computers. Innocent of all this future they sat around the table.

And below, 'the oil trauma had inaugurated the Dark Ages II'. (p. 139.) So, following an account of several major thefts and kidnappings in the tale, Maggie appears dressed in rags in an effort to disguise her wealth.

Long-time enthusiasts were pleased to find that Spark had not neglected humour in this new novel. The dark deeds seem all relieved by the sumptuous setting that Italy affords and by the sense of its sleepily and sophisticatedly having looked on at the human comedy over so many centuries. Maggie herself is a bit like Graham Greene's travelling Aunt: rich and beautiful and comic-ally childish. Characters like Pauline Thin and Coco de Renault gather in more giggles and, all in all it is, as apocalypse, airier and nonchalant in the manner that seems better to suit Spark even when she admonishes.

Maggie, interrupted as she swims off the shore of her property by an invading girl in a rowing boat, is said to be 'aware of her impotence in territorial rights' (p. 114) and this appears to be the artistic idea Spark pursues in her next to latest novel. Fittingly *Territorial Rights* opens on a sunny day in October – an emblem one might feel for the mood of Spark in her genial harvest time. 'Venice', says the narrator, 'changed less than other places with the passing of time', and the two opening chapters evocatively represent the city in a manner that is vintage Spark. Her depiction recalls the Venice of Waugh's Lord Marchmain and L. P. Hartley's *Eustace and Hilda* and the plot is, in the abandonment of Curran, a 62-year-old homosexual, by 24-year-old Robert Leaver, a variation on the Mann tale. The 'territorial rights', referred to here (p. 165), seem less to be political (though the novel has political plaitings – among them espionage and regicide) than the rights humans have, or fail to have, to others.

Lina Pancev is the first girl to interest Robert and he has left
Curran to follow her from Paris to Venice. The city, one can
profitably recall, has the oldest of European opera houses, La
Fenice, and aptly there is much of the operatic about this novel set
there: for instance Lina's Bulgarian father, believed to have
poisoned King Boris, his own body long ago dismembered and
buried in the garden of two sisters who loved him. Spark has lost
none of her conviction that fiction, as she told Victoria Glendinning, 'if it is not stranger than truth . . . ought to be' and so
ironies and coincidences abound as Robert's father and his father's
mistress arrive to the very pensione where Robert is staying and
then by chance move on to Curran's hotel. And the tale is further
complicated by the efforts of Anthea, Robert's mother, back in
Birmingham to discover her husband's doings with the help of a
private investigator. Anthea's nepenthe is the sentimental novel,
and Spark has a delicious time parodying a number of these along
the way.

Generally this novel has been greeted with enthusiasm and its
author thought to be, in Auberon Waugh's words, for instance,
'back to the Spark of the early 1960s'.[36] Readers must judge this for
themselves. No more than the rest of us can novelists be expected
to delight in a judgement that praises them for preserving a
posture that entertained us in the past. Nonetheless this novel has
the celebrated signature of Spark and nicely knits together style,
amusing noticings, profound spiritual and psychological perceptions, and polished technique at every turn. Its virtues can perhaps
be looked at in another way: Spark is a dandy who is ingratiatingly
modest. Style, her narrator says in *The Takeover*, 'needs a certain
basic humility; and without it there can never be any distinction of
manner or of anything whatsoever'. (p. 177.) An insight that no
doubt Newman and certainly Beerbohm helped to waken in her.

Mrs Spark has been at work in recent days on two new novels —
one about Romans in Britain; the other, a novel in the form of an
autobiography (and just published as this study goes to print), is
called *Loitering with Intent* — 'which sort of sums up my life',[37]
says the novelist. In technique and subject, this latest of her novels
(1981) is a mordant kunstleroman, intimately connected to her
first: Fleur Talbot, the autobiographical heroine, quite consciously ponders her earliest work and is in fact a character with
many resemblances to Caroline Rose in *The Comforters*. The
novel is remarkably rich and entertaining in its reflections on the

links between life and art and, by subtext, between the artist and God. 'In her end is her beginning' one is tempted to say, except that critics have hailed *Loitering with Intent* less as a reprise than a creative turn that Muriel Spark has managed. Writing in *The New Yorker* of 8 June 1981, John Updike hopes that *Loitering with Intent* 'may presage a new verve and expansiveness in Mrs Spark's fiction' (p. 149). Updike's review reaffirms what he wrote in 1961: 'Mrs Spark is one of the few writers of the language on either side of the Atlantic with enough resources, daring, and stamina to be altering, as well as feeding, the fiction machine'.[38]

NOTES

All quotations from Muriel Spark's novels, except *Loitering with Intent*, cite page numbers in British editions printed by Macmillan in these years: *The Comforters* (1957); *Robinson* (1958); *Memento Mori* (1959); *The Ballad of Peckham Rye* (1960); *The Bachelors* (1960); *The Prime of Miss Jean Brodie* (1961); *The Girls of Slender Means* (1963); *The Mandelbaum Gate* (1965); *The Public Image* (1968); *The Driver's Seat* (1970); *Not To Disturb* (1971); *The Hothouse by the East River* (1973); *The Abbess of Crewe* (1974); *The Takeover* (1976); *Territorial Rights* (1979). *Loitering with Intent* was published by The Bodley Head in 1981.

1. M. Spark, 'My Conversion', *Twentieth Century* (Autumn 1961) p. 62.
2. *The Dandy* (New York: Viking Press, 1960).
3. M. Beerbohm, *The Works of Max Beerbohm* (New York: Dodd Mead, 1922) p. 108.
4. M. Spark, op. cit., p. 63.
5. J. Felstiner, *The Lies of Art* (London: Gollancz, 1973) p. xix.
6. (Cambridge: Houghton Mifflin, 1965) p. 332.
7. M. Beerbohm, op. cit., p. 159.
8. Muriel Spark, 'The Mental Squint of Muriel Spark', *Sunday Times* (London) 30 September 1962, p. 14.
9. E. M. Forster, *Aspects of the Novel* (New York: Harcourt Brace, 1963) p. 25.
10. M. Spark, *John Masefield* (London: Peter Nevill, 1953).
11. *Child of Light: A Reassessment of Mary Shelley* (London: Tower Bridge Publications, 1951); *Emily Brontë: Her Life and Work* (London: Peter Owen, 1953); *Tribute to Wordsworth* (London: Wingate, 1950); *A Selection of Poems by Emily Brontë* (London: Grey Watts Press, 1952); *My Best Mary: The Letters of Mary Shelley* (London: Wingate, 1953); *The Brontë Letters* (London: Peter Nevill, 1954); *Letters of John Henry Newman* (London: Peter Owen, 1957). In addition Spark has published a children's book, *The Very Fine Clock* (London: Macmillan, 1969).
12. F. Kermode, 'The House of Fiction', *Partisan Review* (Spring 1963) p. 79.
13. D. Stanford, *Muriel Spark* (Fontwell, England: Centaur Press, 1963) p. 58. This biographical and critical study has a bibliography compiled by Bernard

Stone. A more recent bibliography is *Iris Murdoch and Muriel Spark* by Thomas T. Tominaga and Wilma Schneidermeyer (Metuchen, New Jersey: Scarecrow Press, 1976).

14. Sally Fitzgerald (ed.), F. O'Connor, *The Habit of Being: Letters of Flannery O'Connor* (New York: Farrar, Straus & Giroux, 1979) p. 570.
15. D. Stanford, op. cit., p. 123.
16. P. Kemp, *Muriel Spark* (New York: Barnes & Noble, 1975) p. 17.
17. C. Ohmann, 'Muriel Spark's Robinson', *Critique: Studies in Modern Fiction*, 8 (Fall 1965) 70–84.
18. D. Stanford, op. cit., pp. 32–3.
19. F. O'Connor, *Letters*, p. 331.
20. F. Kermode, op cit., p. 80.
21. P. Kemp, op cit., p. 8.
22. See Spark's poem 'Created and Abandoned', *New Yorker*, 12 November 1979, p. 60.
23. S. Smith, 'A Gothic Comedy', *Observer*, 6 March 1960, p. 19.
24. M. Spark, 'How I Became a Novelist', *John O'London's Weekly*, 1 December 1960, p. 683.
25. F. Kermode, op cit., p. 80.
26. K. Malkoff, *Muriel Spark* (New York: Columbia University Press, 1968) p. 26.
27. 'My Conversion', p. 63.
28. 'Muriel Spark', in Richard Kostelanetz (ed.), *On Contemporary Literature* (New York: Avon Books, 1964) p. 594.
29. *Observer*, 17 October 1965, p. 10.
30. Victoria Glendinning, 'Talk With Muriel Spark', *New York Times Book Review*, 20 May 1979, p. 47.
31. *The Novel Now* (London: Faber and Faber, 1971) p. 131.
32. 'Keeping It Short', *Listener*, 24 September 1970, p. 412.
33. *The Collected Poetry of W. H. Auden* (New York: Random House, 1967) p. 18.
34. P. Kemp, op. cit., p. 114.
35. 'Keeping It Short', p. 413.
36. A. Waugh, 'Venice At Canal Times', *Evening Standard*, April 1979.
37. V. Glendinning, op. cit., p. 48.
38. J. Updike, 'Creatures of Air', *New Yorker*, 30 September 1961, p. 161.

9 Edna O'Brien: a kind of Irish childhood

Darcy O'Brien

In 1970 Edna O'Brien said to an interviewer, 'It's amazing . . . childhood really occupies at most twelve years of our early life . . . and the bulk of the rest of our lives is shadowed or coloured by that time'.[1]

Hardly a startling observation, but at the age of forty-one Miss O'Brien was reflecting on the effects of her childhood on her professional as on her personal life. Nearly all of her novels have been, one way or another, about breaking away – from home, family, marriage or love affair – and yet each is also testimony to the impossibility of the clean or permanent break. Childhood, family, husband, and lover live on to haunt heart and memory. Her settings may vary from Ireland to London to sunny Mediter- ranean isle, but one truth hovers continuously near the surface of her prose, and that is the persistence of memory, the impossibility of forgetting. No one ever gets over anything, she tells us; we carry with us till death each broken tie and love and, in Yeats's words, each

>   . . . harsh reproof, or trivial event
>   That changed some childish day to tragedy –

Because memory so dominates her work, it seems worthwhile to consider certain generalities and specifics of Edna O'Brien's child- hood. It will not do to cite the Irishness, cluck tongue over well- documented sexual repression, and reason thence the inevitability of a woman renowned and in some quarters notorious for the

179

sexual frankness of her fiction. For there are many different sorts
of Irish childhoods, each varying as to time and place. The poet
W. R. Rodgers (1909–69) recalled that as a Presbyterian boy in
Belfast he would overhear street-rhymes such as this:

> Holy Father, what'll I do?
> I've come to confess my sins to you.
> Holy Father, I killed a cat.
> You'll have to suffer, my child, for that.
> Holy Father, what'll it be?
> Forty days without any tea.
> Father dear, it's far too long.
> You've done, my child, a very great wrong.
> But Father dear, 'twas a Protestant cat.
> Good, my girl, you did right to do that.[2]

And Rodgers's subsequent life and work were permanently
affected by such verbal explosions of sectarian warfare.

By contrast Seamus Heaney also grew up in the North but as a
Catholic and during a still more complicated time than the Anglo-
Irish war that put its mark on Rodgers. For Heaney, born in 1939,
it was the Second World War that set the course of his passage, and
so complex were the oppositions for a boy of his religion coming
into consciousness in his part of Ireland that he took as a name for
himself *Incertus*, or the Uncertain One. He knew that his people
considered the bitter Orangemen their enemies, or was it the
British? Yet Ulster was British, and the British were at war with the
Germans. He was an Ulsterman, so were not the Germans then
also his enemies? Yet when the family radio was tuned to German
propaganda broadcasts, his relatives listened with approval: 'He's
an artist, this Haw Haw. He can fairly leave it into them'. And on
Sundays a German officer on weekend parole from the nearby
prisoner of war camp would come for lunch, play with the children
and carve them ships in bottles and paint Tyrolean landscapes on
electric bulbs. Was this the enemy? And was it true that when the
German bombs fell they hit the Orange sections of Belfast the
hardest? His own people, he knew, were considered by Protestants
the 'enemies of Ulster'. There was no reconciling all of this, nor has
there ever been, and such complications of definition govern
Heaney's mind and work to this day.[3]

For Edna O'Brien, the Second World War extended through

her later childhood and early adolescence, but for her as for almost
everyone in the southern four-fifths of the island, it was a war of
silence and isolation and considerable ignorance of the calamities
besetting Europe and Britain. Patrick Kavanagh recalled the
period in Ireland as one of peace and hope:

> Gods of the imagination bring back to life
> The personality of those streets,
> Not any streets
> But the streets of nineteen forty . . .
>
> It is summer and the eerie beat
> Of madness in Europe trembles the
> Wings of the butterflies along the canal.
>
> O I had a future.[4]

The butterflies' wings register destruction unseen, unnoticed in
the Irish summer of 1940, but the sense is there that something
terrible is happening and that only the bliss of neutral ignorance
permits hope in a future that is already being shattered. This is the
Ireland of Edna O'Brien's youth. In 1941 she was enrolled in the
Convent of Mercy, Loughrea, County Galway, a place so remote
from the world's strife that the drama of the year is the blooming of
the rhododendrons, there to wait out the war in peace. She had
already thought of writing and her attempts had been encouraged
by her teachers. Her head was filled with such romantic works as
Gone with the Wind, *Rebecca* and *How Green Was My Valley*.[5]
Her earlier years had been spent with her family in the County
Clare village of Scarriff.

Certainly for the urban reader it is difficult to imagine the
protected, remote nature of this childhood that spanned the
distance from a tiny village in one of the least populated districts
of an underpopulated island to a convent set by a lake in the next
county. In their own ways these places are as intricate as London
or New York, but to grow up in them, especially during a time
when one's country was sealed off from the world by political and
military neutrality, was to make inevitable severe shocks later on
when the ways of the rest of the world were encountered. Perhaps
we are all inclined to remember our childhoods as innocent but
Edna O'Brien's childhood truly was innocent in the sense that it
was protected from urban artifice and that it fostered more than

most the clear-cut beliefs in good and evil, truth and falsehood, love and hate. Take someone from such a background, plant them in a modern city, and you can produce a mental case, an energetic entrepreneur, or an artist. Edna O'Brien turned out to be something of both of the latter two phenomena. Her art, dressed out just flamboyantly enough to be eminently saleable, evokes consistently and persistently an innocent past confronted with a brutal present. That she did not grow up a jaundiced, urban sophisticate is everywhere evident in the repeated attempts of her heroines to have it both ways and in their frustration and bitterness at having it neither.

It is easy enough to trace the realities of this childhood through Miss O'Brien's fiction. She describes the convent in *The Country Girls*, and we get glimpses of the village life here and there in the novels and in many of the short stories. It is not a life as remote as that Flann O'Brien gave to his hero in *The Poor Mouth*,[6] a satirical but touching story of growing up absurd in the distant Gaelic-speaking regions of the west. Flann O'Brien's hero seeks to break from his isolation when he discovers a pot of fairy gold and hurries into town to buy his very first pair of boots. He is not exactly sure how to go about the task of buying boots, but when he does, he is arrested for possession of stolen gold and sent to prison. Nor was Edna O'Brien's childhood quite as isolated as that of the woman who had spent her youth on a tiny island off the Dingle peninsula. When she first set foot on the island of Ireland itself, she looked about, astonished, and said, 'I had never dreamed how wide the world was'![7] But Edna O'Brien's was a world whose main link to the outside was the wireless, carefully censored of course during wartime, as were the newspapers, and such books as the proprieties of the place and the most severe, puritannical censorship in the western world would allow. Later her own books would be banned by that censorship. That her arrival in Dublin at the age of sixteen inspired her first novel is enough to suggest the intensity of the occasion. It was not the childhood itself but the confrontation of that childhood with a relatively modern city that was the catalyst, a clash of sights, sounds, feelings and values that would persist in her mind and continue to be the flashpoint of her sensibility and her art.

The theme is a familiar one in Irish poetry, autobiography and autobiographical fiction. It is not a Joycean theme, for he was a suburban-urban child whose psychological jolts came to him as much from his family's descent from the genteel to the shabby as from his conflicts with the Church. It is a theme given modern eloquence first in the *Autobiography* of William Carleton, who made his journey from County Tyrone to Dublin on foot, and next by Patrick Kavanagh, who retraced most of Carleton's trek in the 1930s, coming to Dublin to pay homage to its writers and then getting caught up, used and abused on the Dublin literary scene as an authentic peasant.[8] Edna O'Brien is the first country girl to write of this experience and to make her own kind of poetry of it, and the bravery of the accomplishment ought not to be slighted. A country girl with literary pretentions in the Dublin of the late 1940s and early 1950s would have been a rude intrusion into the male, pub-centred world of the literati, although, to be practical about it, her beauty must have done her no harm. She must have been fairly unusual, buoyed by her ambitions in the sea of radiant typists and shopgirls who even today can be spotted on the Galway road, hitchiking from Dublin home for weekends with their families in the country. She had no literary predecessors, this Catholic, female, literary migrant. Certainly there had been Irish women writers before her — Maria Edgeworth, Lady Gregory, Somerville and Ross, Elizabeth Bowen — but they had been of the Protestant, Anglo–Irish ascendancy, with established families to back them up and with an entirely different, rather aristocratic slant to their lives and works.

Miss O'Brien made some important friendships among the Dublin writers. Benedict Kiely, then literary editor of the *Irish Press*, published her first articles and descriptive pieces, feeling no doubt an affinity with her country background, for he would later write a story describing his first visit to the capital as a humiliated little boy shaved bald by a forgetful barber in Omagh, County Tyrone. At twenty she married Ernest Gebler, himself a novelist, and within three years bore two sons by him. The marriage dissolved in 1964 but by that time she had achieved critical and financial literary success, having moved to London in 1959 and written *The Country Girls* in her first month there.

Her odyssey might serve any ambitious woman as a model of toughness and determination. She survived not only the literary spite and backbiting of Dublin but an unhappy marriage, childbearing, motherhood and uprootedness as well to become, by her thirty-fourth year, that rare thing, a writer earning a living by her craft. *The Country Girls* was followed by *The Lonely Girl* (1962) and *Girls in Their Married Bliss* (1964), and also in 1964 she

adapted *The Lonely Girl* as a screenplay for the highly successful
film, *Girl with Green Eyes*. Novels, stories and screenplays have
flowed freely from her since.[9]

It might be thought of as ironic that these first three novels, all
of them with girls or a girl in their titles, all of them describing the
vulnerability of the female at the hands of an insensitive or brutal
male, were themselves the vehicles by which she travelled to
independence. But if this be an irony, so then is most of Miss
O'Brien's fiction, even after girls vanish from the titles, because
again and again she writes of the vulnerable, mis-used female, girl
or woman, wife or lover, left to dwell in recollections of embraces
and of deep-sworn vows betrayed. But let us push irony aside and
call it simply paradox, the paradox of the strong, independent
woman writing of women as victims. After all, literary success can
often combine with disappointment in love, perhaps most often.

One of Miss O'Brien's heroines, Mary Hooligan of *Night* (1972),
triumphs over these disappointments by means of a Molly
Bloomian burst of lyrical energy and humour. Another, Nora of *I
Hardly Knew You* (1977), smothers her young lover with a pillow.
She goes to prison, feels what seems a great deal like self-pity, as
many murderers do, but appears also to savour her act, as she did
the weeks of lovemaking that preceded it. But more of this novel
further on. If one had to choose an archetypal Edna O'Brien
heroine, one could hardly do better than with Martha, who
narrates the title story of a collection called *The Love Object*
(1968). Separated from her husband and with two young boys to
care for, Martha, thirty, falls for an older gentleman who is
wealthy, famous and married for the third time. She loves him
fiercely, although one is unsure why, because he seems more interested in his public life and in the proprieties of his marriage than in
love. Their relationship diminishes, Martha is tortured by loneliness and a feeling that she has been used, and she contemplates
suicide, pulling back from that brink only when she realises that
her sick son needs her. Martha lives chiefly to be needed, and what
she discovers with her lover is that he does not so much need her as
choose to make use of her. Yet, long after their union has been
reduced to occasional public encounters, she cherishes the
memory of this man, because, she says, not to nourish the memory
of him in her heart would be to live with nothing, and 'nothing is a
dreadful thing to hold on to'.

That a woman has nothing more valuable inside of her than the memory of a broken love affair with a rather self-centred man may or may not be a valid glimpse into the female heart − of this one cannot and dares not speak. What matters here is that it is a condition typical of the Edna O'Brien heroine, and an effect of it is that these women end up looking more sensitive and less selfish than their men and yet also much weaker. The women endure, more or less, depending on this book or that, but the men hurry off to their social and professional engagements, seemingly not much bothered by a severance that may have left the woman close to self-destruction.

One's guess is that many if not most of Edna's O'Brien's readers must have contemplated the relation between these heroines and their creator. Never mind whether such contemplation be indecent, speculative, out of proper bounds, or unworthy of the professional critic: it is a question that arises and begs to be addressed. Two answers to it occur. Either the strong, independent, worldly author is being insincere in her presentation of women as fragile and dependent on men, with only a remembered sense of loss to sustain them, or, alternatively, these heroines do reflect Edna O'Brien's sense of herself in relation not only to men but to the professional world which she inhabits and they control. Unlike her heroines, she has her writing, but like them she dwells on images of a paradise lost and perhaps never even gained. What this suggests is that even in her mature years she continues to see herself as the country girl, equal to the challenge of the city but much abused by it, intentionally innocent, greeting the world with open arms but forced to close up when battered by its aggression and coldness. She might also see herself as goaded into revenge by means of writing books: the initials of the brutal husband in *Girls in their Married Bliss*, Eugene Gaillard, correspond to those of her former husband, and the book was published in the year of their divorce.

> They laughed at one I loved −
> The triangular hill that hung
> Under the Big Forth. They said
> That I was bounded by the whitethorn hedges
> Of the little farm and did not know the world.
> But I knew that love's doorway to life
> Is the same doorway everywhere.
>
> Ashamed of what I loved

I flung her from me and called her a ditch
Although she was smiling at me with violets.[10]

That is Patrick Kavanagh writing of what he called 'Innocence'.
He speaks of the scorn of urbanites for country things and of his
efforts to knock the clay from his boots and adjust to city ways and
values; he speaks also of his regret at separation from the flowery,
innocent, country life of his youth. Like Edna O'Brien he pictured
himself as an innocent made tough, defensive and withdrawn by
the heartless sophistication of the territory that lay beyond the
whitethorn hedges of his little farm. Like Kavanagh, Edna
O'Brien has retained a reverence and wonder for the simple
physical images of her youth, because they mean to her security
and the peace that reigned before the fall, even if from time to
time she writes a story about a lecherous priest or a drunken Irish
father. More and more her novels have become prose-paeans to
the pleasures of the country, the garden, the kitchen or the bed,
and in *Night* she has Mary reflect on the west of Ireland:

The low farm houses were so right, so friendly, so safe and even
then I said to myself what am I missing, and why do stone walls
and white gates and sheepdogs and blond roofs speak so, along
with little bushes and the clotheslines and the garments going to
swirl swirl . . .[11]

It is a passage typical of Miss O'Brien's backward-looking values
and of her lyrical prose, which one cannot help but call Irish and
perhaps Joycean in its mournful music. No surprise at all then that
she, like her heroines, would feel abused by metropolitan life,
whether or not she has endured and flourished professionally. Is
sensitivity meant only for the failures?

Nothing is more telling of her background than her treatment of
sex. Wholly unlike most of her contemporaries, male and female,
she writes of sex explicitly but with a wonder and an awe that is
completely at odds with the modern, urban sensibility, if it can be
termed as such. She does not burden her books with the heavy
theorising of D. H. Lawrence, but like Lawrence she infuses her
sexual passages with a tremulous energy that can only be called
reverence. Unlike Lawrence, however, she nearly always includes
sensations or atmospheres of guilt which heighten the pleasure and

the pain, generating a painful pleasure and an intensity that remind us of how much we lost when we decided that sex was normal and healthy and nothing more to worry about than bacon and cabbage.

> Then suddenly Dee pulling the knickers down, the suspenders still afixed to the charcoal coloured stockings, and the nice lackadaisical way I lay back on my sofa, and lifted my legs right up so that the soles of my feet were facing the cracks on the newly papered ceiling, and shame was banished as I asked for more and more sucks, and just gave into it utterly, as his tongue wound round and round, and I was pleasured in both channels, and in my mind able to bask in the wantonness of it without apologising and thinking of him.[12]

That is from *I Hardly Knew You*, published in England in 1977, and the sexuality described comes right out of the convent, or rather it has all the intense qualities of sex heightened by a rigorously puritannical childhood. Shame, wantonness, black stockings, garter belt, surrender, the lot. The heroine, Nora, may be an experienced Londoner but deep down she is an old-fashioned girl. And why would she mention wantonness and the banishing of shame if she did not in the first place feel wanton and shameful? And the phrase 'pleasured in both channels' has a distinctly archaic ring to it, like something out of *My Secret Life* or Frank Harris's *My Life and Loves*: the explicit description of an act still considered perverse and unmentionable in certain quarters, made more shameful and more a whispered secret by the use of curious, voluptuous euphemisms. The passage reads faintly like an overheard confessional. And how many times, my child? I don't remember, Father. And what did you allow him to do, my child? He pleasured me in both channels, Father. That was not a nice or a good thing to allow him to do, my child. No Father, it was not, not at all nice or good. My child, you allowed yourself to become a slave to the devil.

As it happens, the passage quoted above continues:

> Haven't I always been attending to a him, and dancing attendance upon a him, and being a slave to a him and being trampled on by a him?

It is the characteristic Edna O'Brien view of what occurs between the sexes, a power relationship that the woman loses; but here, in the context of the confessional-sexual effusions that precede it, the metaphors of service and performance and destruction do indeed carry connotations of devil worship. Miss O'Brien's sexual language may, for all its frankness, seem anachronistic in a secular age, but it is no less effective for that. Without shame and shock, writing about sex can be as lifeless as a technical manual on the operation of an electrical generator. One great advantage of her never having severed herself emotionally from her background is that she has been able to preserve a sense of mystery about sex as well as about landscape, weather and all of the mundanities that make up daily life.

It might be said further that all of Edna O'Brien's novels read like confessionals − and in the strict sense of a monologue revealing sins and crying out for absolution. We know from the start in *I Hardly Knew You* that Nora has murdered a lover and that she is talking to us from behind prison bars on the day before her trial. Why exactly she has killed the young man we are never sure, and this absence of credible motive hurts the novel, especially since the gratuitous violence prevalent during the hey-day of existentialism has passed, mercifully, from the literary scene. The only way to understand the crime is to see it as the logical outcome, in Edna O'Brien's terms, of the sexual struggle that has been continuous throughout her novels and stories. Yeats wrote analogously:

> When she, and though some said she played
> I said that she had danced heart's truth,
> Drew a knife to strike him dead,
> I could but leave him to his fate;
> For no matter what is said
> They had all that had their hate;
> *Love is like the lion's tooth.*

But the sentiment works better in a poem than in a novel, where we demand comprehensible and even sympathetic character and motive. One has the discouraging sense that at last Miss O'Brien has wrung dry the withers of her themes, that she has, literally and figuratively, reached a dead end.

It need not be so. Other novelists dominated as Miss O'Brien has been by memory and youth have done well until their deaths.

Proust and Joyce come to mind, but Proust was far more fascinated by social complications and nuances than Miss O'Brien has been, and Joyce became immersed in technical experiment, which is perhaps what a novelist must do of necessity when his subject matter or material is frozen in the past and he no longer has the will or interest to seek out characters, stories and themes in the everyday world around him. It is doubtful that Miss O'Brien is inclined or equipped to travel the Joycean road to experiment, although there are signs that she has considered it. *A Pagan Place* (1970) was set once again in Ireland — she was returning home once again in her fortieth year — but it seems to have been more of a technical experiment than anything else. Not only is the form a free-associating Joycean—Freudian monologue, it is written in the second person: you did this and that, you did, and so on. The form is as awkward as it is self-enclosed and suggests a faltering of outward impulse and nerve on the part of the novelist and a rather unappealing narcissism. *A Pagan Place* resembles her other works in its themes and in its confessional mode, but it is a self-confessional, and confession to the self works no better in a novel than in psychiatry or religion.

Somehow Edna O'Brien must, in future, break free of the self-enclosure to which all of the virtues of her talents and sensibilities have led her. Her pre-lapsarian memory, which can lend to a seduction in a London flat all of the delicious anticipations, fears, guilts and resentments of a country girl fresh from the convent, has served her well but perhaps too long. At times during the past few years one has turned to the first page of a new Edna O'Brien story or novel and had the unexciting idea that one has been there before and often.

To wish for more and different from Edna O'Brien is merely an expression of hope that springs from past pleasures. One does not wish to denigrate a writer whose personal and literary courage has from the start been great and who has already contributed so much to contemporary fiction. But perhaps she should let her familiar fields lie fallow for a season and strike out on a new journey, taking her vivid, precise language and her music with her. She might even write about a man who is neither callous nor powerful: say for instance an abandoned husband.

NOTES

1. Quoted in G. Eckley, *Edna O'Brien* (Lewisburg, Pennsylvania: Bucknell University Press [Irish Writers Series], 1974), p. 79.

2. A Belfast street-rhyme recited to me in 1968 by W. R. Rodgers.
3. See 'England's Difficulty' in Heaney's *Stations* (Belfast: Ulsterman Publications, 1975) p. 16. Part of a collection of prose-poems revealing autobiographical sources of the poet's other work.
4. P. Kavanagh, *Collected Poems* (London: MacGibbon & Keen, 1964) p. 138.
5. See Eckley, p. 25.
6. Hart Davis MacGibbon, trans. from Irish by Patrick C. Power (London, 1973).
7. I do not know the woman's name, but her remark is remembered by Sean MacReamoinn of Radio Eireann, who passed it on to me in 1977.
8. See P. Kavanagh, *The Green Fool* (London: Martin Brian & O'Keefe, 1971).
9. Edna O'Brien's fiction is most readily available in Penguin editions. Quotations in this essay are taken from hardcover editions as indicated. Pagination is identical in British and American hardcover editions.
10. Kavanagh, *Collected Poems*, p. 127.
11. *Night* (New York: Alfred A. Knopf, 1973) p. 98.
12. *I Hardly Knew You* (New York: Doubleday, 1978) pp. 5–6.

10 The Masculine World of Jennifer Johnston

Shari Benstock

In a decade that has seen 'women's fiction' develop as a full-fledged genre, portraying misunderstood and brutalised females struggling against the unjust dominance of males, it is indeed surprising to encounter a woman novelist whose fiction concentrates so exclusively on a value structure supported by patriotism, bravery, loyalty and honour, which focuses specifically on such activities as hunting, drinking, making war and selling property, which examines compulsively the social and religious rites of passage that are the anachronistic inheritance of the modern male. Not that there is not a long and venerable history of women writing about men moving in the world they control – one thinks of Jane Austen, George Eliot, the Brontë sisters, even Virginia Woolf – but that of late women have become exhaustively (some might say neurotically) concerned with themselves. Jennifer Johnston's five novels, *The Captains and the Kings* (1972), *The Gates* (1973), *How Many Miles to Babylon?* (1974), *Shadows on our Skin* (1977), and *The Old Jest* (1979),[1] all focus on the effort to survive the peculiarly masculine claims of worldly responsibilities and each defines the feminine in terms of the masculine. And the feminine, as portrayed in these fictions, is frequently manipulative, cruel, self-protective, and emasculating. But already I have over-stated (and thus mis-stated) the case: if it were true that Johnston's male characters were mere pawns of calculating women, or that the fragile web of her stories could be so blatantly articulated, there would be little to say in their defence. That the relationship between the sexes – as well as between social classes, generations, and political loyalties — is characterised by a complexity involving reciprocal responsibilities and guilts admits a delicately balanced fiction. The tensions preserving these narratives are evasive and thus insidious, even as their locus in time and place is carefully circumscribed: the place is Ireland and the 'time present' of the story is always mediated by 'time past' — Ireland before the Great War, before Independence, before The Troubles. With one exception, the subjects of these tales belong to the Anglo-Irish ascendancy and personify the inherent split between loyalty to English values and location amidst Irish peasantry.

The discussion of these novels hopefully avoids two common avenues of approach: to consider Jennifer Johnston as either a Woman writer or as an Irish writer, although obviously she is both. The genre of women's fiction would seem to have as its salient features not only its creation by women but also its presumption of females as both its subject matter and, until recently, its audience. Those who write Irish fiction are no less constrained by critical expectations that would emphasise the Big House tradition in these works, assuming both a specific historical context to foreground the narrative as well as a determined viewpoint from which it is constructed. Both classifications underrate, I think, that quality of Johnston's fiction which offers complex and often subtle readings, precisely because it is not so easily categorised, that it often defeats efforts at facile assessment, that it calls into question the very premises on which it appears to rest. The thematic and metaphoric elements seem all too obvious (though, perhaps, unusual as tools for a woman writer): hunting games, chivalric and heraldic codes, puberty rites, and the law of primogeniture. But these narrative components are employed as enclosures by which the limits of the individual stories are fixed: compulsively, these narratives turn toward the act of writing and the motivation for storytelling as the premise upon which they are themselves occasioned. The urge to tell stories is the source of this fiction as well as its subject matter: three of the central figures are young people consciously trying to become writers, another 'writes' the story that is Johnston's novel, the last lives in a world of his own invention.

For Johnston, the literary act is not grounded in social convention, nor is storytelling the by-product of a communal (and typically Irish) exchange: in general, these stories eschew the usual settings of pubs and social gatherings as places where stories are told and, therefore, *this* story would be told. Indeed, my desire to discuss Johnston apart from an historical or generic context is supported by fictions which stress in both thematic and structural terms the separation of the writer from the human community. Isolation from rather than membership in the social context is the spur to storytelling. Isolation, by its spiritual and physical vacuity, creates a void in which the writer works, spinning fictitious webs — an image readily available in Johnston's stories — that enclose an open, empty, inviolable space. These stories are spun out of a self that has developed either in seclusion from the world or in reaction against the world and represent Johnston's socially remote commentary on the fictive process.

I should like to begin this examination with the fiction which occurs first historically but third in the writing: *How Many Miles to Babylon?* This story is framed by the final days of its hero's life, the one who identifies himself as the 'I' of the narration and whose opening statement explains the pretext for the storytelling: 'Because I am an officer and a gentleman they have given me my notebooks, pen, ink, and paper. So I write and wait'. The 'writing' and 'waiting' are conterminous and the excuse upon which the re-telling of this soon-to-be-ended life rests. The frame of the story is, as it frequently is in Johnston's work, highly artificial, calling attention to its presence, its function, the necessity of setting off fictional events from 'real' events, of providing the 'I' a voice other than its own. In fact, these frames often provide the speaker a method by which he can deny responsibility for the act of his own creation, separating himself *from* himself, a process that absorbs the energies of this particular narrator:

> I am committed to no cause, I love no living person. The fact that I have no future except what you can count in hours doesn't seem to disturb me unduly. After all, the future whether here or there is equally unknown. So for the waiting days I have only the past to play with. I can juggle with a series of possibly inaccurate memories, my own interpretation, for what it is worth, of events. There is no place for speculation or hope, or even dreams. Strangely enough I think I like it like that. (p. 5.)

It is clear from this opening paragraph that the speaker is soon to die, that the reasons for this dying may be the story he is about to

tell, but that surely he is about to tell *some* story, a version of that
life from which he has begun the process of separation and for
which he feels no responsibility ('there is no place for speculation
or hope'). In the sense of its telling, this story is doubly framed:
first by the separation of the narrator as narrator from the
narrator as fictive person ('I can juggle with a series of possibily
inaccurate memories, my own interpretation'), and secondly by
the unravelling of the story itself which describes, over a number of
years, the process of separation that defined itself as the process of
maturation and which effectively cut off the spiritual self from the
persona to which it was attached. The agent of this second, and
absolutely crucial, separation was the mother, who equated the
child's maturity with the ability to survive without love or affection
– the ability to survive under conditions similar to her own.

The 'fiction' begins, then, with the recounting of the events
which seal and insulate the child against external intervention,
beginning with the withdrawal of the mother's love and succeeding
to exclusion from all other society: 'As a child I was alone. I am
making no excuses for myself, merely stating a fact. I was isolated
from the surrounding children of my own age by the traditional
barriers of class and education.' (p. 6.) Eventually the child
succeeds in pushing aside the barriers of class and education, but
not before it is abundantly clear to him why he has been raised in
total seclusion. The only intruders permitted into this encom-
passed life are his tutors, two of whom are recalled specifically: the
local curate, whose passions are Latin and ear-pulling, and a
nervous, downtrodden piano teacher from Dublin, who is infatu-
ated with the mother, becoming 'almost insane in her presence',
who, when she approached, 'would begin to tear distractedly at
the dark stains of hardened food that decorated the front of his
jacket'. (p. 7.) The mother's treatment of the young teacher serves
as preview and corollary to her demeanour with the child, conveyed by a single episode in which the tutor becomes increasingly
more frantic and distraught as the mother attempts to talk with
him about the child's poor progress: 'His finger picked and picked.
Soon, I thought silently, there will be a hole'. As observer to this
scene, the boy is acutely aware that the teacher 'was ridiculously
out of place', committing a breach of the social code that his
mother could not tolerate. The decision to dismiss him is the
mother's, on the grounds that he is 'dragging his disease and
poverty into my drawing-room', (p. 9) but it is left to the father to

carry out her wishes: 'It was a command rather than a question. I heard a quick sigh from father'. Aware of the teacher's loneliness, the boy is assured that he will never return ('He was a man, I'd have said, who had never felt warm in his life, or well, or momentarily gay'), who retreats into the chill autumn evening looking around the drawing-room 'as if he were trying to memorise it for use during his darker days'.

Indeed, the drawing-room provides the boy with a similar memory of warmth and gaiety that later serves as the synecdochic link with 'home' in its happier aspects, while the dining-room, by contrast, is reminiscent of the chilly atmosphere dominated by his mother:

> The drawing-room smelt of applewood and turf, and, in the autumn, the bitter end-of-the-year smell of chrysanthemums which stood in pots massed in one of the deep bay windows, shades of yellow, gold, bronze and white, like a second fire in the room. (p. 7.)

> The dining-room in the daytime was unwelcoming. It faced north and that cold light lay on the walls and furniture without kindness. Luncheon was the only meal I ate with them. Breakfast and high tea I munched alone in the schoolroom. (p. 9.)

The distinction drawn is between the social setting provided by the drawing-room and the private limits of the dining-room, where the family is secluded against all intrusion, except by the servants. And it is in the chilly atmosphere of the formal dining-room that the child first learns of his father's desire to send him away to school and, years later, of his mother's desire that he join the Irish forces fighting in Belgium. Chronologically, the scenes are separated by seven years; visually, they are joined by the mother's compulsive peeling of fruit as she strips away the father's authority with the child:

> Their words rolled past me up and down the polished length of the table. Their conversations were always the same, like some terrible game, except that unlike normal games, the winner was always the same. They never raised their voices, the words dropped malevolent and cool from their well-bred mouths. Green ringlets of apple peel fell from my mother's fingers on to her plate. (p. 11.)

In the privacy of the dining-room the layers of family secrets are peeled away, the enforced domesticity reveals internal warfare, the burnished dining table becomes a no man's land in which the spoils of battle are the young child. Having 'snapped' a sliver of apple into her mouth, the mother explains to her husband her initial aversion to the child's absence from home: 'I have no intention of remaining alone in this house with you'. (p. 11.) The entire discussion of the child's future takes place as if he himself were not present across the table, as though the parents had forgotten the reason for their argument until his presence is accidentally recalled: 'I must have breathed too deeply or something'. Nearly invisible, his presence is remembered only to be dismissed: 'I could feel their eyes watching me as I cross the miles of floor'.

A parallel dinner scene, some six or more years later, defines the mother's relationship to her child as it reverses her desire to have him present as protection against the father. Taken together, the two vignettes fully approximate the larger isolation that awaits him at the front lines where a stalemated war is being waged between clearly marked boundaries that define a physical and spiritual no man's land.

> Some time later she was peeling a pear. Dinner had been eaten in almost total silence. Only when the maids were in the room had any of us tried to make conversation. Unease was in all my bones.

The question is whether 'your son', 'my son', 'our son' should go to war, a war that Alexander's mother has been unaware of until the receipt of a telegram announcing the death in Flanders of Christopher Boyle, a young man whose relationship with them is never explained. The father's anger at her decision to send Alexander to war results in his banishment from the dining-room; the discussion is contained between the first peeling of the pear with an 'ornately curlicued' knife and its consumption by the mother, between Alexander's mental comments, 'I have never liked pears', (p. 38) and 'I hate pears' (p. 39.)

This scene is followed by one in which Alexander retreats to his father's study ('a room full of shadows, a watching room. I had the feeling always that no matter where I stood or sat someone was just behind me, not just wanting the quick conciliatory smile over the

shoulder, but someone stern and demanding' (p. 40)) to learn that
the father has also been excluded from the circle of self-protection
that wraps his wife ('Now I know she hates me, it is better'), that
her reason for sending the boy to war is to take away from the
father that which he most loves. This scene in the full-shadowed
room is followed by another in Alexander's own darkened room,
down a hallway where 'the light from the huge glass lantern above
the stair-well barely penetrated'. Here, behind 'a thin line of light
shining beneath the door', waits the mother, confiding her hope
that 'when you grew up, my darling, I wouldn't have to be lonely
any more'. (p. 43.) She has infringed upon the privacy of his room,
a place she has avoided during all the years of his childhood, to tell
him now that his father is not his father, that a man 'dead . . .
long since' is his father. The space between mother and son
enlarges in the wake of this announcement: 'It seemed to take a
very long time for her words to reach me, and then to reach right
deep into my mind. Hours perhaps . . . I didn't feel as if it were
happening to me. I was standing aside watching'. The mother is
forced now to admit that her relationship to her son has always
been prescribed by the terms of patriotic loyalty of the sort that has
urged hundreds of Irish youths to battle in Flanders — duty, love,
obedience, but especially sacrifice — 'I could have had a life',
(p. 44) she tells him; her words dispossess him of the land for which
his father only a few moments before had demanded his allegiance
('do what is best for the land' (p. 41)). Although she argues that his
response is 'melodramatic' ('your situation remains unchanged'
(p. 46)), his immediate urge is to escape the atmosphere of the
'inanimate, the inimical', to escape 'the eyes of the ancestors on the
walls, to whom I was now an intruder'. The opening section of this
account closes with a description of Alexander's exit from this
sterile, forbidding environment: 'Through a high narrow gate I
went out into the world, just by the crossroads outside the village'.
(p. 47.)

The exceedingly bleak picture of childhood in an Anglo-Irish
home is mitigated by Alexander's secret, shared, life, the alternative to the closed drawing-rooms and protected context of family
life. Typical of each of the young persons central to Johnston's
fiction, Alexander has a 'private and secret friend', (p. 16)
someone disapproved of on the grounds of class and political per-
suasion. Alexander's friend, like the others, is 'found out' by the
parental figures of the stories; in this case, the friendship with

Jerry, the gardener and stable hand, is the cause of his own death. The scenes of domestic tension which open *How Many Miles to Babylon?* are spliced with Alexander's illicit encounters with Jerry, who shares his passion for riding horses and for swimming nude in the lake behind the house and for whom is established a quasi-homosexual bond. What is remarkable about these secret meetings is that they provide opportunities for Alexander to speak, to discuss with Jerry his feelings about his tutors, his mother, his responsibilities to his father's estate, his plans for the future, while when at home he is consigned to silence, the invisible observer of the war of nerves between his parents. By the close of the novel, Alexander again has retreated into silence ('They will never understand. So I say nothing'); he becomes a narrator who cannot speak, a soldier who cannot explain, much less justify, the murder of a fellow soldier: therefore, he must die.

The account presented by Alexander as he awaits death becomes its own *raison d'etre*; it is not predicated on the need to explain events ('Time enough to do that when it is all over' (p. 5)), or to rationalise actions ('There is no place for speculation'), it merely records an increasing distancing of that self which functions *in* the world from that self which must explain itself *to* the world. The unspoken codes of social class and education which Alexander has consistently refused to acknowledge, against whose restrictions he has strained, whose ensuing isolation he has suffered, find their ultimate enforcement in the military, where men are divided into the categories of 'officer/gentleman' and 'soldier/peasant', and where his breach of conduct brings him before a firing squad. Only when facing the possibility of eternal isolation does he begin to recount the events which have led to this end, remembering the warning of his father against the 'unsuitable relationship' with Jerry: '"The responsibilities and limitations of the class into which you are born. They have to be accepted. But then after all, look at the advantages. Once you accept the advantages then the rest follows"' (p. 30). It may be that Alexander attempts to compensate for these advantages, or perhaps he recognises another code − of friendship − when he agrees to help Jerry search for his father at the front lines. Against the admonition of his commander to 'dissociate' himself from Jerry, Alexander continues to intercede for his friend, eventually killing him in order to spare him the firing squad. The isolation is now doubly enclosed: in order to escape loneliness he must breach social and military

codes, but in doing so he secures for himself a state of impene-
trable solitude out of which is borne the realisation that there is
nothing to do but 'write and wait'. Alexander's account is secured
by the necessity of a passive, contemplative stance − determined
by seclusion and detachment − which can do nothing but reflect
on a life that is in all but one sense 'over', which is presented with
no other alternative but the retelling of a story that can offer only
one telling, precisely because it is the only story known to the teller.
Thus the account opens with a statement predicated on what the
story is about to disclose ('Because I am an officer and a gentleman
they have given me my notebooks, pen, ink and paper. So I write
and wait' (p. 5)) and closes with a statement that is justified by all
that goes before it, the story itself ('Because I am an officer and a
gentleman they have not taken my bootlaces or my pen, so I sit and
wait and write' (p. 141)). The reversal of the terms 'wait' and
'write' suggests another dimension of this artist's isolation, that
which is enforced by time rather than sealed in space; when there
was yet time, at the story's outset, when there was 'no future except
what you can count in hours', the waiting followed the writing. At
the story's close, when there is no time left, the writing has superseded the waiting. This writer has not become a writer by choice
but by chance; his writing is not an idle action with unlimited
possibilities, but one carefully circumscribed by the events of a life
that is closed, finished, 'dead', its ending known before its beginning; his subject has not been determined as a function of his
existence as a social being but has been a record of a reaction to a
determined effort to separate him from that part of him which is
social, to place him in isolation to himself, to establish the most
radical separation of self from self − of speaker from listener, of
the one who lives the life from the one who tells the story of that
life.

The demise of Alexander Moore is the most extreme example of
the story-teller isolated from a social context, although a similar
subject and story-telling method is presented by *The Gates*, the
novel immediately preceding *How Many Miles to Babylon?*, and
The Old Jest,[2] Johnston's most recent fiction. In fact, these two
novels reflect each other almost paratextually in important ways:
each concerns a young girl with aspirations to become a writer;
indeed, each story is compounded of the diary entries written by
the protagonist. The parents of both women are long dead and the
only remaining relations are elderly; central to each story is an old

man (an uncle in *The Gates* and a grandfather in *The Old Jest*) whose seeming disinterest in contemporary events is belied by the painful effort to protect himself against the present moment (Uncle Proinnseas in *The Gates* turns to alcohol and Grandfather Dwyer in *The Old Jest* feigns senility). Importantly, the presence around which the story develops is the land, the estate, on which the old men live, a wealth that has suffered the effects of ill-use and has been eaten away by an encroaching poverty, soon to be sold to wealthy parvenus outside the class structure of Anglo–Ireland. Finally, each young girl develops a secret and special relationship with a man outside her social class, a relationship that is ultimately shown to be the source of the storytelling, subsuming the larger plot structure.

The format for the storytelling in these two novels is even more artificially contrived than in *How Many Miles to Babylon?*, calling attention to the form of its construction from the outset: both novels adopt the diary as the fictional frame, employing a method of narrative that emphasises an arbitrary rigidity, imposing on its subject matter the constraints of recognisable narrative boundaries that seal off subject from setting. While the diary entries remain consistently and precisely dated in *The Old Jest* (the action taking place over a period of ten days), in *The Gates*, each chapter is enclosed by double, conflicting, narrative enclosures: first, by a short titled précis offering historical background in the traditional third person, and secondly by first person diary notes that provide the temporal continuum along which the story moves. These entries are the commentary of Minnie, the protagonist who serves both as the subject of the narrative discourse and – apparently – its first/third person raconteur. (In *The Old Jest*, the narrative is enclosed only by the dated diary entries, but the entries read less like a personalised history than a full-blown fiction, with subtle and constant shifts between the first-person commentary of Nancy and a more objective third-person narrative which assumes a distanced and formal stance to the events being recalled. As in *The Gates*, the young girl's ambivalence to these events and her questioning attitude toward her own developing persona provide an intratextual tension that is supported by the 'plot' line and marked off by the diary notations.) Once the pattern of double distancing has been established in the first two chapters of *The Gates*, the structure begins to disintegrate. The third chapter presents a diary entry, dated, but with no précis; by the fourth, fifth, and sixth chapters, there is only a diary entry, now undated, and no précis. The early intrusions of the précis seem to mirror the traditional 'opening' to stories — but not necessarily the story that is ultimately told here — offering instead other narrative possibilities outside the specific frame-work of *this* story, while in *The Old Jest* the diary entries frequently record the writer's hesitancy at continuing the story at all. What begins in expectation and determination ('Today I want to start to become a person . . . My life is ahead of me, empty like the pages of this book, which I bought myself as a birthday present' (p. 6)) ends on a note of indeterminacy: 'I think I'll stop writing in this book. I find it harder and harder to put down in words my direct thoughts about what happens day by day. It seems to me that I will have to work out some sort of filtering system in order to put ideas clearly on paper'. (p. 143.) Unlike *The Gates*, where the storytelling process is itself highly complex and ambiguous, *The Old Jest* tells a complex story directly, raising the issues of its own production honestly and forthrightly, stating its purposes overtly: 'I'd like to write too . . . but I'm afraid I'll never find anything to write about'. (p. 129.)

The double enclosure of *The Gates* mitigates against any such direct approach to the story proper. For instance, each précis to the diary entry introduces characters who have only tangential import to the actual narrative: the first offers Ireland as 'Cathleen', who weeps her thousand welcomes and farewells (thereby accounting for Irish weather, it would seem); the second introduces a MacMahon ancestor who built the mansion in which the story takes place, whose son designed and built the gates from which the novel takes its title, but whose function in the present moment of the story is ambiguous. The title of the story itself, ironically, seems to provide the most pointed commentary on the process of this story's telling, especially since the selling of the gates is — like Alexander Moore's imminent death — the act which allows the story to unfold. In *The Old Jest*, however, the selling of Ardmore is almost incidental to the more pressing interest of the identity of the mystery man Nancy meets on the beach and her participation in the events which end his life: *her* story is taken over by the events of *his* life and death.

But neither the inconstancy of Irish weather nor the historical accuracy of the gates' construction has much to do with the central account of Minnie MacMahon's desire to become a writer like her journalist father, a desire that is more pointed and more fully articulated than the concomitant interest of Nancy Gulliver, whose reasons for writing are, in a sense, more personal: 'It is not really a dairy, more passing thoughts that give impressions of me, so that in forty years, if, as Bridie would say, I am spared, I can look back and see what I was like when I started out'. (p. 6.) The two introductory 'asides' in *The Gates* are provisional storytelling efforts, comments by voices distinctly different from each other and from those of the diary entries in the text itself, carefully separated from the body of the fiction by special designations ('Run In' and 'A Slight Explanation') and only tangentially related to the central fiction. Indeed, what at first appears to be a tightly circumscribed and limited narration shows itself open to the influences of its own telling, capable of subsuming intrusive voices, following various mental digressions, of adapting itself to its subject. Unlike *The Old Jest*, which is tightly controlled, insistent in its thrust toward the next event, unable to sustain irrelevant intrusions, almost hermetically sealed in its self-justification, *The Gates* is — ultimately — not enclosed at all; what seem to be the boundaries of its narrative possibilities turn out to be open gaps in the configuration through which new stories, in new voices, with new perspectives, slip into the narrative arena. The flat, unassuming prose in which the primary story is told redefines itself effortlessly, cameleonlike, taking on the colouring and intonation of the subjects it surrounds and defines. This porous style accommodates Minnie, the proto-novelist, constantly trying out new stories in her head; unlike Alexander Moore (and Nancy Gulliver, the isolated mental traveller), who has only one story to tell — a story that is very personally and prophetically his own — Minnie MacMahon has some difficulty in deciding which of many stories she wishes to make her own, and her characters frequently endanger her fiction by threatening to tell their own stories: the Major, her uncle, whose story (his career in the army) was 'stolen' by his own father when, as the eldest son, he was forced to take over the estate; Big Jim Breslin, the hotel owner who tells Minnie the story of her father, Red Paddy; Aunt Katherine and Uncle Bertie in Knightsbridge, who want to cast Minnie as a proper upper-class English girl; Mr and Mrs Macguire, the Americans who wish to purchase the MacMahon gates for spurious reasons; and, most slithery of all, the 'silver-faced' ghost in the looking-glass, who sounds for all the world like Ivy, the housekeeper. Minnie's account, then, is a series of trying-outs, of provisional efforts to tell the story she wants to learn by heart, that story which will 'have filled in many of the gaps in my education', (p. 38) and which is gleaned in part from the trunk of mildewed books belonging to her father: in short, a story that is in every respect, except in the persona of its teller, a story that belongs to a man. Like Nancy Gulliver, Minnie MacMahon by *chance* becomes part of a man's story, participates in an account of adventure and intrigue, takes risks and performs deeds that are in no way womanly, appropriate neither to her gender nor to her station in life. This accident provides each woman the subject matter for which she is searching: Minnie tries out several stories before she happens on her own, unforeseen tale; Nancy worries unduly that she will have no story to tell, even as she is telling it. The voices intruding upon Minnie's story recall those she has read, and her characters, 'the children of Lir', now four old men who need constant attention by nurses, (p. 82) are being kept alive by 'wonder drugs in plastic containers', their memoirs being prepared for glossy magazines, their last words recorded in television appearances and press conferences. These representatives of Ireland seem to have lost all identity (as has the nameless, but many-named man who becomes both hero and victim for Ireland in Nancy's account), they are being taken over by people and events more pressing ('All too soon they are no longer news. They slip from the front page to the second, to a tiny sentence in a corner.)' (p. 82.) Minnie admits to having a problem with their stepmother, Eva, who will keep turning into Aunt Katherine'. (p. 82.)

So too, one story slips into another: the story in which Minnie is caught and the one she is trying to tell share similar narrative components and both resemble the one that subsumes Alexander Moore. In all these stories, the past seems overwhelmingly present and the present is kept purposely vague (*The Gates* begins in February, in no specific year, but soon the diary headings become ambiguous and are eventually dropped). *The Old Jest* offers a specific time frame for its story, locking the fictional events into an historical context, manipulating the tenuous line between fact and fiction. But this is a story in which the past invades the present, provides for the account as it is told, fashions events in such a way that the present is always, inextricably, linked to the past out of which it was generated. The nameless man on the beach, the invader of Nancy's private retreat, explains to her that 'the past impinges on me. Nudges its way constantly into my life. Uninvited.

I no longer seem to have time for contemplation. I find it very unnerving. I find I can no longer act unimpeded by voices from the past.' (p. 56.) To a certain extent the mystery of the man's past, its relation to Nancy's family, its juxtaposition to the stark events of the story, become the story itself. And the man who has tried to lose his past only to find it awaiting him at the next corner expresses the frustration of the writer who, trying to tell her own story, ends up telling someone else's: 'So, for the first time in years, everything I do becomes tentative. I have to pretend, fool people. I used to be sure, devastatingly sure; now I have to squash doubts, sharpen constantly the edges of my thoughts.' (p. 56.)

In *The Gates* time present consists for the Major in secret drinking and private memories of the trenches, of Flanders, 'the Somme, the great pushes, the flower of England's youth', (p. 10) of his bitter resentment at being passed over for active service in the Second World War and of his colourful younger brother, Red Paddy, who, according to another wasted old man living in the past, Big Jim Breslin, shocked his nationalist friends by joining the British army to fight fascism and who scandalised his Anglo-Irish peers by impregnating an Irish peasant girl twenty years his junior – Minnie's mother. Time present for the General in *The Old Jest* consists in watching the railway line through field glasses (a line that, like the barbed wire fences marking no man's land, marks the outer limits of the secret battle being waged between the republicans and the black and tans) and in singing the refrain of 'Abide with me'. His memories are of Crimea and the Boer War, of the fight for empire, of the son who died a hero at Ypres. Young Minnie and Nancy are joined by their womanhood and (therefore) by their illegitimacy; with Alexander Moore, they are children 'dispossessed'. These children are spending the present searching for their fathers in the past, for their own personal heritage which remains unknown to them, only to discover that their present is shaped and directed by a past that continues to be both secret and inimical. The stories of the present and the past are strangely intertwined; the story that Minnie now tries to tell in fiction and the one she is presently living in reality are essentially the same: she's the 'spitting image of her daddy' (p. 66) and replays his story by falling tentatively in love with Kevin, the son of her uncle's drunken tenant farmer. Her crime is not the accident of pregnancy but the intentional scheme to sell the family gates, the ones through which her father never again passed 'after the trouble about the girl', (p. 63) a son dispossessed of his inheritance. Nancy Gulliver tries desperately to create a picture of her father, to identify him, name him, fix him in her memory: she fails, but attaches herself instead to another unnamed man in his middle age who is the singular, dedicated, mysterious man she thinks her father to have been. The elements of *How Many Miles to Babylon?* combine in *The Gates* and *The Old Jest* to offer divergent readings of similar tales, reflecting each other ironically: three lives enclosed by ancestral gates, haunted by memories of the past, children whose relationship to Ireland's past and their own past is equivocal; a world dominated by class considerations and distinctions, where men breed horses and protect property, do their duty, serve their country, keep up appearances, enclose themselves against a world that is socially and morally unacceptable. Those who dare bridge the gap become traitors to their class, are corrupted by unsuitable elements, and form attachments with social inferiors.

Third in this series of novels which have as their central subject would-be writers is *Shadows on our Skin*, a story set in contemporary Londonderry. The elements of theme and metaphor closely link this novel to the previous ones: here the family is working-class Catholic rather than upper-class Anglo-Irish, but the alcoholic father feeds his ego on drink and memories of earlier nationalist struggles against the English, the mother survives on religious fervor and a sense of duty to husband and children (any real love for either seems to have been drained off by the exigencies of economic and political realities), and the young son, Joe, develops his poetic talent in secret. The family subsists on the meagre income the mother earns waitressing in Strand's Café; Joe feels guilty about his mother and angry towards his father; he has no illusions about his familial heritage, knowing from the outset of this grim story that he has been in all ways dispossessed. But the novel opens with a poem, scribbled during mathematics class, which belies the young boy's real feelings:

> Father, you had to go away.
> And sadly I have had to stay.
> I am sad we had to part.
> I will miss you in my heart.

The opening pages unveil the creative process of a young poet,

offering four separate versions of the poem against Miss Mac-
Cabe's incessant explanation of the properties of equilateral
triangles.

> You've lived too long, already, Dad.
> And when you go I won't be sad.
> I'll jump for joy and shout and sing,
> Dee da dee da dee da dee ding.

But when the final version of the poem is produced, one worthy of
being printed in the local *Journal*, it is cut short by the intrusion of
an angry teacher: 'One day when it is too late you will regret your
inattention. Regret this incredible waste of time. Your time and, I
may say, my time. You will remain behind after the others have
gone home.' (p. 9.)

If the earlier novels centred stylistically and metaphorically —
even narratively — on the enclosure of space, the separation of
human from the external environment, the schism between public
self and private self, this novel focuses relentlessly on the movement of time. *How Many Miles to Babylon?* took for its title the
refrain of a song that measures distances against time:

> How many miles to Babylon?
> Four score and ten, sir.
> Will I get there by candlelight?
> Yes and back again, sir.

Shadows on our Skin looks at time differently, from the point of
view of something which must be dispensed with, used up, that
which is measured not in distances to be covered but by moments
which must be conquered:

> Now we've got time to kill
> Kill the shadows on our skin.
> Kill the fire that burns within
> Killing time my friend.

As Joe Logan's angry mathematics teacher reminds him, he will
'regret this incredible waste of time'; but Joe Logan already knows
all about time: he measures it ceaselessly every day, trying to 'kill
it'. He measures the freedom he has against the hour that his

'mam' returns from the café or the moment when his father will be
yelling for his tea, waiting for the day that time will be something
other than that which must be endured, killed, measured, burned
up.

For young Joe, time is framed by poetry, and it is poetry that
keeps one day from being like every other day (although the record
of events in the novel appears as an interminable series of days
exactly like each other). Changes in the invariable pattern of going
to school, coming home to make tea for father and to listen to
parental arguments, are recorded by a kind of poetic history, each
new item in the series marking not only a new event, but providing
an account as well of Joe's poetic progress. The poem about the
death of the father, for instance, bears a strongly martial quality
commensurate with Joe's impassioned resistance to paternal bonds:

> When you go to the heavenly land
> I'll hang out the flags and order the band.
> The drums will beat,
> The bells will ring,
> Hail another hero,
> The angels will sing.
> And I will clap my hands and cheer
> Because you are no longer . . . (p. 26–7.)

The 'here' of the final line is suppressed, but the rhythm and
rhyme of the poem are so strongly present that the point is made,
none the less. Joe's poetic commentary on the re-arrival of his older
brother, Brendan, back from England with lots of money in his
pocket, is made through a less insistent and more complex form:

> My brother has come home.
> Why?
> That's what I would like to know.
> That's what I ask myelf from time to time.
> He has money rattling in his pockets.
> Money that folds in his wallet.
> He says he earned it by working very hard.
> Over there he worked.
> Making a packet.
> How?
> My mother says I shouldn't believe everything I'm told.
> Why not? (p. 47.)

This poem is not markedly framed, its rhythms don't insist upon dominating the poetic line; its message is more subtle (and far more complicated) than the childish tune that wishes the father dead. Joe puzzles over the 'problems' of this second lyric: 'It was all much easier if you didn't have to make rhymes. But, then, was it poetry at all. There were people who wrote it like that, he knew that for sure. He had read it. It was rhythms that mattered, so that it didn't sound like ordinary sentences.' (p. 47.)

What remains obscure for the young poet, but rather apparent to the reader, is the developing complexity of his world view. This story is told completely from Joe's perspective, although it is couched in impersonal prose, and the ambivalent feelings that mark the return of Brendan, the son who has escaped the confines of the narrow house, who no longer has to 'mark time', is available in Joe's poem. What makes Brendan different from before is that he has money; it is the money that is 'rattling in his pockets' and the money that 'folds in his wallet' which provides the rhythm and imagery for the poem. It is money which has changed Brendan and which has altered his relationship to his family: because of money, time no longer stands still for Brendan as it does for Joe; money provides an escape. In counterpoint to the observed changes in Brendan, Joe's life is suddenly taken out of a still, infinitely repeatable framework, by the accidental appearance of Kathleen, the schoolteacher: if Joe measures his days by the meter of his poems, Kathleen measures hers by the number of cigarettes she smokes. Because of her, Joe begins to 'steal' time, to measure it by a different process, by counting only the time he is with Kathleen. Although their relationship becomes a 'habit', repeatable, its measure is not the same as the classroom where Joe is painfully aware of time's passage: 'I wasn't listening. I was wasting her time and my time, the whole world's time.' (p. 49.)

The elements of change in the story are Kathleen and Brendan, both intruders from the outside world where time exists for reasons other than to be waited out, where the pattern of daily events seems to hold some purpose. It is inevitable that these two lives will become entangled and that this network will somehow close out the new-found possibilities for Joe's 'time' while restoring the old order where time did not exist or existed only in a negative sense, as that which is 'spent', 'wasted', 'killed', 'overcome'. In Joe's world the absolutes are well known: what was good was the 'way it had always been before Brendan came home'; (p. 113) what was bad was before meeting Kathleen (who 'carried a briefcase that weighed her down slightly as she walked, reminding him, in fact, of the departing back of Brendan' (p. 22)). That these two 'times' are the same time – implying both innocence and restlessness – seems never to occur to Joe. When Kathleen is forced to leave – after a beating from the IRA friends of Brendan brought on by Joe's angered confession that her fiancé is in the British army – Joe finds her 'only just in time', as she is leaving, and he is again reminded of Brendan's earlier departure: 'She handed him a case and he thought of Brendan and the time, the first time, he had gone down the hill, leaning over with the weight of the case in his hand'. (p. 190.) After her taxi has passed into the darkness, he returns to his own dark house to make his father the ritual cup of tea.

The sense of this world as one which is both moving and not moving, where time turns back on itself almost parasitically ('People are always killing time. Some people do nothing else all their lives . . . killing time before it kills them', says Kathleen (p. 56)), is underscored by the confined spatial structures of its events. The action takes place on the street Joe treads daily from home to school and back again, and while there are rumoured 'troubles' which occur beyond the narrow street (frequently heard echoing in the night), the only important events are those bearing an immediate proximity to the central characters. From Miss MacCabe's opening illustration of the equilateral triangle on the blackboard ('EQUILATERAL. Squeak, squeak' (p. 8)) to the final map of Ireland ('Squeak went the chalk. One by one she called the boys up to fill in the names of the towns and rivers' (p. 188)), from Kathleen's introduction of herself ('Kathleen Doherty is my name, / Ireland is my nation. Derry, referred to by some as Londonderry, is my dwelling place / And heaven, my destination' (p. 30)) to her last gift to Joe of *A Golden Treasury of Verse*, inscribed, 'Kathleen Doherty is my name / Ireland is my nation, / Wicklow is my dwelling place, / And heaven, my destination', (p. 191) the setting is carefully circumscribed. Landscape is important to this story by its inescapability, the physical equivalent of the temporal constraint felt by the young poet, and while Joe's poems are consistently about the movement of time toward some goal ('Father, it's time for you to go' (p. 7)), he detours from this subject only once – on the day Kathleen takes him up above the city to the ancient fortress of Grianon, a shelter from danger, a quiet place from another time, a place occupied only 'in times of danger'.

In Joe's present world, the fighting is within, and every route across the portion of Derry he calls his own requires passing 'checkpoints', those visible barriers that keep the city quartered and sectioned, divided and conquered. Having successfully passed the checkpoint on the morning of his excursion to Grianon, he is elated at a new sense of freedom and for the only time in the novel constructs a poem whose controlling image is spatial rather than temporal:

> Gold is the sun
> On a winter's morning.
> Cold is the air.
> Still is the river
> On a winter's morning.
> The hill beyond is black
> Against the gold sun. (p. 85.)

Unlike the bulk of Joe's poems, this one celebrates the beauty (and joy) of the present moment, offering an image of frozen time, a solid, palpable reality that he gives to Kathleen as a present, explaining, 'You don't have to rhyme'. The lyric marks an advance from the heavy, militaristic rhymes of the early poems, a reversal of those first efforts which attempted to kill the temporal present rather than identify and explicate its power. The motivation for this poetic act is rather obvious: the time with Kathleen, away from the tensions of the Derry neighbourhood, represents a sort of time different from the ordinary, meaningless continuum of his daily life. Meaning is here focused on Kathleen as the one for whom the poem is offered: this winter's morning they share together, alone, separate from others. It is not until Kathleen confesses that she has attachments — indeed, a specific liaison with her fiancé, a young soldier — that time reverses itself, returning Joe as it was before Brendan came home and Kathleen appeared: 'She had changed for him. She was no longer one of those solitary people like himself.' (p. 119.) Kathleen's admission returns him again to an isolated world, one which contains only the words in his head ('One day my head will burst and words will spill out and be blown away by the wind and get caught in the branches of the trees. My words. Everybody's words' (p. 140)), and the pressing need to put them in some order, to reify time rather than kill it: 'Can I, with a biro pen and a string of words? Where?

How do you start? What are the rules? Do you just find them out as you go along? Trial and error.' (p. 140.) What Joe is discovering about poetry bears some resemblance to his recent discoveries about human nature: it is unpredictable, often fickle, and frequently malicious. The only defence is self-sufficiency, keeping back that important part of himself which is 'self', steeling oneself against intrusion and violation. But the self too long sealed off against the external world ceases to be, and words too long unused become evasive, silent, untrustworthy, as Joe is beginning to discover:

> Words run
> In and out of your mind
> Like children playing.
> And then
> When you really need them,
> Like children,
> They disappear.
> Maybe tomorrow would be a good day. Maybe . . .
>   maybe . . . He was home. (p. 179–80.)

All of Jennifer Johnston's novels give the impression of time that has been stopped by the forces of history or of personal defeat, against which the plot of the story races to bring what has been a non-story to some kind of dramatic climax. The act of the storytelling is itself an affront to the lethargy of the lives it describes, forcing actions upon settings and people who have resisted action for some indefinite period of time. The first of her novels, *The Captains and the Kings*, is typical in this regard, setting out the method of her storytelling as well as its subject matter. Old Mr Prendergast is waiting — rather impatiently — for death; his life, which 'from the moment of his marriage to Clare until his mother's death . . . had been spent in continuous movement', (p. 10) has now come to a complete halt. Only the inevitable blooming and withering of roses in Clare's garden mark the seasons at Kill House, his family home. As accidentally as Joe discovers Kathleen perched on the road wall, however, Mr Prendergast is invaded by Diarmid, a young boy from down the road whose life is equally empty and bone-bored. The remnants of Johnston's themes are all present here: an old man, drinking his way too slowly toward death, spending long inebriated evenings remembering Ireland before the First World War, suffering ambivalent feelings about a glamorous brother who was a war hero, sealed off from the present, real world by old age and pride. In particular, *The Gates* and *How Many Miles to Babylon?* are anticipated by the world of Mr Prendergast, whose life in his parental home is surrounded by obscure ghosts from the past, scenes from a refined world where a mother's favouritism for one son is veiled by mere toleration of the other, where a father is displaced by a dashing, eldest, son, retreating into the solitude of early senility, where a beautiful mother and her much-loved son share a talent for music.

In the late-afternoon of his life, Mr Prendergast plays the piano at twilight, recalls the clear sound of his brother's tenor voice and the agility with which his mother accompanied him on the piano; he tolerates the drunken gardener, Sean (who confines his drinking to the secrecy of the garden shed), probably because Sean's drinking was accidentally the cause of his mother's death in the family automobile. Relieved now of the responsibility of his mother, his wife, and his daughter whom he has never known, he enjoys his privacy, what the Rector irritatingly refers to as his 'withdrawal'. (p. 77.) Survival is best described as a kind of trench warfare against an unseen but ever-present enemy, ready to attack at the slightest lapse in decorum: Sean's presence is barely tolerated, and it threatens at every moment to take over the private area of Mr Prendergast's life kept only for himself; the well-intentioned but silly local Rector and his wife meddle constantly in an effort to prevent the old man from slipping into total seclusion: 'There seems to be something — well, . . . a little, don't take me amiss . . . unnatural about it. As an old friend, I feel I can speak to you like this,' (p. 77) admits the Rector. But the Rector is not 'an old friend', and his advice is unwanted; Prendergast returns the favour with polite rejection: 'I would like to die as I have tried to live, in private'. (p. 77.) The Rector thinks 'private' means 'alone', a semantic subtlety that Prendergast is willing to admit; but in fact, the old man is not at all alone: his life is peopled by thoughts and events of fifty-some years earlier — of Ireland just prior to and during the First World War, and his admiration is for the father whose total separation from the present moment protected him against its power to invade and occupy, to destroy and hurt, the fragile ego:

Mother had always eaten paper thin brown bread and butter every afternoon at four and taken China tea from a massive silver pot, strained through a strainer into an opaque cup. After Alexander's death she had eaten it on the move, pacing round the drawing room, from one window to another, staring angrily at the unsympathetic sky, at the hateful, constant rebirth of nature. From the piano to the fireplace, her glittering fingers clamped round a fragile piece of bread, she strode every afternoon for over forty years, her mind absorbed by the past, by one man's brief and beautiful life . . . It had been his father's decline into illness that had driven him irrevocably away. The terrible vision that entered his head of having to live with someone who felt love and hate as strongly as she did. His father had protected himself by withdrawl behind a barrier of gentle dignity and silence. He had the strength that his son lacked. (p. 103.)

The present story explicates the son's desire for retreat behind the walls of the family home, his face a mask against the prying eyes of the villagers, his brusque comments a cover for his vulnerability. When his inebriated wanderings of mind are interrupted by the young nephew of his former housekeeper, an Irish lad of thoroughly working class origins, his efforts to protect both the new-found relationship and the young boy become efforts to survive against the intrusion of the outside world: he and the boy retreat, withdraw, into the safety of a circumscribed area, one that becomes smaller and more self-contained as the weeks pass. At first, the boy's appearance at the house is irritating but understandable: his mother wants the old man to give him a post as a gardener. Prendergast refuses, not only because he has no money to pay the boy, but because 'in all fairness to your son, who seems, on a very short acquaintance, far from stupid . . . you should discuss with him any plans you may be making for his future'. (p. 25.) Soon it is evident, however, that whatever plans the parents are making for the boy — the best among them the grim prospect of being sent to Dublin to work for a shopkeeper — the boy is making up his own battle plan. He decides his future is with Mr Prendergast, and slowly, patiently, inexorably, he moves into the house against Prendergast's overt desires, but certainly with his tacit approval and, later, his committed efforts protect the boy from the authorities who wish to return him to his home.

Initially, the boy is intrigued by the collection of war medals Prendergast keeps on his mantle and later by miniature soldiers

hidden away in the old playroom at the top of the house. The
entertainment is soon to become mock military episodes that
engage the wits of opposing generals, and it is the former nursery
(now kept locked) which eventually becomes the last hiding place
against the hunt of the local police and church officials for the
young boy. But before it is evident that this is a 'state of siege'
(p. 90) in which Diarmid's future and Prendergast's past are held
in abeyance, the two have no reason to keep their developing
friendship secret: they freely avail themselves of the vast expanse of
Prendergast's property. Throughout the summer, while Clare's
roses are slowly coming into bloom, the old man and young boy
spend afternoons down at the lake, the old man reading Proust's
Sodom et Gomorrhe (in French, preferring 'to interpret the subtle-
ties of Proust's prose for himself' (p. 26)), the young Diarmid
swimming naked in the water. After tea, they retreat upstairs for a
'game': 'The main part of their time . . . was spent up in the
nursery, the floor covered with soldiers, maps and books. There
they observed military formalities, saluted each other and
addressed each other with military titles.' (p. 61.) It is in this
closed, secret, room that the real world — the one which demands
that both of them come out of hiding and assume their natural
roles, each to accept his respective responsibilities — is put aside in
favour of the fictional landscape of the battlefield. What begins as
a pastime, a diversion, is to become by accident rather than design
a real battle, and military conventions adumbrate the sorry defeat
that is this novel's conclusion:

> 'Are you going to lock me in again'? asked Diarmid as the old
> man began to collect his things.
> 'I think it's best.'
> 'I don't like it.'
> 'I'm not trying to make a prisoner of you. You understand
> that, don't you? It's really to keep other people out. Someone
> just might come prowling around. You ought to trust me. I am
> only trying to do what I think is best.'
> 'I don't like it. You wouldn't like being locked in, either.'
> (p. 101.)

The question posed by this novel, as in the ones that follow, is
whether by one's seclusion, isolation, one is locking oneself in or
keeping others out. Clearly, Mr Prendergast has always seen

himself in the position of locking others out: 'they didn't mix much; in fact, withdrew gently but firmly from the social ramifications created by the past', he remembers of the early years of his marriage; 'Mr Prendergast took to reading. He wandered through books as he had wandered through the world, never quite grasping what it really was that he was looking for.' (p. 12.) But Diarmid's viewpoint is different: first because he is young and has a future rather than only a past, as does Prendergast; second because his desire is to escape the confines of his family life and to enter the world. Mr Prendergast, of course, is not able to secure the boy's safety by locking him in the room, and the two are eventually discovered, wrapped in drunken sleep amidst the debris of their latest battle. Diarmid's mother runs 'across the battlefield, disregarding the gun emplacements, the barbed wire, the redoubts. Soldiers, guns, horses were scattered by her best navy court shoes. She had taken care to dress herself suitably for her visit to the big house', (p. 11.) and Diarmid is taken from one confinement — that of his fictional 'barracks' atop Prendergast's house — to another — the local police station — where he signs a confession to Prendergast's pederasty. That which the old man feared, the invasion of his privacy, and that which he would never have deemed possible, the accusation of immoral conduct, now come together in a fiction that has been written by someone with a mind more diabolical than those of military generals and fighting men. Prendergast's response is to retreat to the piano, alone: 'No Alexander, no mother, not even Clare. No one disturbed his peace', (p. 139) and he played 'as if he had never played like this before', until he falls dead from exhaustion, saving the local police 'a pile of trouble'. (p. 142.) His last retreat, whether the result of strength or weakness, whether merely a need to survive on his own terms, to die as he had lived, 'in private', is a final retreat against the world which has consistently, relentlessly, attempted to circumscribe his life.

The self-contained world that Johnston's fiction describes, the sealed spaces where the storyteller plots his fictions and maps his battle plans, is a world that bears significant resemblance to the separate, isolated, enclosed spaces that have so meticulously been described by women novelists writing about women: a similar atmosphere of exclusion and seclusion has been portrayed with clinical precision by Doris Lessing, Margaret Drabble, Susan Hill, Edna O'Brien, Barbara Pym, Jean Rhys and Elizabeth Bowen. The 'woman's novel' predicates itself on the notion that social separateness is an *a priori* condition of the woman in contemporary society. Johnston's work seems to suggest that such exclusive status is not necessarily peculiar to women: the title of this essay, then, is entirely inappropriate to her subject as I have described it: this world is not masculine, not open, accessible, social, a world of action, but rather specifically feminine: closed, suffocated, lonely, and inward-turning. The apparent suggestion of these novels is that the *male* world is secret, sealed off, plotted by means of battle lines and codes, cut off by arbitrary divisions, checkpoints, military demarcations, that life is perceived to be a series of strategies and diversionary tactics to keep the enemy at bay and that privacy is a retreat to the 'comparative safety of the trenches', while the more social, open stance submits the ego to constant scrutiny and observation. The metaphorical terms delineating this world are certainly masculine, but the world itself — and the condition of those who inhabit it — shares more with Virginia Woolf than with Anthony Powell. While the component elements of her world are certainly drawn from the little-boy games of playing war, which turn out to be the grown-up games of making war, it is not at all clear that the essential subject of this fiction has anything to do with masculinity or maleness. The metaphor of trench warfare, of warfare under conditions where one's loyalties are unclear and one's ultimate goal is held in question, of tracking the enemy through field glasses down the railway line, seems to hold as a kind of statement about the survival of human beings in general and of the literary artist in particular. Against the myth of Irish storytellers, the ebullient, social beings, at home amidst the hard-drinking and long-talking pub patrons, Johnston posits another kind of Irish voice — one that is not clearly even Irish but rather transplanted and misplaced, one that is neither male nor female (there is little difference in tone or style, even in subject matter, between Minnie MacMahon and Nancy Gulliver's tales and Alexander Moore's or between Joe Logan's poetry and Diarmid's battle plans), one that is distinctly separate from and aligned against its origins and impetus. In short, these do not seem to be stories that are told 'naturally', that arise from shared assumptions between speaker and audience as to the efficacy of or the motivations for storytelling; rather, they seem to be bred in spite of the impetus to stop them, against the tactics of the enemy (the larger social intrusion) which would force these to be stories of another kind, to be tales of community rather than the lonely individual, stories of success rather than of stalemate, stories that are shared rather than kept secret. Instead, these narratives are told outside the time frame they delineate, are told from the perspective of an isolation that has been enforced (*How Many Miles to Babylon?* and *Shadows on our Skin*) or by one that has been violated (*The Captains and the Kings, The Gates, The Old Jest*). They exist on a plotted space between the entrenched encampments of the enemy, in a figurative no man's land to which the reader has gained access by being an accomplice to the intrusion these stories resist, but to which they bear testament. That the common denominator of these fictions should be the activity of war suggests that they serve to explicate the furthest reaches of artistic alienation.

NOTES

1. Citations are from the following editions of Johnston's books: *The Captains and the Kings* (London: Hamish Hamilton, 1972); *The Gates* (London: Hamish Hamilton, 1973); *How Many Miles to Babylon?* (London: Hamish Hamilton, 1974); *Shadows on Our Skin* (London: Hamish Hamilton, 1977); *The Old Jest* (London: Hamish Hamilton, 1979).
2. Jennifer Johnston was born in Dublin on 12 January 1930, the daughter of playwright Denis Johnston and of Shelagh Richards, actress and producer. She was educated at Trinity College, Dublin. She is married to Ian Smyth, is the mother of four children, and now lives in Northern Ireland.

Index

Abbess of Crewe, The, 172–3, 174
About Chinese Women, 103
Abrams, M. H., 7
Accidental Man, An, 31–3, 38
Adler, Renata, 166
Albatross and Other Stories, The, 90–2, 94
Andersen, Hans, 101
Aspects of the Novel, 70, 74, 155
Auden, W. H., 168
Austen, Jane, xi, 191

Bachelors, The, 164
Bainbridge, Beryl, xvi
Balkan Trilogy, The, xv, 39–58
Ballad of Peckham Rye, The, 163–4
'Basement Room, The', 164
Beckett, Samuel, 101
Beerbohm, Max, 153–4, 161, 176
Bell, The, 21
Bell Jar, The, 84, 99
Bennett, Arnold, 131
Bird of Night, The, 82–3, 94
Bit of Singing and Dancing, A, 95–7
Black Prince, The, 35–7
Bowen, Elizabeth, 183, 215
Briefing for a Descent into Hell, 2–5, 10
Brontës, the, xi, 155, 170, 191

Browne, Thomas, 92, 93, 102
Bruno's Dream, 28
Burgess, Anthony, 167

Captains and the Kings, The, 191, 211–15, 217
Carleton, William, 183
Cecil, David, 154
Change for the Better, A, 86, 87–9, 95
Charterhouse of Parma, The, 41
Chesterton, G. K., 156
Children of Violence, 6
'Choice, The', 95
Christie, Agatha, xiv, 110, 120
'Cockles and Mussels', 91
Cold Country, The (radio plays), 81, 100–1
Comforters, The, 155–9, 176
Compton-Burnett, Ivy, 158, 165, 170
Conrad, Joseph, xi
Country Girls, The, 182–3
'Custodian, The', 97

Dickens, Charles, xi, 86–7
Dr Faustus, 94
Do Me a Favour, 84–6, 89
Donleavy, J. P., 20

218

Drabble, Margaret, xii, 130–52,
174, 215
Garrick Year, The, 131–2, 136–7
Ice Age, The, 130–2, 138–9
Jerusalem the Golden, 131–2, 135
Millstone, The, 131–6, 139–45
Needle's Eye, The, 135, 138, 145
Realms of Gold, The, 133–4,
145–51
Summer Bird-Cage, A, 130–1,
133, 135, 139
Waterfall, The, 131, 133–4, 137,
139: children as a thematic
and moral focus, 137ff.;
feminist issues, 133–6;
imagery, 148–50; literary;
roots, 130–5
Review of Spark's *The Takeover*,
174–5
Driver's Seat, The, 159, 169

Eckley, C., 179, 181
Edgeworth, Maria, 183
Eliot, George, xi, xiv, 25, 145, 191
Middlemarch, xiv
Mill on the Floss, The, 131, 134
Eliot, T. S., 163, 166, 168, 171, 174
Enclosure, The, 82, 84–5, 92
Endgame, 101
End of Summer, The, 100
Eustace and Hilda, 175
Excellent Women, 63, 66–7, 70, 73

Fairly Honourable Defeat, A, 28–31
Fanfarlo, The, 155
Fire and the Sun, The, 16
First World War, xiv, 193ff.
Flight from the Enchanter, 21
Forster, E. M., 70, 74, 93, 155, 167,
171
Four-Gated City, The, 1–3, 5
Frazer, Sir James, 174
Friends and Heroes, 45, 51–3, 54–8
'Friends of Miss Reece', 91

Garrick Year, The, 131–2, 136–7
Gaskell, Elizabeth, xi, 87, 99
Gates, The, 191, 199–205, 217
Gentlemen and Ladies, 86–7, 89

Ginger Man, The, 20
Girls in Their Married Bliss, 183,
185
Girls of Slender Means, The,
166–7, 171
Girl With Green Eyes, 184
Glass of Blessings, A, 69, 70, 73
Glendinning, Victoria, 167, 176
'Gods, the Gods, The', 170
Golden Bough, The, 174
Golden Notebook, The, 2, 6
Great Fortune, The, 39–48
Greene, Graham, 156, 164, 175

Hardy Thomas, xi, 143
Hartley, L. P., 175
Hawthorne, Nathaniel, 131
Heaney, Seamus, 180
Henry and Cato, 16, 27, 35
Hill, Susan, xv, 81–103, 215
Albatross and Other Stories, The,
90–2: 'Albatross, The',
90–1, 94; 'Cockles and
Mussels', 91; 'Friends of Miss
Reece', 91; 'Somerville',
91–2
Bird of Night, The, 82–3, 94
Bit of Singing and Dancing, A,
95–7: 'Bit of Singing, etc.',
95; 'Custodian, The', 97;
'How soon can I leave?', 96;
'Peacock, The', 96–7
Change for the Better, A, 86–9,
95
Cold Country, The (radio plays),
81, 100–1: *Cold Country,
The*, 100–1; *End of
Summer, The*, 100; *Lizard
in the Grass*, 100
Do Me a Favour, 84–6, 89
Enclosure, The, 82, 84–5,
92
Gentlemen and Ladies,
86–7, 89
I'm the King of the Castle,
88–90, 94
In the Springtime of the Year,
97–9, 102
Land of Lost Content, The, 82

Hill, Susan—*cont.*
  Strange Meeting, 82, 86, 92–3,
    102
  Strip Jack Naked, 101–2: awards
    won, 81; humanist tradition
    in her work, 81–103;
    imagery, 82ff.; metaphysical
    v. feminist concerns,
    81–103; polarisation of male
    and female qualities, 81–103
Hopkins, Gerard Manley, 166,
  172
Hothouse By the East River, The,
  171–2
'House of Fiction, The', quoted,
  155, 161, 163–4, 170
How Many Miles to Babylon?, xiv,
  191, 193–9, 205–6, 217
'How soon can I leave?', 96

Ice Age, The, 130–2, 138–9
'Idiot Boy, The', 138
'I Had a Future', 181
I Hardly Knew You, 184, 187–8
I'm the King of the Castle, 88–90,
  94
'Innocence', 184–5
Innocent Blood, xv
In the Springtime of the Year,
  97–9, 102
Italian Girl, The, 19

James, Henry, xi, 92, 93
James, P. D., xiv, 104–29
  Black Tower, The, 108, 110, 112,
    114, 116, 118–19, 122,
    125–7
  Cover Her Face, 105, 110, 112,
    115, 120–1
  Death of an Expert Witness, 109,
    114, 117, 119, 127–8
  Innocent Blood, xv
  Mind to Murder, A, 107, 112–13,
    121–2
  Shroud for a Nightingale, 107–8,
    112, 116, 117–18, 123–4
  Unnatural Causes, 110–11, 113,
    117, 119, 122–3, 128

Unsuitable Job for a Woman, An,
  106–7, 110, 113, 124–5,
  128: characterisation, 119ff.;
  the detective hero, 111–19;
  indebtedness to D. Sayers,
  113, 128; setting, 105–10
  and *passim*
Jane and Prudence, 62, 64, 66–70,
  73–4, 76
Jerusalem the Golden, 131–2, 135
Johnson, R. Brimley, xvi
Johnston, Jennifer, xiv, 191–217
  Captains and the Kings, The,
    119, 211–15, 217
  Gates, The, 191, 199–205, 217
  How Many Miles to Babylon?,
    xiv, 191, 193–9, 205–6, 217
  Old Jest, The, 191, 199–205, 217
  Shadows on our Skins, 191,
    205–11, 217: isolation and a
    self-contained world,
    191–217; the storytelling
    format, 192–217; temporal
    considerations, 192, 203–11
Joyce, James, 172, 189

Kavanagh, Patrick, 181, 183, 184–5
Keats, John, 145
Kemp, Peter, 157, 160–1, 163, 169,
  170
Kermode, Frank, 155, 161, 163–4,
  170
Kiely, Benedict, 183
Kristeva, J., 103

Landlocked, 2
Land of Lost Content, The, 82
Lawrence, D. H., xi, 22, 170, 186
Leavis, F. R., *The Great Tradition*,
  xi
Les Liaisons Dangereuse, 22
Lessing, Doris, xv, 1–15, 215
  Briefing for a Descent into Hell,
    2–5, 10
  Children of Violence, 6
  Four-Gated City, The, 1–3, 5
  Golden Notebook, The, 2, 6
  Landlocked, 2
  Memoirs of a Survivor, The, 2, 4,
    13

Lessing, Doris — *cont.*
　Summer Before the Dark, The,
　　4–15: cataclysmic view of
　　the future, 1–15; energy,
　　9–10; influence of Jungian
　　therapy, 13; spiritual and
　　psychic evolution to a higher
　　state of consciousness –
　　transpersonality, 3, 7–8ff.
Less Than Angels, 62, 64–5, 69, 70,
　75–6, 77
Levant Trilogy, The, 58n., 59
Life's Little Ironies, 143
Lizard in the Grass, 100
Loitering with Intent, 176–7
Lolita, 35
Lonely Girl, The, 183–4
Love Object, The, 184
Lurie, Alison, 5, 11

'Macao', 168
Malkoff, Karl, 164
Mandelbaum Gate, The, 167–8,
　172
Mann, Thomas, 1, 94, 175
Manning, Olivia, xv, xvi, 39–59
　Balkan Trilogy, The, xv, 39–58:
　　Great Fortune, The, 39–48;
　　Spoilt City, The, 43, 48–54;
　　Friends and Heroes, 45, 51,
　　52–3, 54–8
　Levant Trilogy, The, 58n., 59;
　　affinities with Orwell, 41;
　　affinities with Stendhal, 41,
　　50; characterisation, 43ff.;
　　the importance of place,
　　39–58; a weakness in the
　　trilogy, 56
Masefield John, 155
Max, 154
Memento Mori, 159, 161–3,
　170
Memoirs of a Survivor, The, 2, 4, 13
Meredith, George, xi
Middlemarch, xiv
Millet, Kate, 65–6
Mill on the Floss, The, 131, 134
Millstone, The, 131–2, 133–6,
　139–45

Mind to Murder, A, 107, 112–13,
　121–2
Mrs Dalloway, 85
Moers, Ellen, xi, 153
Murdoch, Iris, xiv, 16–38
　Accidental Man, An, 31–3, 38
　Bell, The, 21
　Black Prince, The, 35–7
　Bruno's Dream, 28
　Fairly Honourable Defeat, A,
　　28–31
　Fire and the Sun, The, 16
　Flight from the Enchanter, 21
　Henry and Cato, 16, 27, 35
　Italian Girl, The, 19
　Nice and the Good, The, 25–7
　Red and the Green, The, 24
　*Sacred and Profane Love
　　Machine, The*, 33–4, 37
　Sartre, Romantic Rationalist, 20
　Sea, The Sea, The, 31
　Severed Head, A, 21–4, 28, 38
　Sovereignty of Good, The, 20
　Under the Net, 20
　Unicorn, The, 17, 25
　Unofficial Rose, An, 24
　Word Child, A, 34–5: concern
　　with upper middle class
　　manners, 21–4; use of the
　　'enchanter' figure, 20, 28,
　　30, 32–3; use of the Gothic,
　　18, 19, 20, 33; theme of
　　guilt, 27; 'moral muddles
　　and muddlers', 16–38; as a
　　philosophical novelist,
　　16–38; her 'reversals', 17,
　　19, 22, 24, 27, 33; influence
　　of *The Underground Man*,
　　34–5
'Mystery of Job's Suffering', 157

Needle's Eye, The, 135, 138, 145
Newman, John Henry, 153, 155–6,
　176
Nice and the Good, The, 25–7
Night, 184–6
No Fond Return of Love, 63, 65–7,
　70, 73–6
Not to Disturb, 170–1, 172

Novel Now, The, 167

O'Brien, Edna, xv, 179–90, 215
  Country Girls, The, 182–3
  Girl With Green Eyes, 184
  Girls in Their Married Bliss, 183, 185
  I Hardly Knew You, 184, 187–8
  Lonely Girl, The, 183–4
  Love Object, The, 184
  Night, 184, 186
  Pagan Place, A, 189: importance of childhood and memory, 179–89; the confessional mode, 187–9; her treatment of sex, 186–9
O'Brien, Edna, by C. Eckley, 179, 181
O'Brien, Flann, 182
O'Connor, Flannery, 156, 161
Ohmann, Carol, 159
Old Jest, The, 191, 199–205, 217
'On First Looking into Chapman's Homer', 145
Ordeal of Gilbert Pinfold, The, 157
Orwell, George, 41

Pagan Place, A, 189
Passage to India, A, 167
'Peacock, The', 96–7
Plath, Sylvia, 84, 99
Poor Mouth, The, 182
Prime of Miss Jean Brodie, The, 164–6, 167, 172
Proust, Marcel, 153, 160, 189
Public Image, The, 168–9
Pym, Barbara, xiii, xvi, 61–80, 215
  Excellent Women, 63, 66, 67, 70, 73
  Glass of Blessings, A, 69, 70, 73
  Jane and Prudence, 62, 64, 66–70, 73–4, 76
  Less Than Angels, 62, 64–5, 69, 70, 75–6, 77
  No Fond Return of Love, 63, 65–7, 70, 73–6
  Quartet in Autumn, xiii, 62, 63, 70, 77–9

  Some Tame Gazelles, 64, 67, 70–2, 74–5, 77
  Sweet Dove Died, A, 67: fiction misrepresenting life, 61–79; love idealised in fiction, 61–79

Quartet in Autumn, xiii, 62–3, 70, 77–9

Realms of Gold, The, 133–4, 145–51
Red and the Green, The, 24
Rhys, Jean, xi, xvi, 91, 215
Richardson, Dorothy, xi, xii
Robinson, 159–61
Rodgers, W. R., 180
Room of One's Own, A, xiii, 61

Sacred and Profane Love Machine, The, 33–4, 37
Sandcastle, The, 21, 24
Sartre: Romantic Rationalist, 20
Sayers, Dorothy, xiv, 113, 128, 156
Scarlet Letter, The, 131, 140
Scott, Sir Walter, xi
Sea, The Sea, The, 31
Second World War, xv, 39–59, 165–6, 171
Severed Head, A, 21–4, 28, 38
Sexual Politics, 65–6
Shadows on our Skins, 191, 205–11, 217
Shah, Idries, 3
Showalter, Elaine, xi
Shroud for a Nightingale, 107–8, 112, 116–18, 123–4
Sinclair, May, xi
Smith, Stevie, 163, 170
Snow Queen, The, 101
'Somerville', 91–2
Somerville and Ross, 183
Some Tame Gazelles, The, 64, 67, 70–2, 74–5, 77
Sovereignty of Good, The, 20
Spark, Muriel, xiv, 153–78
  Abbess of Crewe, The, 172–3, 174
  Bachelors, The, 164

Spark, Muriel — *cont.*
  Ballad of Peckham Rye, The,
    163−4
  Comforters, The, 155−9, 176
  Driver's Seat, The, 159, 169
  Fanfarlo, The, 155
  Girls of Slender Means, The,
    166−7, 171
  Hothouse By the East River, The,
    171−2
  Loitering with Intent, 176−7
  Mandelbaum Gate, The, 167−8,
    172
  John Masefield (and other non-
    fiction), 155
  Memento Mori, 159, 161−3, 170
  'Mystery of Job's Suffering', 157
  Not to Disturb, 170−1, 172
  Prime of Miss Jean Brodie, The,
    164−6, 167, 172
  Public Image, The, 168−9
  Robinson, 159−61
  Takeover, The, 173−5, 176
  Territorial Rights, 168−70, 175:
    affinities with Beerbohm,
    153, 161; Catholicism,
    156−9, 164−5, 172, 174;
    cinematic techniques, 160,
    170 and *passim*; 'dandyism',
    153−77; death in the later
    novels, 169ff.
Spark, Muriel
  biography by Derek Stanford,
    155−6, 159−60, 164
  critical study by Peter Kemp, 157,
    160−1, 163, 169−70
  study by Karl Malkoff, 164
Spoilt City, The, 43, 48−54
Stanford, Derek, 155−6, 159−60,
  164
Stendhal, Marie-Henri Beyle, 41, 50
Strange Meeting, 82, 86, 92−3, 102
Strip Jack Naked, 101−2
Sufies, The, 3
Sufism, 2−4, 8, 11, 12, 15n.9
Summer Before the Dark, The, 4−15
Summer Bird-Cage, A, 130−1, 133,
  135, 139
Sweet Dove Died, A, 67

Takeover, The, 173−5, 176
Territorial Rights, 168−70, 175
Thackeray, William M., xi
Time of the Angels, The, 19−20

Under the Net, 20
Unicorn, The, 17, 25
Unnatural Causes, 110−11, 113,
  117, 119, 122−3, 128
Unofficial Rose, An, 24
Unsuitable Job for a Woman, An,
  106−7, 110, 113, 124−5, 128
Updike, John, 176

Ward, Mrs Humphry, xi
Waste Land, The, 163, 170−1, 174
Waterfall, The, 131, 133−4, 137,
  139
Waugh, Auberon, 176
Waugh, Evelyn, 157, 175
Wescott, Roger, 6, 7, 8
White, Antonia, xvi
White, John, 4, 6
White, Phyllis Dorothy, *see* P. D.
  James
Wilde, Oscar, 154
Wimsey, Lord Peter, 113−14
Women Novelists
  change in status 1960s and 1970s,
    xi, xii
  creation of male characters, xiv,
    16−38, 191−217
  creation of microcosm, xv and
    passim
  detective fiction, 104−29
  First World War, 193ff.
  problems and frustrations, xii,
    179−90
  problems of old age, 77−9
  Second World War, 39−58,
    165−6, 171
  sexual dimensions of women
    characters, xv, 179−90
  themes emerging from
    experience, xii, 130−52
  willingness to confront
    cataclysmic questions, xv,
    1−15
Women Novelists, The, xvi

Woolf, Virginia, xi, xii, xiii, 157,
    163, 191
  Mrs Dalloway, 85
  review in *TLS*, xvi
  Room of One's Own, A, xiii, 61

Word Child, A, 34–5
Wordsworth, William, 138, 155
Wreck of the Deutschland, The, 166

Yeats, W. B., 95, 161, 167, 188